Lampasas

1855–1895

Biography of a Frontier Texas Town

BILL O'NEAL

EAKIN PRESS ❧ Fort Worth, Texas
www.EakinPress.com

Dedicated to my favorite Lampasans:
My sister, Judy O'Neal Smith
Our mother, Jessie Standard O'Neal
Our grandparents, W. W. and Lucile Standard

Contents

Preface and Acknowledgments

Lampasas was my mother's home town. She grew up in the old fire house, because her father was the only paid employee of the Lampasas Volunteer Fire Department. My grandmother operated the town's photography studio, and she avidly reproduced images of our ancestors, of other local pioneers, and of venerable community buildings. My family traveled regularly from our home in Corsicana to Lampasas to visit my grandparents, aunt, uncles, and cousins.

I heard stories of my great-grandfather, who cowboyed for trail driver Pink Higgins during the 1870s and 1880s. I was told about the notorious Horrell brothers, and about the Horrell–Higgins Feud. I was shown where the Horrells gunned down four members of the Texas State Police in the deadliest of Lampasas's numerous saloon fights. At my uncle's sheep ranch I learned that his grandfather had killed a cowboy during the classic range conflict between cattlemen and sheepherders.

My first teaching job was in Lampasas, and for three years I continued to learn from history-minded citizens, especially about Lampasas's Victorian heyday, when tourists came by the thousands and events of statewide importance regularly occurred at the "Saratoga of the South." Years later I wrote about Lampasas as part of my biography of Pink Higgins. Now I've made Lampasas the subject of a biography—the biography of a colorful and fascinating frontier community.

I was given crucial assistance by several Lampasas grassroot historians. My sister, Judy O'Neal Smith, has served as president of the Daughters of the Republic of Texas chapter and as board member of the Keystone Square Museum in Lampasas. Judy embraced this project from the first. She opened a great many doors for me, secured photos and artifacts on my behalf, and accompanied me on numerous field trips.

Jane McMillin is the daughter of Dr. Rush McMillin and LaVerne Gary McMillin, who was a classmate of my mother at Lampasas High School. From her parents Jane, along with her sister, City Attorney Sue Faulkner, inherited a passion for Lampasas history. Jane collected a mountain of books, file folders, and other research materials accumulated by her father. Jane and Sue generously agreed to let me transport this invaluable collection to my office in Carthage for the duration of this project. I am deeply indebted to Jane and Sue for their trust and encouragement. Furthermore, as the manuscript developed, Jane read it chapter by chapter and provided me with countless helpful suggestions.

Carol Northington Wright, a descendant of prominent Lampasas pioneers and a longtime friend, is past president of the Keystone Square Museum, and she graciously opened to me the archival resources of the museum. Robert Gantt, current president of the Keystone Square Museum, generously provided me with numerous photographic images. Jerry Goodson, Lampasas County Surveyor, loaned me maps and books, and shared many observations from his lifelong interest in county history.

I am grateful to Shanda Subia, head librarian at the Lampasas Public Library, for permitting me to take important newspaper microfilm with me to my home in Carthage, where I worked with them at length on the microfilm reader of the M. P. Baker Library at Panola College. At Panola, inter-library loan specialist Sherri Baker once again obtained for me various obscure resources. Sheryl Housmann, chairman of the board of the Lampasas Public Library, was kind enough to read the manuscript and offer useful comments.

Donaly Brice, senior research specialist at the Texas State Archives in Austin and a valued friend, responded to a phone call for help with his customary resourcefulness. When we met at the Archives Building he produced petitions from the 1850s, miscellaneous documents, and obscure reports which amply filled several gaps. For researchers, Donaly is a Texas treasure.

Chris Ford of the Lampasas Fire Department generously granted access to the old LFD horse-drawn fire wagon, enlisting several of his colleagues to maneuver the historic vehicle into position for photography. Sylvia Eddy, descendant of early county pioneers, permitted me to photocopy her invaluable collection of McCrea family correspondence.

Charles E. Stokes, Jr., is the son of Charles E. Stokes, grandson of M. Y. Stokes, and great-nephew of Charlie Stokes. Continuing in the tradition of the Stokes brothers and of his father, Charles Stokes, Jr., had a distinguished career in business. He spoke at length with me about the Stokes brothers and their personalities and methods, and shared valuable materials with me.

Bonilee Key Garrett regaled me with delightful stories about her ancestors, and provided heirloom photographs. Kay Briggs, archivist and past president of the Keystone Square Museum, expertly guided me through the museum's archival collection. Jeff Jackson, superb local historian, generously shared materials on Pink Higgins with me. David Johnson, author of the first book-length account of the Horrell–Higgins Feud, allowed me to read his manuscript and to ask questions about aspects of the conflict.

Robert Oliver is a rancher, member of the Lampasas County Historical Commission, and a former student of mine. Robert spent an afternoon touring me around his ranch and the surrounding countryside. Robert's ranch includes the ghost town of Senterfitt, and he has maintained the few remaining buildings, which he allowed me to photograph. Another area rancher, my cousin Andy Feild, let me handle and photograph the revolver with which his great-grandfather—Andy Feild—killed a cowboy in self-defense.

Eakin Press published my first two studies of the urban frontier, about Cheyenne, Wyoming (in 2006) and the last railhead of the Chisholm Trail, Caldwell, Kansas (in 2008). They urged me to provide a third volume to complete a trilogy, and I am grateful to Kris Gholson, Director of Eakin Press, for publishing this study of frontier Lampasas. I also deeply appreciate the expertise of Pat Molenaar, who improves every manuscript that passes through her proficient hands.

My youngest daughter, Causby O'Neal Henderson, spent countless hours preparing the manuscript, and I am deeply grateful for her conscientious efforts on my behalf. My wife, Karon, also helped with the manuscript as well as photography. She made several trips to Lampasas with me, and served as a sounding board throughout the project. My appreciation for her assistance with this and other books is boundless.

—BILL O'NEAL
Carthage, Texas

CHAPTER ONE

Early Settlers

*"Myself and brother, Nimrod Hughes, were the
first families that settled in the county. . . ."*
—Moses Hughes

There were no roads, but the little party of pioneers plunged resolutely into the rocky wilderness of the Texas Hill Country. The family group was led by thirty-four-year-old Moses Hughes, a lean, bearded man with sharp features. His wife Hannah, and their younger children rode in their wagon. Nimrod Hughes, twenty-three, and his young family followed the lead of his older brother. Fifty-two-year-old Rebecca Hughes, the widowed mother of Moses and Nimrod, rode in one of the wagons.

It was November 1853, and the Hughes party was on the move from Williamson County, Texas. Hannah Hughes, at the age of thirty, recently had given birth to her seventh child. Hannah understandably was run down, and it was decided that she was suffering from "dropsy," an accumulation of fluid in her overworked body. Medical treatment was inexact and scarce in Texas during the 1850s, but there was an age-old—and slightly desperate—belief in the curative powers of mineral waters. Moses Hughes heard about a collection of sulphur springs to the northwest where Native Americans long had camped.

The site was only fifty miles from the Hughes farms, but it was up and over the Balcones Escarpment, where there were no white settlers.

Friendly Tonkawas, who probably told Hughes about the sulphur springs, had been driven out of the Hill Country by ferocious Comanches. In the 1850s Comanches dominated West Texas, and would plague Lampasas County settlers for two decades. But Moses Hughes was not intimidated by Comanche raiders. Besides, Comanches almost never raided during winter months, because their grass-fed war ponies were undernourished until spring arrived.

Watching his sickly wife grow weaker, Hughes came to hope that the sulphur springs would be a "fountain of life" for her. Moses persuaded his brother Nimrod to move with him to unsettled country. The Hughes brothers were from pioneer stock, and another move west into a new frontier was part of the pattern of their lives.

Even though there were no roads, Moses Hughes understood the approximate location of the springs, near the source of the Sulphur Fork of the Lampasas River. Confidently he had led the little emigrant train onto the hilly Edwards Plateau above the Balcones Escarpment, relying on what he called "hog knowledge" to find the way. Soon the Hughes party struck the Sulphur Fork at its confluence with the Lampasas River, and Moses realized that he was too far to the east.

Following a buffalo trail, Hughes led the way west and upstream along Sulphur

Moses Hughes led his family to Lampasas Springs in 1853. He built a cabin and a mill, and was active in community affairs for forty years. —Courtesy Keystone Square Museum, Lampasas (hereafter cited as KSM)

Fork. After a final trek of several miles, a spring soon to be called Hughes Springs was discovered. But further travel brought the party to a ford of Sulphur Fork, and the party crossed to the north bank beside a dense thicket that would become the Lampasas townsite. The Hughes brothers erected tents, and for a time the two families lived out of their wagons and beneath the tents.[1]

A quick exploration revealed several springs, which had created marshy bogs around each water flow. North of their campsite and within a bog was a spring which produced strong sulphur water. In time it would become known as Hanna Springs, and just to the east was a lesser spring, soon called Cooper Spring. To the southwest, in a magnificent grove of shade trees, was a bubbling spring with the greatest flow in the area. Because of the location it was often called the Upper Springs; because of its bubbling action (not its brisk, cool temperature) it was sometimes known as the Great Boiling Spring; it also occasionally was called Rock Springs. But within a few years it would become famous as Hancock Springs, after settler John Hancock acquired the property. Each spring offered a slightly different taste, and Hannah Hughes soon was consuming large quantities of the sulphur water.[2]

Wood and water were necessary for frontier settlement, and both commodities were plentiful. The Upper Springs grove was dominated by oak trees with outstretched branches. Most of the timber was hardwood: cedar, post oak, live oak, pecan, mesquite and, along the streams, cottonwood. But branches of all varieties were brittle, and most trees were short and stunted, indications of an arid

Hannah Hughes gave birth to seven children by the age of thirty. In failing health, she was brought to Lampasas Springs for the restorative qualities of the waters.
—Courtesy KSM

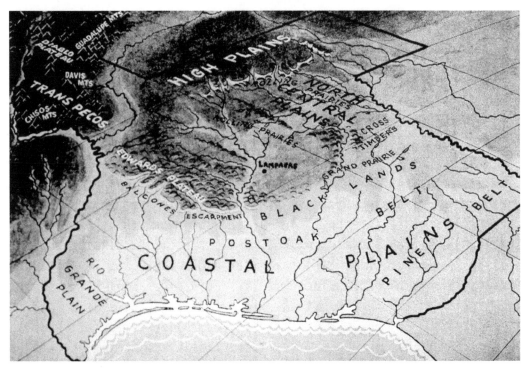

The step-like topography of Texas is defined in this illustration from the Texas Almanac of *1939-1940. Note the Balcones Escarpment and the location of Lampasas, just east of the Colorado River.* —From the *Texas Almanac,* 1939-40

The spring-fed Sulphur Fork of the Lampasas River. —Courtesy Jane McMillin

climate, making the springs and spring-fed Sulphur Fork all the more important. The thin soils coating the limestone had never been broken to the plow and seemed promising as farmland. Much of the countryside was open prairie, and the grasses clearly would support livestock. Moses Hughes eagerly formed plans for his family's future.

The combination of mineral water, a strong constitution, and a lighter-than-usual workload restored Hannah Hughes to health. "She soon become [*sic*] hearty," and within a year resumed her schedule of a birth every other year. Word of her recovery spread, "and from the time that it became known, hundreds flocked to this place, seeking relief from their infirmities."[3]

Moses Hughes built a cabin at his campsite, on the north bank of the Sulphur Fork and just east of the future site of Lampasas. He began erecting a grist mill on the north side of Sulphur Fork, and he acquired title to the land. Well aware that others soon would follow him to this promising new area, Moses Hughes fully intended to capitalize on the opportunities that opened in the wake of his wife's recovery.

Moses Hughes was born in 1819 in South Carolina, but while he was still a baby his family moved to Alabama, which had just become a state and where new cotton lands beckoned. When Moses was fifteen the entire clan—a total of seventy people, all related—decided to join the pioneer migration to Texas.

"We had with us tradesmen of all kinds—millwrights, wagonmakers, blacksmiths, gunsmiths, shoe and hatmakers," reminisced Hughes half a century later.[4] There also was a Baptist preacher, and almost everyone farmed. The great attraction of Texas in 1834 was land—vast amounts of land. An American farmer who moved west could purchase 80 acres of federal land for $100 under the Land Act of 1820, but if he moved to Mexican Texas he could qualify for as much as 4,605 acres. So the Hughes clan migrated to Texas, arriving in Stephen F. Austin's colony in January 1838 and settling near Washington-on-the-Brazos. It was heady adventure for a fifteen-year-old.

Just over a year later Moses' family was part of a desperate retreat from the invading army of Santa Anna. "Father carried the second child and mother the youngest," recalled Hughes. "I carried the meat house, which was an old-fashioned rifle gun." The crisis ended with the Battle of San Jacinto, and the Hughes family returned to their land. Moses and his parents became charter members of the first missionary Baptist church in Texas, organized at Washington-on-the-Brazos in 1837 by the redoubtable Baptist missionary Z. N. Morrell. The next year the family moved to what would become Burleson County. In 1840 Moses married sixteen-year-old Hannah Berry, and in 1841 children began to arrive like clockwork every other year. In 1847 the young couple lost their third son at the age of two, and Moses restlessly moved his family west into what would become Williamson County.[5]

For twenty-eight-year-old Moses Hughes, it was his fourth move to new country since the age of fifteen. Four times in thirteen years he experienced the pioneer's adventure of creating a new home in sparsely-settled territory. But Texas was admitted to the Union as a state in 1846, and in 1848 Williamson County was organized. As the countryside began to settle up, Moses Hughes must have felt stirrings of the adventurous restlessness that had driven him since adolescence.

Certainly he was intrigued by descriptions of the beautiful Hill Country springs beyond the Balcones Escarpment. By the time his wife's health weakened in 1853, Moses was eager to see new country again. His oldest sons, John and Joseph, were twelve and ten, old enough to help with building a new cabin and establishing a wilderness home. Enlisting his younger brother in the venture, Moses again embraced the challenges of a new frontier. "Myself and my brother Nimrod Hughes, were the first families that settled in the county. . . ."[6]

The Hughes families soon were followed by other pioneers with the same lust for new land and adventure. Robert McAnelly, a veteran frontiersman, already had penetrated the area, and he came to stay just after the Hughes brothers. A native of Kentucky, McAnelly came to Texas in 1835, served in the Revolution, and was awarded a land bounty of 1,476 acres—one-third of a league—by the Republic of Texas. McAnelly worked as a surveyor for German immigration companies. These surveying crews advanced in an east-west line from the south to the north, creating a grid of surveyed sections. Frontier surveyors generally worked in uninhabited country, occasionally came in contact with Native Americans, and learned the lay of the land. McAnelly took his land bounty at a bend of the Colorado River which boasted excellent soil— and which would form part of the western boundary of Lampasas County. McAnelly purchased other bounty certificates from Texas army veterans who had no intention of settling in this remote area, and his

Andrew Bell Burleson was the oldest son of John Burleson, who provided the townsite for the county seat, first named Burleson, but soon renamed Lampasas. At the age of twenty-five in 1856, A. B. Burleson became the first "chief justice" (county judge) of Lampasas County. —Courtesy of Sylvia Eddy

holdings grew to 3,212 acres beside the river. In 1850, when he was forty-four, McAnelly married twenty-year-old Sarah Jane Rowe. The couple would have nine children, and as McAnelly began his family he plunged again into the Hill Country to create a wilderness home.[7]

John Burleson, a noted veteran of the Texas Army, played a key role in the creation of Lampasas. Burleson fought with the volunteer army at the siege of San Antonio in 1835 and with Sam Houston's force during the final campaign of the war, serving under his distinguished brother, General Edward Burleson. After the Revolution John Burleson served the Army of the Republic of Texas and rode with Colonel John Moore against Comanches. Of course, he qualified for his own land bounty certificates, but he was given one for 1,280 acres by an older first cousin, also named John Burleson, that would provide the townsite for Lampasas. Originally dated April 26, 1838, this certificate was delivered to John Burleson (the younger) in July 1854. Burleson lived in Travis County, and was aware of the movement to the springs about seventy miles northwest of Austin. But his wife had just died, and he turned the certificate over to two daughters and their husbands: Elizabeth and George W. Scott, and Martha Jane and Robert Moore.[8]

The Scotts recognized opportunity. Following the restoration of Hannah Hughes' health after quaffing the sulphurous spring waters, a large number of health-seekers came to the springs to camp in the summer of 1854. The Burleson land certificate was two square miles and included several of the springs. A townsite was surveyed, including lots and a—presumed—courthouse square. There was not yet a county, so a courthouse was not yet required, but Elizabeth Burleson Scott insisted upon a square. The town would be named Burleson.

It was announced that town lots would go on sale on July 4, 1855. Early in the summer people began coming to the springs by the hundreds. By July it was estimated that six hundred campers and potential settlers had arrived at the springs. There were at least seventy-five tents in the grove beside the Upper Springs, and several ramshackle cabins were assembled. A preacher named Childress delivered the community's first sermon to campers.[9]

Many campers purchased fresh venison from a hunter named Pleasant Cox. Three years earlier Cox had migrated to Texas from Missouri with his wife, Martha, their three little boys, and other family members, settling in Williamson County. In 1855 Cox and his family joined the parade to the springs in a covered wagon. An energetic frontiersman in his mid-thirties, Cox hunted deer to supply meat to the campers, which allowed him to scout the countryside for a promising homesite.[10]

Everyone who came was struck by the handsome country. "The scenery is rather picturesque and romantic, than grand or wild," reported a journalist from LaGrange, east of Austin. "In approaching the springs by the Austin road the valley of the Sulphur Fork Lampasas, opens the door to view at once; and in prospective view arises the beautiful array of the 'Lampasas peaks.' Way off to the south are seen two or three oval shaped hills, and just before you the tremendous cone or pyramid looms up, while away to the north you behold a large flat top mountain—all well defined against the sky. . . . The valley is all timbered apparently as if it were covered with a carpeting of cloud green. But the most striking feature that we observed on the road was a peculiar mountain off to the right. It is seen during a whole days [*sic*] travel . . . continually changing its form and dimension. . . . It is called 'Beason's Hill.' By ascending the side of the valleys we can command a panoramic view—worth a trip of fifty miles to see. Yonder to my right is the 'wagon and team' mount, for the clusters of trees thereon remind me of a loader wagon—with a long team and driver, winding over the summit. And yonder to the east are the 'Buffalo Hills,' for there still grazes a prodigious herd of the prairie monsters."[11]

The "Lampasas peaks," "oval shaped hills," "pyramid," "a large flat top mountain," "a peculiar mountain," the "Buffalo Hills"—none of the promontories that so impressed the LaGrange journalist loomed more than 1,500 or 1,600 feet above sea level. There were no "mountains," only hills, but the Hill Country was no less "picturesque and romantic"—and often beautiful. The topography of Texas is step-like, and the lower step encompasses the eastern third of Texas, where there are no elevations comparable to the rugged peaks of the Hill Country. (The next "step" is onto the Cap Rock Escarpment and the High Plains of the Panhandle, or the actual mountains of far West Texas.) The ravines and plateaus and rocky streams of the Hill Country offered a striking variety of scenery that Texans had not seen before they ventured across the Balcones Escarpment.

There was not a single town in the Hill Country until 1846, just seven years before Moses Hughes headed for the Lampasas springs. Seventy miles southwest of the springs, Fredericksburg was founded as a German colony by orderly farmers who were exposed to Comanche attacks. When F. M. Cross, a bold young frontiersman, rode across the land that became Lampasas County, "there were no white men. . . ."[12] But by the 1850s Texas was the fastest-growing state in the Union. The population of the Lone Star State nearly tripled from 1850 to 1860, soaring from 212,592 to 604,215. Population pressure sent Texans into the Hill Country in the 1850s, and Burnet County, just south of Lampasas Springs, was organized in 1854.

A year later, on Wednesday, July 4, 1855, town lots went on sale for the new community of Burleson. Eighteen blocks were laid out with eight lots per block, with each lot measuring sixty-nine feet by one hundred twenty-eight feet. Streets were sixty feet wide.[13] This site was north of the Sulphur Fork and just south of Hanna Springs, as it would become known, which was the second most prolific of the Lampasas springs, behind only the Upper Springs. The odor of sulphur was even stronger at Hanna Springs than at the Upper Springs, and some campers were beginning to pitch their tents near Hanna Springs.

The new townsite therefore would be located in a basin, with Sulphur Fork flowing from the southwest just below and past the eastern edge of the townsite on its way toward the Lampasas River, several miles to the east. A lesser stream, named Burleson Creek, meandered north of Hanna Springs and adjacent Cooper Springs, before joining the Sulphur Fork of the Lampasas River. The elevation of the townsite is just over one thousand feet above sea level.

Town lots were priced at $5.00, $7.50, $10.00, and $12.50. Within a few days about $2,000 worth of lots had been sold, including a few lots in a hastily-expanded townsite. The urban pioneers who ventured into the unsettled Hill Country to help form a frontier town wasted little time once they secured lots. Many who had been camping immediately moved their tents to their town property. Almost overnight "ten stores and shops" opened, mostly in tents, along with "two Daguerran rooms" (operated by photographers who soon moved on after the initial boom ended). "There is a market open all the time with the necessaries, and occasionally some luxuries—for the camp," reported the LaGrange journalist. George Scott hauled a load of lumber and merchandise from Houston by ox-drawn wagons and erected the town's first commercial building south of the square. About "8 or 10 dwelling cabins" went up, each housing "about four inmates. . . ."[14]

Sadly, the community already had a cemetery. On March 10, 1854, Rebecca Hughes died, no more than four months after she arrived. The Hughes family matriarch was buried south of Sulphur Fork in the first recorded grave in the region. Before the year ended Rebecca was joined by her twenty-year-old daughter-in-law, Nimrod's wife, Mary Frances. The new burial ground appropriately was named Pioneer Cemetery.[15]

Rebecca Hughes, mother of Moses and Nimrod, died in 1854 at fifty-two. She was the first person buried in Pioneer Cemetery, now called Cook Cemetery. —Photo by the author

While the fledgling town was taking shape, hundreds of campers stayed in the grove for summer recreation and to drink mineral water. "The drinking springs—called the 'box spring,' is always surrounded by a crowd of persons, 'drinking to their own health,' late and early" observed the reporter from LaGrange.[16]

There was such solid activity at the Upper Springs that George Scott decided to develop the big spring just north of the townsite. He cleaned out the marshy residue around the spring, uncovering buffalo bones from animals that had bogged down while seeking water. Accessibility to the spring was created with boards across the mire, a small hotel was built, and the name "Scott's White Sulphur Springs" was assigned. Several years later, John Hanna acquired the property, and following further development the facility became permanently known as "Hanna Springs."[17]

Meanwhile, Moses Hughes finished his small mill, a story-and-a-half structure on a rock foundation, along with a dam of logs and stones to channel the waters of the Sulphur Fork. The flimsy dam soon was swept away, so Hughes erected a substantial dam of rock and mortar that stood for decades before being dynamited to clear the way for twentieth century waterway improvements. Hughes ground both corn and wheat, because every household needed meal and flour. Business was steady, and soon Ambrose Bradley and John Casbeer each built a mill on Sulphur Fork near town.[18]

The town was only a few weeks old when a violent summer storm nearly flooded Sulphur Fork within a few hours. A house with eight people inside was struck by lightning, "smashing a table and killing two boys outside." Lightning also struck

The stone mill built by Moses Hughes stood for decades on the north bank of the Sulphur Fork at the east end of Fourth Street.
—Courtesy KSM

and killed a horse hitched to a buggy in town.[19] The fatal storm and near flood of the town in a basin was a portent of future cataclysm.

John Burleson came up from Austin to visit the new community that bore his name. Undoubtedly Burleson, a man of reputation and influential contacts, helped to advance plans that were being laid to organize Lampasas County. As Texans moved further west, new counties were created with extensive boundaries, so that still newer counties could be carved from existing counties. Burnet County, for example, was organized in 1854 from Bell, Travis, and Williamson counties. Also in 1854, Coryell County was created from Bell County. In this manner, Lampasas County would be created from Bell, Coryell and Travis counties. And in later years Hamilton County, in 1858, and Mills County, in 1887, would be organized in part from Lampasas County.

A key step in creating a new county was the submission to the state legislature of a petition signed by as many citizens as possible. The legislature of Texas met in regular session once every two years, and the Sixth Legislature convened in early 1856. Among the items under consideration was a "Petition of the citizens of the territory of Coryell County asking the creation of a new county." The petition respectfully pointed out that "the population of said territory has been rapidly increasing and is now sufficient to justify the organization of a new county. . . ." Mention was made of "the celebrated Lampasas Sulphur Springs" and that the adjacent town of Burleson was "the most logical point for the seat of justice for said County. . . ." Of course, there was no other town in the proposed county.[20]

The petition was signed by 135 male citizens of the region. The first man to sign was George Scott, who had laid out the townsite. Moses and Nimrod Hughes signed, and so did John Burleson and Robert McAnelly and Pleasant Cox, the hunter who already had settled his family on a choice homestead north of town on Lucy Creek. Dr. Hillary Ryan, the first physician to arrive at Lampasas Springs, signed the petition, along with pioneer miller Ambrose Bradley. John N. Gracy arrived in town in time to sign the petition; for decades he would operate a prominent hotel and be a key member of the community. Surveyor W. E. "Bill" Willis added his signature, then surveyed the boundaries of the new county and served as the first county surveyor.[21]

Texas already had a Burleson County, named after John Burleson's noted brother, Gen. Edward Burleson. The most prominent feature of the new county was the Lampasas River, which ran north to south through

the eastern part of the county before angling into Bell County and joining the Leon River a few miles below Belton, where the two rivers formed
the Little River.

The most likely men to have discovered and christened the Lampasas River, probably at or near its confluence, were scouts of the 1720
Aguayo Expedition, a force of 500 soldiers led by Governor Miguel de
Aguayo from San Antonio to the vicinity of present-day Waco. Later there
were other expeditions, associated with the establishment of Franciscan
missions among various tribes of Texas Indians. Another Franciscan mission recently had been founded in the pueblo of Lampazos in the
Mexican state of Nuevo Leon. Perhaps a priest or soldier thought of
Lampazos when naming the Texas river. Another possibility stems from
the meaning of the Spanish word *lampazos*—"burdock," one of several
plants with burs, large leaves, and a strong smell, which may have lined
the riverbank. A less likely possibility is the suggestion that Lampasas
derived from a Native American word for "water lily." Whether Spanish
or Native American, the word was Anglicized to "Lampasas."[22]

So on February 1, 1856, the Sixth Legislature authorized the formation of Lampasas County, and designated the town of Burleson as county
seat. But the name Burleson never caught on. "Lampasas Springs" was
a common designation, and Lampasas was an obvious name for the seat
of Lampasas County. When the Sixth Legislature officially organized
Lampasas County on March 10, 1856, the town of Lampasas was
named as county seat.[23]

Funding was not available to build a proper courthouse. Indeed, a
quarter of a century would pass before a courthouse would be erected on
the square—and it would be a magnificent structure. But at first a small
frame building on the south side of the square served as the seat of justice, while county officials operated out of any office space they could
find. The square offered shade trees, parking for wagons and saddle
horses, and, in time, a water well for the public.

But there was a growing number of merchants and artisans, lawyers
and doctors, as more and more urban pioneers tried their luck in the new
frontier town. There were mills, small hotels, and boarding houses to accommodate the hundreds of summer campers who flocked to the springs
each "watering season." The Lampasas business community enjoyed a
spurt of activity and revenue each summer comparable to the modern
Christmas season. For Lampasas the future offered growth and excitement—and danger.

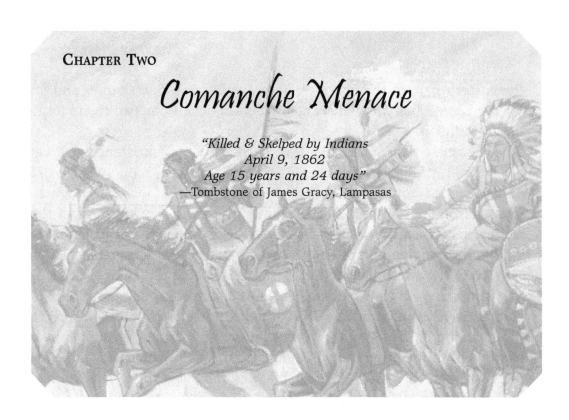

CHAPTER TWO

Comanche Menace

"Killed & Skelped by Indians
April 9, 1862
Age 15 years and 24 days"
—Tombstone of James Gracy, Lampasas

It did not take long for Comanche warriors to notice the growing community of settlers around the Lampasas springs. Comanches knew the location of every source of water within the vast range of their raiding expeditions. Decades earlier these ferocious warriors had expelled Tonkawas from their longtime campsites around the springs, and since then Comanches doubtless had utilized the waters regularly on their far-ranging journeys.

"In 1857 the Indians became very troublesome, killing people and stealing horses . . .," related Moses Hughes, who came to Lampasas Springs in 1853. He built the town's first cabin, but in 1856 he moved his family to a two-story, four-room stone house he erected seven miles west of Lampasas Springs. The structure could be defended, and Hughes was a good shot. He was not scared back into town despite several encounters with warriors. "I have been chased by the redskins seven times, and once had my horse shot out from under me. I was surrounded by seven of them and outran them by working in the lead for a mile and a half. Then I thought that a good thicket would beat a bad run, so I made for the thicket, and on stopping, I found that my horse had an arrow in his flank. . . ."[1]

Hughes drew a bead on a warrior riding about seventy yards away, "and at the crack of the rifle, I saw him straighten himself and he gave a yell." Unwilling to challenge his marksmanship further, the raiders galloped out of sight. Hughes led his wounded mount to the nearby home of Thomas Espy, who had medical training, but the horse died.

Hughes survived this and half a dozen more encounters with Comanches. Other Lampasans would not be so fortunate. From 1857 through 1874, usually in the spring and summer, Comanches raided at will in Lampasas County. The raiders stole large numbers of horses, often at night under a "Comanche Moon," and sometimes murdered and mutilated unwary settlers. This long Comanche menace retarded population growth, forced many settlers to leave for a safer county, and filled others who stayed with a nagging fear. The *Lampasas Dispatch* reported that in 1871, the year the newspaper was founded, "the population of the county was only about fifteen hundred, and they lived in constant dread of the murdering savages of the plains. . . ."[2]

Comanches terrorized the Texas frontier for forty years, beginning with the Parker Massacre of 1836. For the next four decades settlers near the Texas frontier line were subject to vicious attacks. As Spanish and Mexican Texans already had learned, Anglo Texans discovered that Comanches were ferocious warriors, superb horsemen who appeared without warning, descending pitilessly upon homesteads or travelers. Men and older boys were slain, often after torture and mutilation and scalping. Men taken alive were staked out on their backs with eyelids removed, with genitalia and extremities and tongues amputated, with fire applied to their worst wounds. Women invariably were gang-raped by the raiding party, and sometimes mutilated. Infants were killed in front of their mothers, but children were taken captive—Comanches had learned that Anglos would pay dearly to ransom captured children. Many young captives—such as nine-year-old Cynthia Ann Parker—were forced to grow up among Comanches.[3]

Comanche warriors were magnificent horsemen, riding down opponents on foot with lances, or firing arrows at the gallop—their bows and arrows a repeating weapon that could be used from horseback. The principal weapon of Spanish or Mexican or Anglo adversaries was a single-shot, muzzle-loading firearm, and Comanches mounted on quick war ponies usually could charge before such guns could be reloaded. This advantage began to be lost during the 1840s, when Samuel Colt's new invention, the revolving pistol, was utilized by Texas Rangers in combat against Comanches. Early Colt revolvers were small weapons, difficult to reload and with only five chambers in the cylinder. But Texas Rangers under Captain Jack Hays carried two five-shooters each, and from horseback they had ten rounds without reloading. Soon Rangers obtained improvements: larger pistols with larger caliber balls, six chambers, a hinged ramrod-loader beneath the long barrel, a plow-handle grip that ideally fit the shooter's hand. Now Texas Rangers had twelve rounds that could be fired in a running fight, and other improvements were made in revolvers during the 1850s. Counties—including Lampasas—that became the target of Comanche raids often requested a supply of revolvers from the state.

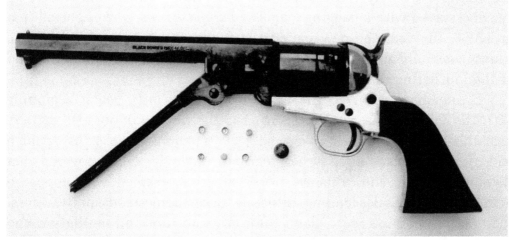

Utilized by Texas Rangers in horseback combat against Comanche warriors, Sam Colt's early, awkward five-shooters soon evolved into six-shooters with plow-grip handles and hinged loaders which rammed powder and shot into each of the six chambers in the revolving cylinder. Nipples behind each chamber were capped with fulminate of mercury percussion caps. Armed with two cap-and-ball revolvers, Rangers or citizen members of pursuit parties could fight effectively from horseback. —Photo by the author

Comanches measured wealth in horses, with a warrior often possessing more than one hundred and a chief more than one thousand. Comanches therefore became incomparable horse thieves. Just after the Civil War Georgiana Greenwood moved to Lampasas from Belton as a young bride, and she quickly learned that Comanches "made frequent and terrifying raids on the settlers." When a traveler stayed overnight at a small cabin beside the home of her brother-in-law, Columbus Greenwood, he was warned to secure his horse carefully. The traveler tied his mount to the doorknob of the little cabin, "but to his amazement next morning the horse was gone." Georgiana added that "Indians were so stealthy that they could do a trick like this and the victim never be aware of their presence."[4]

When the War with Mexico ended in 1848, the U.S. Army was able to turn its attention to protecting the frontier of the State of Texas. A line of forts was erected to screen the settlements, from Fort Worth on the north down to Fort Martin Scott at Fredericksburg. The nearest outpost to Lampasas Springs was Fort Croghan, a small cluster of log buildings a little more than twenty miles south of the springs. In the other direction, about fifty miles northeast, stood Fort Gates. Frontier "forts" were unfortified, because the army found that hit-and-run horse raiders had no intention of attacking a military base. Unique to Texas frontier forts, Gates was enclosed by a stockade.[5]

This line of forts was built in 1848 and 1849 by garrison labor and at little cost to the government. By 1853, when Moses Hughes led his family to Lampasas Springs, the westward movement in Texas had passed by the original line of protective forts. These posts were abandoned and a new line farther west was built and garrisoned. Fort Mason, Camp Colorado, and Fort Phantom Hill were closest to Lampasas Springs, but all were a ride of two days or more away, and presumably formed a protective screen well to the west of Lampasas.

But hard-riding Comanche raiders easily slipped between the forts and struck unguarded settlers, murdering and riding away with captives and livestock. Settlers rode in pursuit, and so did any Texas Rangers within the vicinity. The army tried to cut off these raiding parties, but the forts were garrisoned with infantry. Military pursuit was conducted in wagon or on muleback, and offered scant deterrence to horseback warriors.

The Secretary of War from 1853 until 1857 was Jefferson Davis, a West Point graduate and a combat hero of the War with Mexico. Davis was the ablest secretary of war the nation had yet seen, and he upgraded the army significantly. His innovations included the U.S. Camel Corps, introducing camels as pack animals to Texas and the arid Southwest. Assessing the operations of Comanches and counter tactics of Texas Rangers, Secretary Davis decided to organize a regiment of cavalry, an elite fighting force that attracted ambitious officers and non-commissioned officers. Although a cavalry regiment cost three to five times as much as an infantry regiment—for horses, hay and grain, saddles and bridles, revolvers and sabers—in 1855 Secretary Davis secured funding for the "Second Cavalry" (curiously, there was not a First Cavalry).

The Second Cavalry was commanded by Col. Albert Sidney Johnston, a Texan and future Confederate general. There were twelve future generals—more than in any other regiment in army history—among the officers of the Second, including Lt. Col. Robert E. Lee, Major William Hardee, and such aggressive captains and lieutenants as John Bell Hood, George H. Thomas, Edmund Kirby-Smith, Earl Van Dorn, and Fitzhugh Lee. The Second Cavalry, 750 men strong, was deployed to the outposts of the Texas frontier in 1856. The strategy called for constant patrols and instant pursuit of raiders. These relentless patrols and pursuits "were punishing to man and beast, and they used up corn and horses—but they were even more punishing to the Indians," stated Texas historian T. R. Fehrenbach. "By the end of 1856, the normal patrol traversed six hundred miles and remained in the field for thirty days."[6]

All of these military operations took place well to the west of Lampasas. Regimental headquarters was located at Fort Mason, more than eighty miles to the southwest, and other outposts were even more distant. If small raiding parties could make their way past the outposts, the still sparsely-settled communities—like Lampasas—lay unprotected. During the spring and summer, with their war ponies in prime condition, Comanches could ride hundreds of miles. Often they traveled long distances on moonlit nights—under a bright "Comanche Moon"—then concealed themselves throughout the day, before riding on the next night. Raiders regularly used the illumination of a Comanche Moon to steal horses at night while settlers slept.

As raiders descended upon Lampasas County, many settlers refused to be intimidated. The pioneers who ventured into unsettled territory steeled themselves to face hardships and a certain amount of danger. Thomas Espy spoke for many others when he wrote the governor, in the wake of a series of raids: "Our people are not alarmed [,] the time for fear has passed and now we want revenge [.]" How to seek revenge? How to retaliate? "The whole frontier wishes to engage in expeditions against the Comanche. . . ."[7]

Early in 1858 Comanche raiders captured a number of horses in Lampasas County, then headed northwest with the stolen herd. An impromptu pursuit party caught up with the raiders and killed some of the thieves. When the raids continued through the summer, more than eighty Lampasans—including Moses Hughes and R. D. McAnelly and a redoubtable new settler, Samuel W. Sparks—signed a petition requesting "aid & protection" from Governor Hardin Runnels. A month later, when word reached Lampasas "of a horrid massacre" of the family of Joshua Jackson, more than fifty men signed a petition to the governor volunteering to form a company "for six months Service on our immediate frontier—" Governor Runnels respectfully declined their offer, but promised to call on the commander at Camp Colorado (near Coleman) for military assistance.[8]

Lampasas County "Chief Justice" (county judge) Williamson Jones informed the governor that Lampasas had to organize "a vollentier [sic] company" in order "to ward off the tomehawks and scalping knife from our wives and children [sic]." But Lampasas fighting men needed to borrow "State arms." A week later Lampasas Notary Public B. S. Whitaker reported to the governor that he had ridden to the site of the Jackson massacre and had seen the corpses of Mr. and Mrs. Jackson and a son, while a younger son and two daughters had been taken captive. About thirty citizens rode after a large party of raiders who had captured several horses, but the Lampasas men "are poorly mounted and worse armed."[9]

Soon the appeal for help from the governor's office was taken up by Dr. Hillary Ryan, who was a personal friend of Governor Runnels. Apparently Dr. Ryan had been in Austin attempting to obtain authorization and assistance for a company from Lampasas, but he returned only with a letter of polite refusal. "Your letter was read to the Citizens [and] they seemed disappointed that I did not get a company." Dr. Ryan wrote the governor on October 30, 1858, the day he returned to town. He learned that one of the Jackson sisters had been found murdered. "One of her Breasts was cut off and her person otherwise badly butchered."[10]

Dr. Ryan was dismayed that conditions had worsened during his absence. "Today I arrived home and found our people much more alarmed than when I left—large numbers have moved on into Counties below this. . . ." Several families who abandoned their homesteads had been persuaded to stop in Lampasas, "and every house in town is full—all free of rent [.]" Families that stayed in the countryside forted up—"None daring to attend their business." Dr. Ryan immediately rode to Camp Colorado, where he was impressed by the commander of the little outpost, Lt. John Bell Hood. But Hood had only thirty men, and they were busy erecting barracks. When Dr. Ryan reported this trip to the governor, he repeated that "the citizens above Lampasas had either left or forted up. . . ."[11]

A few weeks later, eight raiders stole horses along the Colorado

River, then drove the stolen animals northward. Eight men pursued promptly, catching up with the raiders soon after they crossed into Hamilton County. A running fight ensued and the raiders were mauled, with two killed and three wounded, and sixteen horses were recovered. Both dead Comanches were scalped, and the scalp of the mutilated "Miss Jackson" was taken from a dead warrior. All three scalps were sent to the military.[12]

Dr. Ryan helped to organize a militia troop, "the Belton company," in May 1859, asking the governor for four mules and pack saddles, and "for some Six Shooters." Then, on the Fourth of July, beleaguered Lampasans organized "a Military Company to be known as the Lampasas Guards." Dr. Ryan doubtless was the guiding force, and he was elected captain, while Moses Hughes was elected first lieutenant. A brief constitution and by-laws were drawn up, and more than sixty volunteers affixed their signatures. Seven squads of eight or nine men apiece were organized, with the objective of week-long "Scouts," or patrols, throughout the county. Each scout would commence on a Thursday. Captain Ryan would lead "Scout No. 1" the first week, First Lieutenant Hughes would lead Scout No. 2 the second week, and so on through all seven squads, when the rotation would begin again. "If we do not catch the Indians we may keep them out of our immediate frontier.   H. RYAN *Captain*"[13]

The aggressive efforts of the U.S. Army and the Texas Rangers at last began to drive Comanches back into the northern depths of Comancheria. But early in 1861 Texas seceded from the Union and joined the Confederate States of America. (There was only a handful of slaves in Lampasas County, and many Lampasans agreed with the pre-Union sentiments of Governor Sam Houston, voting for secession by a turnaround margin of only six votes, 85-75.) Federal troops in Texas, a significant contingent of the pre-Civil War U.S. Army, withdrew from the Lone Star State, abandoning the frontier outposts. The Civil War erupted in April 1861, and during the next four years more than 60,000 of 92,000 Texas men between the ages of seventeen and forty-five served in military units. Texas was the only Confederate state with a frontier exposed to Indian attack, but the C.S.A. was compelled to focus all of its military resources to battle vast Union armies.

Comanches seized this opportunity to return to their familiar raiding grounds. In November 1861 the Texas State Legislature created the Frontier Regiment to protect the frontier counties. Some of the old army outposts were used as patrol and pursuit bases, but the Frontier Regiment was spread thinly across the vast expanse of the Texas frontier. Small war parties began to appear everywhere, and raids increased after the Frontier Regiment was incorporated into the manpower-starved Confederate Army late in 1863.

Defense of the frontier would fall upon local militia units. In 1861 more than forty Lampasans formed the "Lampasas Minute Men." Former county judge Williamson Jones was elected captain, and the Minute Men operated scouting squads like the Lampasas Guards of 1859.[14] Indeed, in September 1861 Captain Jones led a hot pursuit of Comanches who had just stolen sixty-five horses, and the stolen animals were recovered, although the eight raiders escaped. Also in 1861 the multi-county 27th Brigade of Texas Militia was organized, including such Lampasans as Second Lieutenant Moses Hughes, Dr. Hillary Ryan, Nimrod Hughes. R. D. McAnelly, Pleasant Cox, John N. Gracy, and future sheriff Albertus Sweet. In 1862 Captain Hillary Ryan commanded a company including Lampasas men in Col. R.T.P. Allen's Regiment of Texas Infantry. Later Lampasas was designated part of the Second Frontier District patrolled by Texas State Troops. All able-bodied men in a tier of frontier counties from the Red River to the Rio Grande were organized into militia units, and at least one-fourth of the men were to be in the field at all times. Off-duty soldiers could protect their own families, but following a Comanche raid as many men as possible rode in hot pursuit. Militia members had to furnish their own mounts, guns, ammunition, and rations.[15]

The roster of these militia companies fluctuated constantly, in large part because so many frontier families moved to safer counties. John Higgins, who moved to Lampasas County with his wife and five children in 1857, retreated east into Bell County in 1859. But the Higgins family returned to Lampasas County in 1862, and John became a thirty-nine-year-old private in the Second Regiment of the 27th Brigade of Texas Militia.[16] When John was away from the family on militia duty, responsibility for protecting the home fell on the shoulders of his oldest son, John Calhoun Pinkney "Pink" Higgins. Pink was eleven in 1862, fourteen when the Civil War ended, but he was tall for his age and an excellent rifle shot. Shortly after the Civil War, John began to protect his home while teenaged Pink rode with pursuit posses. Boys grew to manhood early on the frontier.

For years Pink rode with pursuit posses, later reporting that he "fought [Comanches] all over the western part of Texas." During these combats he was wounded twice, once in the leg and once in the foot. Pursuit parties often used Tonkawas as trackers. Having been driven from their homelands by the Comanches, "Tonks" were eager to help white men hunt their longtime enemies. Tonkawas were known to be cannibals, but they ate the flesh of Comanches not for nourishment but to absorb the courage of these ferocious warriors. Following one fight against Comanches, Pink broiled a piece of buffalo meat over coals. When a Tonkawa scout squatted before the fire with a piece of meat on a stick, Pink ordered, "Quit letting that greasy beef drip on my buffalo."[17]

"Him no beef," replied the Tonkawa. "Him Comanche."

One of the saddest trage-

John H. Higgins brought his family to Lampasas County in 1857, when he was thirty-four. Comanche depredations forced a retreat to Bell County, but the Higgins family returned to their ranch in 1862. John and his oldest son, Pink, took turns riding with pursuit posses or guarding the family home. —Courtesy Betty L. Giddens

dies of the early years of Lampasas began to unfold in April 1862. Fifteen-year-old James Gracy was sent by his father, John Gracy, owner of the Star Hotel in Lampasas, to gather horses west of town. John was a militia member and knew the dangers lurking in the countryside, but he seemed to feel that James, second oldest of his seven children, could perform the chore safely.

James spent Thursday night, April 10, at the cabin of Thomas Dawson, nine miles from Lampasas. The next morning Gracy and thirteen-year-old John Stockman, who lived with Dawson, went out on foot to round up the horses. A couple of miles from the cabin, Stockman ventured into a grove of scrub trees to hunt turkey.[18]

Suddenly a party of about fifteen warriors appeared, driving at least one hundred horses. Spotting young Gracy, three warriors galloped to him, dismounted, stripped off his clothes, and scalped him where he stood. Then they released him, but as Gracy frantically ran away, they filled him with arrows.

Just as the Comanches were about to go after Stockman, a party from Austin blundered onto the scene. George Baker was astride a horse, while his wife, baby, and elderly father-in-law rode in a buggy. Several warriors stayed with their horse herd, but the others charged Baker and his family. Armed with a rifle and pistols, Baker covered a retreat to a thicket of timber and brush about two hundred yards away. Baker killed one warrior and wounded another, although he was repeatedly struck by arrows. An arrow passed through a blanket and pierced his baby, but the arrowhead only broke the flesh.

As his family found cover, Baker collapsed from his wounds. Mrs. Baker pulled the arrows from his body and tried to stop the bleeding. Then she took up her husband's weapons.

Meanwhile, the buggy horse bolted in the direction of Dawson's cabin, dragging the careening vehicle behind. Dawson caught sight of the pursuit. He mounted one of his horses and galloped toward Lampasas for help. Within a mile of his home he encountered a four-man hunting party, who galloped to the rescue and drove off the warriors.

Baker was carried in a litter to the nearby cabin of Thomas Espy, where John Stockman already had fled. The wounded man spent several weeks in bed, then he was taken to his home where he finally recovered. On the evening of the fight a party went to find Gracy, but he could not be located in the darkness. The next morning the nude corpse was found and taken into town to his grief-stricken family. The murdered youngster was buried behind the Star Hotel. His tombstone proclaimed: "Killed & Skelped by Indians."

At fifteen James Gracy was scalped, then murdered by Comanche raiders. He was buried behind the Star Hotel, owned by his father, but in recent years his remains and gravestone were moved to the family plot at Oak Hill Cemetery. —Photo by the author

The raids continued in the vicinity throughout the war years and be-yond. Even after the Confederate surrender in 1865, the U.S. Army did not regarrison the Texas frontier. During the first two years of Reconstruction, Federal troops served as an occupation army in the set-tled portions of Texas. Frontier Texas, therefore, continued to be ravaged: from 1865 until July 1867, at least 163 Texans were killed by warriors, another two dozen were wounded, and forty-three were taken captive. In addition, more than 3,000 horses were stolen, as well as over 30,000 head of cattle. There was a voracious market for cattle on the new ranches of New Mexico and Arizona territories. Comanchero traders from New Mexico sought out Comanches, exchanging repeating rifles for cattle. Comanches began to steal more cattle in Texas than horses. In re-turn they could offset the Texas advantage of revolving pistols in combat with Spencer and Winchester rifles. Admittedly their new rifles were more complex weapons that often fell into disrepair, and the right caliber of ammunition could he hard to obtain, but Comanche raiders now went after cattle as much as horses—and settlers.

In 1867 the state of Texas compiled "A Tabular Statement" of forty frontier counties, requesting from the county judges specific information regarding damages from "Indian Depredations" during the two years since the end of the Civil War. Montague County on the Red River was just south of the Comanche Reservation in Oklahoma, and in two years 11,620 head of cattle were stolen, along with 191 horses. Jack County, adjacent to Montague County on the south, lost an estimated 5,000 cattle. Uvalde and El Paso counties each reported twenty-nine deaths. Lampasas County reported eight settlers killed, the fifth highest total among the forty counties, and 409 horses stolen, the second highest total, after Parker County's 454. Lampasas County also reported one captive taken and 400 stolen cattle.[19]

Speaking of the years immediately after the war in Lampasas, Georgiana Greenwood reminisced that: "We were compelled to tie our horses up at night to prevent the Indians from stealing them. They stole most all of our horses at different times but one horse in particular which my husband was foolish about we hated to lose. This horse he had named 'Hannibal' and had been offered $500 for. One night the Indians slipped in and stole him. My husband and the pursuing party found him later in the day dead on the trail with all legs cut off."[20]

C. C. Carter raised horses on his ranch northwest of Lampasas. The father of sixteen children, Carter was in his forties during the Civil War, but he served with the Lampasas Minute Men and in the Texas State Troops. On April 22, 1866, Carter was out looking for horses when he was jumped by Comanches. Badly wounded by an arrow, he eluded the war party and made it to a neighbor's house. Carter staggered onto the front gallery, collapsed and died. Buried on his own property, Carter's grave was the first in what became Center Cemetery. On the same day, Comanches also killed a settler named Joseph Bond.[21]

Later in the year, on July 7, a sweeping raid by a "horde of Indians" gathered a herd of ninety-two stolen horses. One of the victims was T. H. Adams, who rode with a pursuit posse; another member of the posse was Mary Cochran, whose husband was away from home. In frustration Adams dashed off a letter to Governor J. W. Throckmorton. "Depredation[s] are bring Committed by them dayley [sic]," fumed Adams. A week later Adams, along with Moses Hughes and fifty-seven other Lampasas County citizens, signed a petition to Governor Throckmorton "that for more than one year past the frontier has received no protection from the General Government," and that Comanche "raids have increased [sic] in number [,] boldness and Violence. . . . Whole settlements have been broken up, families reduced from affluence to want, the rewards of a lifetime of industry have passed off before their eyes [,] the scalping knife not unfrequently [sic] used. . . ."[22]

A few weeks later W. B. Pace, Chief Justice of Lampasas County, and four other Lampasas citizens sent a report of recent Comanche raids, "which are now of almost daily occurrence. It is not our wish to exaggerate, the reality is bad enough. It will be observed that these depredations are now extended to Cattle, and not confined, mostly, as heretofore, to horses. . . . This county used to count its horses by thousands, now scarcely a hundred can be mustered, and still the work goes on, each moon, diminishes the number of stock and settlers. . . ."[23]

Reports such as these and appeals for help continued to pour into Austin from Lampasas and other frontier counties, and finally the Reconstruction government responded. In 1867 the army returned to the frontier, upgrading and re-garrisoning many of the older forts, and establishing three new outposts: Fort Richardson, Fort Griffin, and Fort Concho. But none of the reopened or new forts were near Lampasas, and Comanches continued to raid throughout the county. So a cavalry detail sometimes was assigned to Lampasas, camping in the grove at Hancock Springs. There were no permanent buildings, so this little outpost was not designated "fort" or even "camp." Beginning in 1867 and off and on for the next few years, the encampment at Hancock Springs was known to the military as "Post at Lampasas."[24]

But the sporadic presence of soldiers at Lampasas did little to halt Comanche raiders. On January 30, 1868, a Lampasas youngster named Prince Ryan was sent to find a cow that had strayed away from the house. Not far from town he was jumped and killed by raiders. Buried at the Pioneer Cemetery, Ryan was murdered six days after his fifteenth birthday.[25]

More than a year later a man named Peacock was killed while riding with a militia patrol, "Guard Group Number Five," north of Lampasas. A band of Comanches was encountered, including a warrior who wore a red shirt. Spurring his mount, Peacock shouted, "Watch me plug that red shirt." Peacock surged ahead of the patrol, but a warrior suddenly turned and loosed a fatal arrow. A seven-man pursuit force intercepted the raiders about ten miles from the murder site. During the subsequent running fight, Joe Straley closed in on a warrior. Suddenly Straley's stirrup strap broke and he tumbled to the ground. His adversary, thinking he had wounded Straley, charged Joe, who shot the warrior off his pony. Three warriors were killed in the fight, but none of the posse members was wounded.[26]

In August 1870 a large Comanche party "made a raid near our town, and drove off quite a number of fine horses." Several days later Lampasan P. H. Healy was returning to town in a wagon. About ten miles west of Lampasas he was attacked "by the red fiends of hell." Armed only with a revolver, he was killed and scalped. "His body was found a few days afterwards most horribly mutilated. . . ." Little wonder that "people are warned to keep on the lookout for the lurking, murderous, thieving red skins."[27]

One pioneer family wrote about the long years of danger in Lampasas County in a series of lengthy letters to each other. James and Sarah McCrea moved with their growing family (ten children were born between 1840 and 1863) from Brenham to the Lampasas frontier in 1855. James had received a land grant bequest of 1,400 acres, and the McCreas established a pioneer home on Yancey Creek, about nine miles west of the new community at Lampasas Springs.

Immediately the family learned to stay alert for Comanche raiders: "we all keep on the look out for there is no telling when they will come. . . ." In February 1861 Sarah McCrea wrote to her daughter, Mary Frances "Frank" Supple, a young bride, about recent alarms: "We

James and Sarah McCrea came to Lampasas County in the 1850s, erecting a log cabin west of town. Within a year a second cabin was built nearby, but in 1867 the large family moved into a big cedar log cabin which still stands. For nearly two decades the family was exposed to Comanche raiders. —Courtesy Sylvia Eddy

was surrounded for thre[e] days" by three raiding parties. "Ther[e] was nine indiens [*sic*] and a white man in each party." Benjamin Van Hook and a man named Skaggs were slain, a neighbor saw his bell cow and her calf killed, James McCrea was cut off from his cabin for a time, and the raiders stole a number of horses. "Thay made a clean sweap purty near [*sic*]. [I] never hav[e] felt like they wo[ul]d get my skelp till now." Sarah sent a lock of hair so "you may hav[e] it if the indiens gets oure skelps [*sic*]."[28]

Sarah managed to keep her scalp, and the next year wrote to Mary Frances that again they were "in a bad way with the indiens [*sic*], the co[u]ntry is full of them." Sarah graphically described the murder of James Gracy and the subsequent fight between Comanches and the Baker family. The next year a description of one of the escapes of Moses Hughes was recorded, along with nearby thefts. "The Indians are worse than ever; the[y] have stolen all the horses in the country. . . ." By October 1865, although the Civil War had ended, there was no relief from Comanches in Lampasas County. A McCrea son, Len, wrote to a brother and sister that "the County is fool [full] of Indians. . . ."[29]

Margaret McCrea Ayns-
worth, the oldest daughter,
wrote to a brother and sister
about an incident that happened early in 1870. "The
Indians have been in a good
deal lately and stolen a good
many horses, [and] our men
had a fight with them . . .
two weeks ago but did not
kill any of them. There were
too many Indians for them;
but they took about a hundred head of horses from
them. . . ." The next year
Len wrote his brother John
about conditions in 1871.
"The Indians is in the country. They kild 2 Beeves
about 2 miles from here."
Sarah agreed that nothing
had improved, reporting
that the country remained
"full of indens" and that

*Sarah Baldwin McCrea (1821-1914) pioneered
Lampasas County with her husband while in her thirties. Sarah gave birth to ten children, she was an excellent horsewoman, and she was known as a healer.
She handed down memorable family correspondence
about frontier experiences in Lampasas County. —*
Courtesy Sylvia Eddy

there had been "2 fites below hear. 2 men woonded wone [one] Boy kyld
[*sic*]."[30] Sarah and her family had endured the mortal peril of Comanche
raiders for a decade and a half.

When he was eighty-three, in 1934, W. L. Bradley provided an account of a Comanche raid and subsequent pursuit that started at his
home on the outskirts of Lampasas in 1872. Bradley was twenty-one
and lived a little over one mile east of Lampasas on the road to Belton.
"Our horses were hobbled and one was staked just back of our house.
We stood guard until midnight, then we decided that the danger was over
for the night and went to bed."[31]

About two hours later everyone was awakened when two of their
horses ran back to the house. Bradley caught one of the mounts, saddled
up, and rode to Hancock Springs. "The U.S.A. soldiers were stationed
there and I reported the Indians to Major Greene," who organized a thir-
teen-man detail and appointed Bradley as guide. At dawn the pursuit

force took up the trail along the Belton road. The cavalry detachment was joined by six civilians listed by Bradley.

After fifteen miles the Comanches left the road and drove their stolen animals north into Coryell County. After another twenty miles Bradley found two mules and three horses belonging to his uncle. Then he spotted a warrior heading "off across the prairie riding my bay mare."

A moment later about seventeen Comanches climbed into position on a mountain and opened fire. A fight erupted, and Major Greene led a charge. A soldier was thrown from his horse near several warriors, but he managed to scramble on foot down the mountain to safety, "the happiest man I ever saw." Bradley's horse fell in the brush and rocks.

"I jumped up with my pistol in my hand," looked back for Indians, "and would have shot anything in sight," Bradley remembered. "I was scared good and proper."

Major Greene was the only casualty. Wounded in the side, he died two days later, according to Bradley. But there is no record of a Major Greene being killed in action in Texas in 1872, or in any other year during the Indian Wars. It is also unusual that a major would lead thirteen men into the field; normally a sergeant or perhaps a lieutenant would ride at the head of such a small command. Of course, Greene might have been a brevet major during the Civil War, then reverted to his regular army rank of lieutenant or captain after the war (George Armstrong Custer was brevetted a major general during the Civil War, but in 1866 he returned to his regular army rank of captain). But there is no record of an officer of any rank named Greene—or Green—who died in action in Texas.[32] Perhaps W. L. Bradley's memory played a few tricks when he reached his eighties.

Conditions were so bad by 1872 that "Company M of the Minute Men" was formed in August in Lampasas. There was a lieutenant, two sergeants, two corporals, and fifteen privates. The original volunteers included brothers Tom, Mart, Merritt, and Ben Horrell, as well as their brother-in-law, Bill Bowen. But by 1873 the clan left Company M because they were busy with cattle rustling and with serious difficulties with officers of the law. Indeed, the roster was reorganized in February 1873 and again in September 1873. Like the Lampasas Guards of 1859 and the Lampasas Minute Men of 1861-62, the Minute Men of 1872-73 tried to keep rotating patrols in the field.[33]

The final Comanche depredation in Lampasas County was the murder of Charles Peel on February 13, 1874. Peel, a native of England, was

riding from Coleman County to the town of Lampasas when he was attacked by eight warriors. Peel galloped away, but he was wounded, and
after a mile he fell from his horse. The Comanches stripped Peel and rid-
dled him with bullets. Two men witnessed the fatal chase from a distance, and Peel was buried in a lonely grave in the shadow of San Saba
Peak in northwestern Lampasas County. (In 1887 this portion of the
county was broken off to help form Mills County.)[34]

By 1874 buffalo hunters virtually had destroyed the immense bison
herds that provided the staff of life for Comanches and the other horseback tribes. In June 1874 Comanches launched an attack in force against
a group of hide hunters at Adobe Walls in the Texas Panhandle. Although
these heavily-armed professional marksmen beat off their attackers, the
Battle of Adobe Walls ignited the Red River War of 1874-75. The army
launched a four-column convergence onto the High Plains of Texas, the
heart of Comancheria. In 1875 the last bands of Comanches were
hounded onto the reservation at Fort Sill. Afterward, even when small
parties of would-be warriors broke off the reservation, there was no way
for them to subsist, and soon they reluctantly returned to reservation
life.

At last the seemingly endless procession of Comanche raids came to
an end. Lampasans of the 1850s, 1860s, and 1870s had lived in dread,
year after bloody year, of Comanche war parties sweeping through the
countryside, stealing horses and cattle, and committing brutal murders.
Growth of Lampasas and of the county long had been retarded by recur-
ring Comanche depredations. Now, two decades after Lampasas was
founded, an important step in civilizing the region had been accomplished, and development of the frontier town could proceed in a notably
more secure environment.

CHAPTER THREE

Watering Seasons at Lampasas Springs

*"A goodly number are still at the hotels,
but the watering season may now be said to be over. . . ."*
—*Lampasas Daily Times*, August 29, 1878

When Moses Hughes sought the healing powers of Lampasas Springs for his wife in 1853, there already were several mineral springs in Texas where ailing Texans went to find cures by bathing and imbibing the waters. Lampasas Springs soon took its place in the long tradition of drinking and bathing at mineral springs in America and around the world.

"In classical Greece, waters with distinct tastes, smells, or colors often represented the abodes of gods and spirits," asserted Dr. Janet Valenza in her masterful history of the mineral springs and resorts of Texas. "People erected altars near sacred springs where they celebrated recovery by placing crutches, bandages, and replicas of diseased organs around their edges. Coins or small objects thrown into the water served as tokens of supplication or gratitude."[1]

Romans founded hundreds of bathing establishments throughout their vast empire. As many of these baths as possible were built where there were mineral waters, including, most famously, Bath in England. Temples and military hospitals were erected near these "sacred water sources." Along the Rhine River more than twenty "Bad" (bath) designations (Bad Hoffen, Bad Tonnistein, Bad Ragaz, etc.) indicated bath locations, including Bad Munster in the cliff-lined Nahe-Valley, a thermal spa and climatic health resort for people suffering from rheumatism and respiratory complaints.

By the 1700s Bath and other watering resorts were centers of social and recreational and gambling activities, along with taking the waters. English colonists in America brought bathing traditions with them to the New World, where Native Americans already frequented mineral springs. During the 1700s Saratoga Springs in New York became America's best-known mineral springs, and during the 1800s Saratoga Springs became famous not only for watering resorts but for gambling and horse racing. In the South, many watering resorts were in rural areas, where there might be a single hotel with adjacent rows of cottages, such as White Sulphur Springs in western Virginia. In addition to taking the waters, Southerners enjoyed dancing, card games, billiards, shooting, boxing, and horse racing. George Washington and Thomas Jefferson took the waters, and in the summers after the Civil War Robert E. Lee brought his family for leisurely vacations at White Sulphur Springs and other resorts.

Most early Texas settlers were natives of the South and were well aware of the Southern traditions of taking the waters and of the presumed healing qualities of mineral springs. One of the earliest resorts in Texas grew up at Sour Lake, in what became Hardin County. Development began at the springs around the lake, and by the 1850s there was a hotel, bath houses, and more than two dozen other buildings on the grounds. Hoping to relieve the discomfort of old wounds, Sam Houston came to Sour Lake in 1863—only a few weeks before he died.[2]

Several miles north of Sour Lake the discovery of another spring led to the development of a modest resort named Saratoga, an optimistic reference to Saratoga Springs, New York. Another hopeful reminder of a famous resort was White Sulphur Springs, opened in Anderson County in the 1830s. Comparatively large resorts were developed at Dalby Springs in Bowie County and at Sutherland Springs in Wilson County, both in the 1840s, and Hynson's Iron Mountain in Harrison County during the 1850s. Indeed, nearly a score of health resorts began to develop, generally as campgrounds, during the 1850s—most notably at Lampasas Springs.

Springs form when surface water—rain or snow—seeps through pores and cracks in the soil into layers of rock. Finally reaching a layer through which it cannot pass, the water—now termed ground water—collects underground until it finds a way through a crack or channel in the rock. Flowing to the surface, many of these springs contain minerals dissolved from rock by the moving water. The Lampasas area boasted at least seven mineral springs, with a high content of sulphur and other minerals.

"There are seven springs of different mineral qualities—Sulphur predominating it all," reported a journalist from LaGrange in 1855. "There are also two chalybeate springs [containing salts of iron, and tasting of iron], and two called pure. There is another beside that has a soft salt taste."[3]

"We believe the Lampasas Springs of this county equal to any Sulphur water in the world," stated Dr. Hillary Ryan in 1858. As perhaps the most articulate community leader and booster of the 1850s, Dr. Ryan described the principal springs of Lampasas: "Hancock's, or the upper Springs, were those first used. . . . The largest one is used for bathing—the others for drinking. Mr. Scott's Spring, one mile below Hancock's, contains more salt than the others, and may suit some better. It is not so pleasant to drink. Persons drinking the water of the Hancock's Spring, became very fond of it, and will not drink any other willingly."[4]

Dr. Ryan, the first physician in Lampasas, evaluated the medical effects of the springs: "The diseases most readily relieved are those incident to a malarious country, such as chronic diseases, intermittent fevers, biliary and gastric derangements. One case of diabetes has been relieved. Diseases of the kidneys are readily relieved. As a place of resort, for pleasure, these springs offer every inducement, and merchants and planters will find it less expensive and more pleasant to spend the season here, than to go North."[5]

Certainly it was inexpensive to come to Lampasas Springs. Families came by wagon, camping en route, then camping without charge near the Lampasas Springs. "I have seen as much as 20 acres of ground solidly covered at one time with tents . . ., especially during the summer season," reminisced F. M. Cross, an adventurous frontiersman who saw Lampasas in its earliest days.[6]

In the summer of 1855, the second watering season at Lampasas Springs, there were as many as seventy-five tents near the Upper Springs and an estimated total of six hundred people gathered around the new townsite. The drinking springs were "always surrounded by a crowd," and early each day "the beautiful grove around is occupied by persons who retire there to respire the gaseous sulphur, with which the air seems to be more replete at that time." The reporter from LaGrange also observed that the sulphur water and gasses "are somewhat offensive to the newcomer but soon become rather pleasant than otherwise after a few days—in fact he will prefer it to any other. The water is of rather bluish color, and even in the darkness of night looks clear as if phosphorous was a component."[7]

Three years later, in October 1858, brothers T. P. and R. A. Dawson arrived in Lampasas from Tennessee with a couple of wagonloads of tobacco. Two days later, on Sunday, October 24, they attended a camp meeting, and their Sabbath experiences were recorded in a diary: "Clear and pleasant. All went to church at the Springs. Saw some of the Texas girls of Lampasas. Some talk and excitement of Indians above here."[8]

For decades preachers found Sunday summer crowds among the campers at Lampasas Springs. The Texas population was predominantly rural. In 1860, with a population of more than 600,000, Texas had only twenty towns with more than 1,000 citizens, and the largest "cities," Galveston and San Antonio, could boast a population of no more than 7,000 to 8,000. Most Texans lived on farms or ranches, or in farm villages. These isolated Texans welcomed camp meetings or preaching services by circuit-riders, as much for social as for religious reasons. With summer crowds of campers numbering in the hundreds, a preacher could ride to Lampasas Springs and address an assemblage far larger than his usual congregation. And if a preacher was not available, a man of learning or position—a doctor or judge—might be drafted to conduct a Sunday service.

On July 15, 1856, Rev. Richard Howard organized the Lampasas Baptist Church at Scott's Hotel, "At the White Sulphur Springs," north of the town square. Reverend Howard was employed by the Mission Board of the Southern Baptist Convention, and he moved his family to Burnet from Georgia to found churches in the area. During the watering season of 1856, with hundreds of campers at the village of Lampasas, Reverend Howard conducted services, then organized a Baptist church. Reverend Howard was nominal head of Lampasas Baptist Church until 1860, but he had other churches, and the congregation stabilized at just seventeen permanent members. For years no other denomination even organized a congregation, and the little group of Baptists did not have the resources to erect a church building until 1872. But as each annual watering season approached, Lampasas Baptist Church members could provide a religious nucleus for the large number of summer visitors who were spiritually inclined.[9]

The shady grove at Hancock Springs was an ideal location for camp meetings, and in time a sizeable brush arbor was fashioned. An energetic circuit preacher, Major William Penn, conducted successful revivals there in 1879 and in 1885. "At Lampasas we had a large brush arbor which seated several hundred people—perhaps a thousand. It was full every meeting, and many were in seats for prayer at each meeting. . . . There were over three hundred conversions in eleven days, and nearly all of them joined the church in Lampasas, were baptized, and some took letters and joined at their country churches."[10]

Dr. Janet Valenza perceived a deep spiritual connection between "the sacred waters" and ailing healthseekers. "Symbolically, the waters represented life. Healthseekers believed that the Creator gave them as a gift to mankind, to be used judiciously and wisely." The great attraction for Texans journeying to mineral springs "lay in the potency of the waters, which the invalid and healthy alike considered 'fountains of youth.'" The waters of Lampasas Springs were regarded as potent, and sometimes restored certain functions of youth, so that many healthseekers could "once again chop wood, churn butter, walk the hills, and enjoy life and all its daily bodily demands." Therefore "journeys to these places indeed became pilgrimages, sometimes necessitating travel that was painful and inconvenient." Successful healthseekers often repeated their pilgrimage year after year, and "camp meetings at these watering holes reinforced the idea of a consecrated journey." If taking the waters "proved successful in alleviating pain, a strong connection with the spa and its physical location easily took hold."[11]

Another alluring attraction of Lampasas Springs was the sociability of camp life. Campers usually stayed for a period of weeks. Friendships developed, women—usually isolated on the family farm—visited one another to heart's content, and children—unaccustomed to so many playmates—ran through the campsites in large groups. "Eat and play, and play and eat was all they did from dawn to bed time"—and one of their favorite games was "Indians," including "stealing" babies!"[12] Families combined their resources and ate together; there was group singing during the evenings; and horse races were staged. The pilgrimages to healing waters, for many families, also were enjoyable vacation trips. Health was not the only reason some families returned, year after year, to Lampasas Springs. And young men, like the Dawson brothers, were attracted to "the Texas girls of Lampasas," including girls who were camping with their families.

There was an understandable dropoff in visits to the springs during the Civil War, but after the war healthseekers returned to Lampasas in large numbers. In 1867 Dr. Gideon Lincecum, an eccentric but highly knowledgeable pioneer naturalist, visited Lampasas Springs during a sweeping expedition undertaken when he was seventy-four. "These springs gush forth from the split rocks in the bed of the sulphur fork of Lampasas river. . . ." Lincecum was mesmerized by the largest spring, the "uppermost" spring; its basin was filled with pebbles which are being rapidly worn and polished into all manner of shapes and forms, from being incessantly thrown to the top by the gushing waters." He estimated that the upper spring threw out two barrels of water per second.[13]

"Many bushels of pebbles are perpetually dancing and audibly tinkling in the upward rush of this great column of water," reported Lincecum in awe. "Nothing can sink in it. A child or stone or anything else thrown into it is instantly thrown out again. I have seen hairpins and finger-rings that had been dropped by the ladies while bathing picked up amongst the whirling pebbles. Fifty or sixty yards from this wonderful fountain of water . . . is another very flush spring. . . ." Although this spring produced only a fraction of the water as the big spring, the "smaller spring is the one from whence the invalids dip the water they drink, using the larger one to bathe in." Along the creek many smaller springs oozed from the banks, and about a mile away Lincecum noted another large spring. "This splendid fountain of mineral water is situated at the north-east end of the town of Lampasas, and is the spring, on account of the accommodations afforded there, that is principally resorted to by the afflicted."[14]

In 1867, the year that Dr. Lincecum saw the "splendid fountain of mineral water . . . at the north-east end of the town," this location became known as Hanna Springs. George W. Scott had built "Scott's Hotel" in the 1850s, a ten-room facility, adding a log kitchen, two bath houses, and two stables. But Scott and his wife moved away to North Texas just before the Civil War, and the hotel and spring were sold in 1863. Four years later the property was purchased by John Hanna, who had come to Lampasas from Illinois with his father and sister. John, a bachelor with health problems, thus acquired his own mineral springs resort. He launched repairs to the buildings, which had become dilapidated during the Civil War, and he assigned new names to his resort: Hanna Hotel and Hanna Springs.[15]

Dr. J. N. Adkins, in 1866, moved his family and medical practice to Lampasas from Florence, a trek of about thirty miles. On the afternoon of the second day on the trail the Adkins wagons pulled into the grove at Lampasas Springs. Dr. Adkins rented two tents for his family, while word quickly spread that a physician was in camp. Supper for the Adkins family was collected from several campers: "A loaf of bread from one, a piece of meat from another, honey, eggs, and a bucket of buttermilk." Dr. Adkins was told about an enterprising family across the creek who had brought milk cows and sold sweet milk to campers.[16]

Before bedtime that first day Dr. Adkins was called on to pull a tooth, then he delivered a baby. The new father paid the doctor fifty cents, all the money he had, and promised "a little more" when he had it. The man with the tooth problem had no cash at all, but offered to help the doctor with anything he might need—a promise Dr. Adkins would often hear, and just as often redeem. On Sunday morning "campers brought their benches, chairs, children and hymn books to the doctor's tent and had singing, prayer, and Bible reading," according to his daughter. As everyone expected, Dr. Adkins delivered inspirational remarks. After less than a week in Lampasas, the new town doctor was on his way to becoming a local institution.[17]

Most early campers pitched their tents in the big grove near Hancock Springs. But some campers preferred to spend watering seasons near Hanna Springs, as shown above. —Courtesy KSM

W. H. Webber, a carpenter who settled in Lampasas several years after the Civil War, recalled seeing "campers all up and down the creek through the whole summer, spending hundreds, yes thousands of dollars here in Lampasas, at that time with the public square and a few stores and dance halls." The "few stores and dance halls" of the little town, as well as hotels and boarding houses, enjoyed a lucrative economic impact every watering season.[18]

"For years after I came here at almost every hour of the day or night people were going and coming to and from the Hanna Spring," said Webber, "and the only way one could get to the water was to walk on poles and rails laid on the boggy ground to keep from sinking in the bottomless mire, where thousands of buffalo had lost their lives in struggling for water. . . . The only places to bathe were half-screened from public gaze, and . . . only two or three at that, but in use night and day."

Webber reflected thoughtfully upon years of watching healthseekers who left Lampasas "apparently cured." Although he conceded that the sulphur content in the springs could have a beneficial effect on skin problems, and even though he had witnessed in his own home a boarder from Arkansas notably improve during a month of taking the waters, Webber remained skeptical. "I realized the effect mind has on mind where a community believe[s] alike, and how a stranger may become affected so that his or her mind believes so strongly that cures are effected . . .," he mused. "In fact the general belief was that these waters were curative for almost any affliction of the human body, and this mental condition probably was a greater help than the use of the water." Such views would not have been popular during the hayday of watering seasons in Lampasas.

By the 1870s the widespread belief "that those waters were curative for almost any affliction" was bringing healthseekers to Lampasas from all over Texas, as well as a few from out of state. Organizing a community-wide effort to enrich recreational experiences for watering season visitors, Lampasans also found increasing opportunities to profit from summer crowds.

In 1875 the "Lampasas Agricultural and Mechanical Association" organized a county fair, to be held toward the end of the summer. Horse races were scheduled, along with speeches and musical performances. Prizes were offered for hundreds of competitions: ten dollars, five dollars, four dollars, three dollars, two dollars, one dollar, or "diplomas." Lampasas businessmen provided the cash prizes: "MOSES HUGHES,

Proprietor of Lampasas City Mill, Best half bushel of wheat . . . $5.00."
"LADIES HANDIWORK" included more than twenty categories, from
"Best three yards of flannel" to "Best cotton quilt" (one dollar and two
dollar prizes, respectively). "SHOP, MILL AND FACTORY" rated three
dozen categories, from "Best stubble plow" to "Best churn" to "Best
bridle." There were fifty categories of food, from canned goods to pick-
led goods to jellies. Almost every category of livestock would be rated,
such as "Best aged bull, Best three years old bull, Best two years old bull,
one year old bull, calf," etc.[19]

Most of the county's population came into Lampasas to attend and
participate in the activities at the fair grounds and race track on the outskirts of town. Of course, all of the summer tourists were in attendance,
as well as large crowds from other counties. Gate fees were fifty cents
for anyone over fifteen, twenty-five cents for children six to fifteen, and
children under six were admitted free. "No spirituous liquors will be
allowed to be sold within the Fair Grounds," and betting also was prohibited. The fair was a huge success, the highlight of the 1875 watering
season, and the event was repeated in 1876. In the spring of 1877 the
Lampasas Agricultural and Mechanical Association scheduled four days
of fair activities, August 21-24, and anticipation was high for an exciting summer.[20]

*On Sulphur Creek boating always was a popular recreation, as enjoyed by the couple at left.
Meanwhile, the cow at right has found a familiar crossing.* —Courtesy KSM

"Visitors are pouring into our city from every quarter," reported the weekly newspaper, the *Lampasas Dispatch*, in May 1877. "Some ten or a dozen camps are pitched at the Gooch Spring, while as many have stopped at the Hancock Spring, besides the great members seeking quarters in town. We anticipate a larger gathering here this summer than at any former year."[21]

A few weeks later the *Dispatch* happily observed that "wagons by the dozen are coming filled with living freight." The *Dispatch* regularly announced the arrival of tourists and their home towns or counties. "Every sort of shop, store, tent, trade and occupation can be found at our springs," but a warning was issued. "Many people expect to grow rich from the sales of their wares, tricks, and wits. A good deal of Humbugging will be done during the summer. Look out for all sorts of people."[22]

By July Dr. S. K. Smith, a dentist from Comanche, arrived in Lampasas to spend a couple of months doing dental work, as he had for the past several watering seasons. Dr. Smith set up shop at the "boarding camp" of G. E. Wood, conveniently located near Hancock Springs and the fair grounds. A Union Sunday School welcomed camper children. Six dances per week were staged, "and still many of our young folks are not

Built shortly after the Civil War as a stagecoach stop, the Hart Hotel later was expanded, and still stands today. —Photo by the author

happy." The public square was filled with wagons, and on Tuesday, July 26, one hundred visitors arrived in town. Gov. Richard Hubbard came on Monday, August 20, just in time for the Third Annual Lampasas Fair. It was a banner season, and 1878 promised to be even better.

There was sufficient promise for 1878 to attract an enterprising journalist from Waco, D. B. Kennedy, and his partner, John Hubby. Kennedy and Hubby decided to run a daily newspaper in Lampasas during the watering season of 1878, from June 1 through the end of August. Kennedy and Hubby, along with a printer's devil named Smith and the necessary equipment, arrived in Lampasas on May 20. Welcomed "with uniform courtesy," the partners signed up most of the businessmen and families in town to a subscription, at fifty cents per month. To businessmen in Lampasas, Austin, and Round Rock (site of the nearest railroad), Kennedy and Hubby offered bargain advertising rates, promising to deliver the *Lampasas Daily Times* "every morning, fresh and newsy, to visitors, both campers and boarders," and to mail it "in every direction." The publishers did not work on Sundays, but the six issues a week of the *Daily Times* throughout the summer of 1878 offer the most complete coverage of any Lampasas watering season.[23]

By 1878 Lampasas boasted a population approaching 1,200, with three hotels "and, during the summer, ten to twenty boarding houses." The recently refitted Lampasas House boasted carpet in every room, along "with cane-bottom chairs, tables, mirrors, bedstead, soft bed, and in fact everything necessary to comfort and convenience." John N. Gracy, who had operated hotels in Lampasas for two decades, had built the Star Hotel, a two-story stone structure with a big wagon yard, located a block northwest of the square.[24]

Although Dr. S. K. Smith from Comanche did not come to Lampasas for the 1878 watering season, dental work was provided by Dr. M. Martin, who established an office at the Star Hotel. E. W. Hammons came from Waco and set up a barber shop at Hancock Springs. The *Daily Times* began to print a ditty advertising their fellow Wacoan:[25]

> When you wish an easy shave
> As good as barber ever gave,
> Call on Hammons, Hancock spring,
> At morn or eve, or busy noon.
> His shop is neat and towels clean,
> Razors sharp and scissors keen.[26]

There was so much foot traffic between Hancock Springs "camp-town" and Lampasas proper that several Lampasans hitched up vehicles and worked as hackmen. In July one hackman imported a horse-drawn omnibus. Appalled at the dusty streets, the editor of the *Daily Times* called for someone to employ "a sprinkling cart." In addition to dust, the editor also noticed a profusion of pesky insects: "7,999,333,001 fleas, by actual measurement, have emigrated from Lampasas within the last month."[27]

Lampasans organized an Arrangements Committee for the upcoming watering season. The Lampasas Brass Band was formed under the direction of Professor George Smith, who was an accomplished violinist. When Professor Smith requested a snare drum, funding was provided to purchase the instrument. By May Smith relentlessly was conducting practice sessions "almost twenty or thirteen times a week," stated a mathematically-challenged reporter. And in late May serenaders, some playing stringed instruments, began making periodic visits among the campers.[28]

On Friday, June 14, a "General Picnic" was held at the fair grounds for campers, as well as for citizens of Lampasas and the surrounding countryside. On Friday morning, Professor Smith led the Lampasas Brass Band through town and on to the fair grounds. A crowd followed the band, and latecomers arrived in a steady stream. Beneath shade trees the assemblage listened to speakers while the ladies of Lampasas prepared the noon meal, dinner. "And such a dinner," recounted a *Daily Times* representative. "Well, long tables groaned beneath the weight of good things, both delicacies and substantials. Everybody was provided for, and all had enough. . . ." Afterward "the floors were cleared and music begun, to which was soon added dancing."[29]

Serenaders—a brass band—a free picnic and dance. In these and other ways Lampasans rapidly built a camaradarie with the campers and boarders of 1878.

As everyone began to make their way home late in the day of the General Picnic, "an impromptu dance was gotten up." Young ladies and gentlemen, already in a festive mood, secured the services of a fiddler named Bass, who arranged to use Northington Hall for the dance that night.[30]

Alex Northington, one of the most industrious and innovative of Lampasas entrepreneurs, in 1870 erected a two-story stone commercial building on the southwest corner of the square. The second floor was called Northington Hall, and the facility often was rented for dances. Sometimes Northington announced a dance, lined up fiddler Bass or another musician, and charged admission at the door.[31]

In June Northington purchased a large number of roller skates and announced that his hall was a skating rink. Roller skating was an increasingly popular pastime with young people, and Northington helped organize a skating club. Admission was fifty cents for those who brought their own skates; twenty-five cents for those without skates (and who would have to rent a pair); and young ladies were admitted free (they would attract young men). On Friday night, June 28, "the hall was crowded, and of all the ridiculous, laughable sights, it is to see twenty great, awkward men start out as hard as they can go, meet each other, bump and go to meet the floor. Some of them bumped without any assistance. . . ." Within a few weeks Northington began to stage an hour of skating followed by a dance, usually with fiddler Bass and another musician on duty. But on Tuesday evening, August 2, Northington scheduled skating from eight to nine, followed by a dance: "A full string band, led by Prof. Gay, from Austin, will furnish elegant music. . . ."[32]

When plans were made, as usual, to conclude the Fourth Annual

In 1870 Alex Northington built what is today the oldest two-story building (at left) on the square. He operated a store on the ground floor, while "Northington Hall" upstairs housed dances, a skating rink, and church services. —Photo by the author

Lampasas County Fair with a ball at the Exhibition Hall on Friday night, August 9, Northington decided to claim his share of the immense crowd that would be in town. On Tuesday night, the evening of the fair's opening day, the Skating Club would skate for prizes, followed by a dance. "A splendid string band will furnish music for the occasion."[33] In 1878, as well as in other years, Northington Hall provided a lively social site for the Lampasas watering season.

Northington Hall did not hold a monopoly as a location for dances. A platform built at Hancock Springs was utilized for several dances, as well as for preaching services. The Exhibition Hall at the fairgrounds was used for the General Picnic early in the summer, then for the "grand ball of the season" at the end of the fair. When Prof. Geo. Smith resigned from the Lampasas Brass Band early in July, band members promptly wrote to a teacher in Austin to obtain his services. During Lampasas watering seasons, music and dancing were of paramount importance.[34]

Also important to campers, as well as to many Lampasas residents, were preaching services, "protracted meetings," and worship services of local congregations. In 1878 there was only one house of worship in Lampasas, the First Baptist Church, but by now small congregations of Methodists, Disciples of Christ, Episcopalians, and Catholics had been formed. The Methodists and Disciples of Christ sometimes used the Baptist Church or the Aten College building, while Catholics held services on occasion in Northington Hall. On Sunday evening, July 16, Rev. Abram Weaver, the new First Baptist minister, preached to campers at Hancock Springs, then "extended them a cordial invitation to attend services at his church[.]"[35]

Most of the sermons to campers were delivered by visiting preachers, usually at Hancock Springs. A large group camped north of Hanna Springs and largely kept to themselves: "They don't mix with other people much." Fortunately a preacher was camping in their midst, and he occasionally conducted services.[36]

The most popular visiting preacher in the summer of 1878 was Rev. H.S.P. Ashby, who rode over from Belton, about fifty miles to the east, where he was pastor of the Methodist Church. Reverend Ashby stayed in Lampasas a month, preaching often and making a host of friends. At the General Picnic in June he was asked to speak, delivering brief remarks that drew laughter from the crowd. In mid-June Ashby's horse threw him during a hunting foray. Badly bruised, the preacher was confined to his bed for a few days, before taking the sulphur waters. Soon

Reverend Ashby resumed preaching ("His fund of anecdote is inexhaustible . . ."), before riding back to Belton early in July.[37]

Aside from preaching services and dances and picnics, recreation for campers included croquet between couples and mumble-peg—also between couples! A game was invented at Hancock Springs: a board was nailed to a tree; four nails were driven in part-way; iron rings were tossed at the nails. On the Fourth of July more than three hundred people, including the Lampasas Brass Band, trekked to a scenic site on the Lampasas River, about fifteen miles north of town, for a picnic and an afternoon of patriotic speeches and music.[38]

Occasionally parties of spirited young men and women ventured on horseback over a rough trail to the Colorado River at the southwestern end of the county to enjoy magnificent scenery which included a cavern and a waterfall. The first group of the summer, comprised of five men and five women, left town in mid-July. "It is a party of beauty and gallantry," observed the *Times*, "and the trip is sure to be pleasant."[39]

In mid-August a party of eighteen youthful campers from Waco rode to the Colorado River. A few miles out of town they stopped to enjoy water without sulphur. "Of course," insisted a young woman named Eugenia who reported on the expedition, "we have nothing to say against Lampasas water: it is *awfully medicinal, beneficial* and all that, but we don't like the taste of it." Pushing on through the rugged countryside, the friends camped near the mouth of the cave. By "the weird light of the camp-fires," some of the "Waco mob" (as they were nicknamed by the bath-house keeper at Hancock Springs) cooked, some prepared fishing tackle, some cleaned and loaded revolvers and hunting rifles, and some played cards, pulling kernels from an ear of corn for poker chips. The next day everyone hiked up to the waterfall, constantly snagging their clothes. There was fishing, and hunters were sent out to replenish the larder, returning with: "one wild turkey, twenty or thirty squirrels and any number of juicy birds." They explored the cavern by the illumination of candles and lanterns. "In some places we (the ladies) had to be carried over streams of water, and of course we selected the ones to carry us, and . . . how we had to cling around their necks!" But they were awed by the lofty rooms, the beauty and grandeur. Eugenia urged, "Let no one who visits Lampasas miss going to the cave."[40]

The fun-seeking "Waco mob" was only part of a large delegation of citizens from Waco. The Waco journalists who opened the *Lampasas Daily Times* ran a great many ads from Waco businessmen, and Kennedy and Hubby doubtless encouraged many of their acquaintances to visit the Lampasas springs. "A considerable party, headed by Prof. F. P. Maddin, arrived from Waco last evening and will spend the summer here," welcomed the *Daily Times* on July 6. "Prof. Maddin is a citizen of whom Waco is justly proud, for more perfect gentleman has never quaffed the limpid waters of Lampasas springs."[41]

The Maddin group departed on August 1, but the next day Dr. W. H. Wilkes of Waco led a party of nine family members and friends into camp at Hancock Springs. Dr. Wilkes brought "a splendid tent and a very conveniently arranged dining-table." Like many campers, Dr. Wilkes offered his tent and camp gear for sale when he left for home a few weeks later. Soon after returning from their expedition to the Colorado River, the "Waco mob" departed Lampasas. When another small group broke camp, only one Waco family remained in Lampasas. Editor Kennedy of the *Daily Times* was proud to observe "that Waco has sent the largest delegation to the springs this season."[42]

Summer visitors in 1878 were exposed to a sizeable dose of frontier violence. There were two murders within a week of each other in July. On Monday night, July 15, James McMasters was killed in a field near his home seven miles east of Lampasas, and the following Sunday Walter Harcrow was slain in town. At noon on Tuesday, June 5, a transient known as "Coffee" fired three revolver rounds at bartender Newt Cook, inflicting a leg wound. Later in the month, "the first genuine burglary ever committed in Lampasas" was a late-night break-in of Justo's Gun Shop north of the square. On an evening in mid-July, someone fired a gun around Hancock Springs, and the bullet struck a tree about ten feet from a family at dinner. There were at least two fistfights in town that summer.[43]

Lampasas was still a rough town. On June 7, 1877, at the height of the Horrell–Higgins Feud, a lengthy and murderous shootout erupted on the town square. But the 1877 watering season continued, and so did the season of 1878 with its murders and brawls. Nearby violence did not send campers retreating to their homes. There were more gunfights in Texas during the 1870s than in any other decade, and news of shootouts and murders spread rapidly across the state. Texans of the era were rugged and not easily frightened, and it took more than a few shootings and fistfights to make them cut short their vacations.

When the Fourth Annual Lampasas County Fair was announced, on June 9, organizers defiantly declared their intention to "show that there is something else in this country besides long-horned steers, cow-ponies and six-shooters." Organizers were determined to make the Fair "of 1878 excel any heretofore held." A great deal of work was devoted to putting the race track in top condition. "Two fat men" from Lampasas challenged each other "to run a foot-race at the fair for $25." On July 13 it was announced that those "desiring to erect private exhibition stands on the fair grounds, should select locations as soon as possible."[44]

With the four-day fair scheduled to open on Tuesday, August 6, on Saturday, August 3 ladies of Lampasas "are requested to meet at the fair grounds this morning, to aid in decorating the exhibition hall." On Saturday several horse races were run (since the fair had not yet begun, betting was permitted). The *Daily Times* offered a succinct account of the results: "The fastest animal won each race."[45]

The fair grounds opened at eight each morning. "The attendance was large and the interest unflagging," reported the *Daily Times*. The Friday ball closed the fair and "was one of the most brilliant occasions of the kind ever known in Lampasas. . . . The lovely daughters of this cozy little town were out in full force, supported by beauties and belles from far and near, the toilets of all being unusually elegant."[46]

The weeks after the Fair were anti-climactic, and tourists began to go home. The primary post-Fair excitement unexpectedly took place at a mill pond on Sulphur Fork. A few boys were swimming in the ten-foot waters, and Jimmie Finney tried to jump in from a small boat. He slipped and fell across the side of the boat. A protruding nail ripped into the under part of his thigh, and Jimmie was suspended with his head beneath the water. His ten-year-old friend, Willie Matthews, was standing on the bank in his clothes. Instantly Willie jumped in and saved the drowning boy. Dr. J. N. Adkins sewed up and dressed Jimmie's nasty wound, while Willie, son of former county judge John C. Matthews, was hailed as a hero.[47]

Late in August the *Daily Times* continued to report on various people breaking camp and heading back to their homes. "A goodly number are still at the hotels, but the watering season may now be said to be over . . .;" stated Editor Kennedy, two days before shutting down his newspaper and returning to Waco, "and not until the warm season of next year will there be a return of the gay and festive scenes of this summer."[48]

The next year there was indeed a return of the gay and festive—and profitable—scenes of 1878. Each watering season seemed to be better, year after year, as many regular visitors returned to their familiar summer recreation site, and as new tourists tried out the health and pleasure opportunities offered at Lampasas Springs. But it was not easy to reach Lampasas; the nearest railroad was at Round Rock, fifty miles away. Lampasas community leaders continued to seek and hope for a railroad connection. And when railroad tracks finally reached Lampasas, for a few years the watering seasons soared to spectacular heights of opulence, of "gay and festive scenes" on a level never before imagined—the level of the "Saratoga of the South."

CHAPTER FOUR

Urban Pioneers

*"I can just grow up with the town,
and our children can have better advantages."*
—Dr. J. N. Adkins, 1866

Mountain men, gold prospectors, farmers in covered wagons, and cowboys riding an open range were not the only pioneers in the West. Indeed, the settlement of each successive frontier was concluded by urban pioneers who created towns in a wilderness. Like fur trappers, prospectors, and land-hungry farmers and ranchers, urban pioneers sought opportunity in an undeveloped West while relishing the adventure of a new land.

"The attitudes of urban pioneers differed from those of eastern city dwellers," stated frontier historian Ray Allen Billington. "Most were restless seekers after wealth who . . . deliberately selected a promising frontier community as the site of their next experiment in fortune making. There they built a mill, opened a general store, set up a portable printing press, or hung out a shingle as a lawyer or . . . teacher, confident that the town's rapid growth would bring them affluence and social prominence. When they guessed right and the village did evolve into a city they usually stayed on as prosperous businessmen or community leaders. . . . Their mobility and restlessness distinguished them from the more stable souls who filled the eastern cities."[1]

The first risk-taking frontier entrepreneurs to try their luck at

Lampasas Springs established mills, general stores, hotels, saloons, livery stables, blacksmith shops, and other businesses. Lampasas soon attracted other urban pioneers: lawyers, doctors, preachers, teachers, editors, and their wives, who would shape the culture of the new community.

Moses Hughes was the first urban pioneer to venture to the Lampasas Springs. He built the first home, a log cabin on Sulphur Creek, near the community's first grist mill, which he erected on the creek. Hughes bought a large number of lots in East Lampasas, which he sold for home sites through the years. Although he built a two-story stone residence for his family a few miles west of town, he continued to operate the Lampasas City Grist Mill, along with a sawmill he opened. He sold his log cabin to John Gracy, who moved it to his Star Hotel grounds. He was elected an officer in the Lampasas Guards in 1859 and later in two militia companies. By 1878 Hughes had established a cotton gin.

Hannah Hughes, who was the first white woman to use the Lampasas springs in 1853, died in 1863 while trying to give birth to their twelfth child. With a houseful of children, Moses married a young widow, who gave birth to four more Hughes babies before passing away

Grocer J. B. Messer, like most early merchants, attempted to operate on a strictly cash basis.
—Courtesy KSM

in 1872 at the age of thirty-one. Moses married again in 1875, but his third wife died the next year. Hughes also survived a fourth wife. Several of the Hughes children made their homes in Lampasas, carrying on the forty-year legacy of their father to the town he founded.[2]

Another founding father of Lampasas, energetic George Scott, had the townsite surveyed, conducted the sale of town lots, erected the town's first commercial building, built a hotel and began to develop the springs just northeast of town. But in addition to energy and aggressiveness, Scott had another trait of the urban pioneer. Restlessly he and his wife Elizabeth soon moved from Lampasas Springs to a more promising town.

Dr. Hillary Ryan was a similar case. The community's first physician was assertive and a natural leader. He signed the 1856 petition to create Lampasas County, in 1857 he was elected county treasurer, and the next year he provided the *Texas Almanac of 1859* a descriptive article which enthusiastically promoted the county. Also in 1859 Dr. Ryan was elected captain of the Lampasas Guards, and later he traveled to Austin to generate support from the state government for militia to battle Comanches. In 1862, now thirty-nine and with a wife and four children, Dr. Ryan agreed to command a Confederate infantry company. But this able town-builder, like George Scott, soon was lost to Lampasas.[3]

Shortly afterward, however, a physician came to Lampasas who would stay for the rest of his life. Dr. J. N. Adkins was thirty-two in the summer of 1866 when he brought his wife, Josie, and their growing family from Florence to Lampasas. He knew that the sulphur springs would attract many health seekers, and he felt that Lampasas had more potential as a community than little Florence. "I can just grow up with the town," he said to his wife in a classic expression of the urban pioneer, "and our children can have better advantages."[4]

On the day he arrived at Lampasas Springs, Dr. Adkins delivered a baby, the first of hundreds in and around Lampasas. But the father of that first Lampasas baby paid only fifty cents, and often Dr. Adkins would receive no fee at all from cash-strapped patients. At the end of the summer of 1866 Dr. Adkins had enough money to order lumber from Austin, and when the freight wagons arrived, a carpenter and several other men who owed medical fees were notified to lend a hand. John Casbeer had donated to the doctor a large lot atop a hill east of the square, and a two-room box house was completed in two weeks.[5]

Within two years a two-story stone house was erected atop the hill.

Dr. J. N. Adkins erected a two-story home atop a hill east of the Lampasas business district. The building stone and labor were provided by men who owned medical fees to the doctor.
—Photo by the author

Dr. Adkins had intended to build a low rock fence around his home and he asked those who owed him to cut and deliver native stone. The rock supply became so great that Dr. Adkins hired a stone mason who, with a workforce comprised of medical debtors, built a sturdy house that still stands today. One man paid his doctor bill by crafting for the house a long dining table and six chairs from white pine. The house was opened to everyone with a Saturday night candy pull.[6]

To stay abreast of professional developments, Dr. Adkins left to spend three months working and studying in a Cincinnati hospital. For years he advertised himself as an "Eclectic Physician," and indeed he treated everything from measles to gunshot wounds. When new doctors began to arrive in town, some patients who were in debt to Dr. Adkins switched to a different physician. One girl repeated a complaint to Dr. Adkins' daughter Ettie Aurelia. "We're not going to have your papa when we get sick, for he don't give enough medicine."[7]

"I've doctored that family for many years and they've all gotten well," smiled Dr. Adkins. "If they wanted more medicine they should pay their drug bill."[8]

More gracious were the patients who gave him a saddle horse, a milk cow, a new buggy, a pair of black horses to pull the buggy, and countless smaller gifts and services.[9] Dr. J. N. Adkins came to Lampasas the year after the Civil War when Comanche raids and gunfights were all too frequent. The first physician to make his permanent home in the community, he devoted himself to the well-being of Lampasans—and he became a beloved community mainstay.

Another prominent urban pioneer arrived in Lampasas two years after Dr. Adkins. Alex Northington came to town in 1868 with a wife and two babies. A young man of ambition and drive, Northington sought a town on the grow where he could exercise his abilities as a capitalist, where he could attain wealth and position.

Alexander Jesse Northington was born in 1841 in Red River County, but a year later the family moved to Georgetown. When the Civil War broke out, Alex joined a company that was attached to Hood's Brigade, which meant that he saw heavy combat. By 1864 he was ill enough to be sent home to Georgetown. Manpower was in short supply on the home front, and Northington promptly was hired by two experienced business partners. While learning the mercantile business, Northington married Maria Louisa Knight, daughter of a Georgetown physician. The young couple soon sought opportunity in Burnet, where Northington took a job in a general store.

But Reconstruction officials were oppressive in Burnet County, and by 1868 Northington, now twenty-seven, decided that nearby Lampasas offered greater opportunity and a more hospitable environment. Northington opened a small general store on the north side of the Lampasas public square. Within two years he moved his operations to the southwest corner of the square, when he built a two-story building. Northington and a laborer quarried and cut the building stone from a pasture four miles north of town. On the ground floor Northington installed his mercantile business. The second floor became Northington Hall and was used for dances, performances, church meetings, and as a skating rink.

Northington prospered rapidly, and he erected a large home on South Live Oak Street for his growing family (Alex and Maria became the parents of four sons and two daughters). The family belonged to the First Methodist Church of Lampasas, and he joined the Masonic Lodge. Northington engaged in cattle ranching, and the family moved to a 4,000-acre ranch four miles east of Lampasas. (In time Northington descendants would engage in business, banking, ranching, and Lampasas civic affairs.)

With such obvious abilities, Alex Northington was voted into public leadership. He was a county commissioner when the handsome courthouse was built, and he spent two terms, years apart, in the state legislature. "He was no ordinary man . . .," lauded the *Lampasas Leader*, adding that "in public life, he was a gentleman. . . ."[10]

Gentlemen—and ladies—were needed in education as well as business in any frontier community. "Frontiersmen believed that schools were the salvation of democracy and ladders to personal advancement," explained frontier historian Ray Allen Billington. "The principal hope of all pioneers was self-betterment, and this meant equipping the children to rise in the social circle."[11] "Professors"—the universal term for male teachers—and "school ma'rms" were among the most important of urban pioneers.

Most schools in frontier towns were private "subscription" schools. Indeed, more than three decades would pass before Lampasans would fund and organize a free public school system, and not until 1895—forty years after the town was founded—would a public school building open. In 1854 the Texas Legislature provided the first state funding for schools, authorizing payment of 62 cents per pupil per year. This paltry amount was raised to a still inadequate $1.50 per student in 1855. If a professor in a rented town building or a country school ma'rm in a one-room school taught twenty students in a school year that lasted perhaps four to six months, they were eligible to receive a total of thirty dollars in state funding.

In that year of 1855,

Portrait of rancher-businessman Alex Northington, who served two terms in the state legislature. —Courtesy Carol Northington Wright

Professor E. W. Holler opened a school in a one-room clapboard building that measured twelve by fourteen feet. Holler taught fifteen to twenty students, but at the close of school he became a wagoner to support his family. M. D. Sherman was the next teacher, and among his students were brothers John and Martin Van Buren Sparks, whose father was an incurable pioneer who had just moved his family to a farm near Lampasas. Van Sparks was nineteen and had a thirst for knowledge. In 1859 he taught the Lampasas school, which was located near the modern site of the public library. Van served throughout the Civil War as an infantry sergeant. Returning to Lampasas after the war, he became a businessman, justice of the peace, county judge, family man, and deacon of the First Baptist Church. His younger brother, John, became a cattle king in Nevada and governor of the state.[12]

There were three other teachers at the Lampasas school during the late 1850s, including a young woman named Fannie Foster. The primary reason that there was a new teacher every term was because it always proved difficult for teachers to collect the modest tuition. Like doctors, teachers often received chickens or a pig or a bushel of corn instead of cash. During the Civil War Rev. D. M. Lewis and R. G. Pidcoke tried to keep the school open as teachers.[13]

When the war ended Major Martin White moved with his family to Lampasas. Soon it became known that Major White had teaching experience, and he was approached by several fathers who asked him to head a school. White agreed, on condition that a school be built on his Casbeer Street property. A double log cabin quickly was erected: two log rooms separated by a "dog trot," or breezeway, with a single roof spanning the entire building. A long table with split pine log benches served for student desks, with boys on one side and girls on the other.[14]

While Major White taught in the log schoolhouse, citizens organized a joint-stock company to build a two-story rock school that also could double, when needed, for town meetings, church services, and miscellaneous gatherings. The company collected funds through subscriptions and acquired property on Sulphur Creek between Pecan and Elm streets. Begun in 1869, the structure faced west, with two doors on the front, an outside wooden stairway on the north, and chimneys on the north and south walls. There were two rooms, one on each floor, with a small bell tower atop the roof. The new school was grandly named "The College."[15]

Major White closed his log school, which he expanded into a residence, and began teaching at The College. He taught for a few more years, assisted by other teachers, including his daughter, Betty White. (Years later his son, Martin White, Jr., taught at the first public school building in Lampasas.) Ettie Aurelia Adkins started school at The College, and on her first day, wearing a bonnet and carrying a book satchel and a syrup bucket with a lunch biscuit, she followed big brother Joe to school. At recess the girls played "Ring-Around-a-Rosie and Hide-And-Go Seek," while the boys played "town ball" (baseball swept the country after the Civil War). During Ettie Aurelia's second year someone was stricken with smallpox, and county officials decided to pay for the vaccination of the schoolchildren. At the "taking-up bell," the children formed three lines and were marched to the offices of the three doctors, including Doctor Adkins, who were practicing in town. During the spring an epidemic of mumps struck Lampasas. When Ettie Aurelia and two boys were the only pupils still attending the lower classroom, and the upper room was similarly depopulated, the school finally was closed.[16]

In 1872 Professor R. A. Jones "secured the College building for the period of five years" and established the "Lampasas Male and Female High School." All ages were welcome: there was a $10 per term tuition for primary students; $15 per term for the intermediate department; $20 for collegiate classes; and $25 for instrumental music instruction. Payment was expected in "specie" or "Produce at market rates." But the school did not flourish.[17]

Another experienced educator, A. V. Aten from Austin, brought his wife and son to Lampasas to take the waters in 1876. Lampasas was growing, and Aten purchased the College building. Professor Aten renamed the school Aten College, but once again management soon changed hands.[18]

In 1877 Professor H. G. Niblo and his colleague, Miss Eva Gillett, established Lampasas College in the Aten building, with a Primary Grade ($2 per month), Intermediate Grade ($3 per month), High School Grade ($4 per month) and Collegiate Grade ($5 per month). Dr. and Mrs. N. Friend also rented a building and opened a school, and so did Miss M. M. Bradford. "All these teachers are popular as educators . . .," remarked the *Lampasas Dispatch*, "and it affords everybody an opportunity to send their children to a teacher of their choice." Year after year since the 1850s at least one or two adventurous, dedicated teachers had been willing to try their luck at Lampasas, and by 1877 there were

The first substantial school building in Lampasas was erected in 1869, above the north bank of Sulphur Fork between Pecan and Elm streets. There were two rooms, one above the other, and the building became known as "Aten College," after one of the many private schools that were conducted here. —Courtesy KSM

enough educators to staff *three* schools in the growing town. "The people of the frontier can now educate their children at Lampasas without being obliged to send them off to other schools."[19]

A succession of Gracy children were taught in the Lampasas schools. John and Harriett Gracy were Tennesseans, but as a young couple they moved to Missouri, where their first three children were born. The next move was to Texas, where Harriett gave birth to the rest of their babies. There would be thirteen Gracy children, although three died in infancy. The Gracy family had seven children when they moved again, this time to Lampasas, in 1856.[20]

John and Harriett were urban pioneers who, in their thirties, at last had found their home. John was a hotel keeper who saw opportunity in a town which had a large tourist population every summer, and which had regular stagecoach traffic from Austin. Harriett would become known for serving fine meals and, within the family, "as a strong willed woman who ruled her children with an iron hand." John opened the Star Hotel and a wagon yard one block northwest of the square. During the Civil War John served with militia units against Comanches, but in 1862 the Gracy's fifteen year-old-son, James, was killed and scalped by marauding warriors. Also in 1862 a ninth child, Harriett Rebecca Frances, was born blind, even though she would overcome her handicap and marry twice as a young woman.

A few years after the war Charles Royston Green, who had been wounded while fighting Comanches, checked into the little frame Star Hotel and began taking healing sulphur baths, probably at nearby Hanna Springs. Green was a stone mason, and he was engaged by the Gracys to build a two-story rock hotel. Green, who would marry a Gracy daughter in 1872, hired two stone cutters to help him quarry building stone three miles from town, and there was enough left over to erect a small annex, the "Little Hotel," across the street to the northwest. Each room in the new Gracy Hotel had a fireplace, and a dinner bell was brought in from the East. The Gracys raised their own vegetables, fruit, and meat, and the formidable Harriett demanded that any armed man in her hotel dining room had to remove his revolver. The oldest son, Jasper, ran the Gracy livery stable across the street from the hotel, and a Gracy son-in-law operated a stagecoach line to Austin.[21]

"A large rock, cut like steps, accommodated people to step from the high step out of the coach, to a walk leading to the door," stated granddaughter Dorothy Belle Gracy. In the east wall of the new hotel "J. N.

John Gracy built the Keystone Hotel in 1870, and Mrs. Gracy made the hotel famous for its meals. Later a long wing was added to the west (out of view to the right). —Photo by the author

Gracy" and "1870" were carved.[22] The grave of murdered son James was behind the hotel. Gracy roots ran deep in Lampasas.

The new Star Hotel, also called the Gracy Hotel, opened in 1870, the same year as the Northington building on the square. These sturdy new, two-story stone buildings, were erected by urban pioneers who planned their futures in Lampasas. But these and other new buildings around town soon would be tested by a catastrophic force of nature.

After midnight on Saturday morning, September 27, 1873, "rain began to fall with considerable force," reported the *Lampasas Dispatch*. The downpour continued until Saturday afternoon. By noon on Saturday Lampasas was beginning to flood "with water from the branches around town and the back water from Burleson and Sulphur Fork." About one o'clock Saturday afternoon Sulphur Creek overran its banks, and raging floodwaters swept dozens of buildings from their foundations and engulfed the town with several feet of water.[23]

"Women and children went from their falling houses, wading up to their waists, screaming for help . . .," described *Dispatch* editor W. P. Beall, who lost his own house. "Some took refuge in trees, where they were obliged to remain for three or four hours before help could get to them. One sick lady with a child three weeks old in her arms stayed in a tree until rescued after the waters subsided."[24]

Lewis C. Philips was drowned on the public square. Philips had a crippled hand, and when roiling waters swept him through tree branches, he could not pull himself to safety. His brother, clinging to another tree, saw Lewis sink below the violent waters. Philips's body was found the next day beside Burleson Creek half a mile from town.

A couple of miles east of Lampasas, Judge W. H. Garrett and a hired man named Jones watched the floodwaters of Sulphur Fork threaten their homes. They loaded their families into a wagon and headed across a flat plain toward higher ground. On the plain onrushing waters toppled the wagon. Judge Garrett and one of his children were drowned, along with Jones and two of his children. Mrs. Garrett and Mrs. Jones and their surviving children were saved. The water never reached their homes. "Had they remained at their houses they would have been perfectly safe," lamented the *Dispatch*.[25]

Houses on high ground in town were filled with wet, shivering women and children. When the waters began to subside, about four o'clock in the afternoon, men in wagons and on horseback went on rescue missions all over town. "Dozens of families are left with not a change of clothing, a pair of shoes or a morsel of food." But wagons loaded with provisions and clothing soon began to arrive from Burnet, Austin, Waco, Georgetown, Gatesville, and far away Galveston. Four years later, *Dispatch* editor W. P. Beall continued to express his appreciation: "to those people we will ever feel a grateful remembrance."[26]

More than fifteen families were rendered homeless, and many commercial buildings were wrecked, including a general store "in which there was the Post Office, with all the contents. . . ." Grocery stores, a meat market, a blacksmith shop, two law offices ("with all their papers and books"), were gone. On the south side of the square, the large frame commercial building owned by Henry Hill and "used as a Court House, was washed 10 or 12 feet and many of the records lost and the balance badly injured." Ramshackle frame buildings had vanished, with almost no wreckage left behind. It can hardly be imagined what would have happened if campers and tents had been in the Hancock Springs grove. All three mills were badly damaged, and the mill of John Casbeer was destroyed. "Mr. Casbeer waded out with a six year old son on his shoulders and barely escaped with his life."[27]

For nearly three decades there was no courthouse on the Lampasas square. But there were shade trees and a public well, and wagons regularly were parked on the square. This view looks west up Third Street. The infamous saloon where four state policemen were gunned down and where Merritt Horrell was slain stood just to the left, or south, of the two-story building on the corner of the square. —Courtesy KSM

But Aten College still stood, rock solid, and so did John Gracy's new stone hotel building. Alex Northington's two-story commercial building downtown and his substantial new home both survived, as well as several other residences. The lesson was clear that the flimsy construction of the early years of Lampasas needed to be replaced with stout rock structures. Building stone was abundant near town, and stone masons soon were advertising their services in the newspaper. John Casbeer rebuilt his mill across the creek on higher ground, and other citizens replaced wrecked homes and business houses with solid, improved buildings, Lampasas began to take on a more permanent look.

One of the town's most progressive urban pioneers steadily expanded his holdings as Lampasas grew. Charles N. Witcher was a native of Georgia who became a Confederate sergeant during the Civil War. The year after the war the twenty-three-year-old veteran and his father-in-law, Judge John C. Rasbury, brought their families to Texas, and by 1868 they had settled in Lampasas. Charlie and his wife, Mahalia, had a baby boy, and in time there would be twelve more children. Witcher developed a cattle ranch, then used his profits to open a wholesale grocery and dry goods business on Third Street. He bought land all over town, and rent houses added to his income.[28]

Witcher had no desire to hold public office, but he promoted Lampasas with business and political friends. Charlie and Mahalia were devout Baptists known for their generosity to the poor and needy. Former Sergeant Witcher served on the board of the Texas Confederate Home. As a businessman he believed in advertising, running large newspaper ads for the Texas Trading Company.

In 1888 a typical Texas Trading Company ad dominated the front page—top to bottom and three columns wide. There were long lists of fabrics and clothing and prices, including: "Over 2000 suits for Men, Youths and Boys for $3 and upwards" and "Women's Shoes, 85 cts. And upwards," as well as "Our $2.50 Stockman's Hat, equal to any $4 hat in Lampasas or elsewhere, is a rouser." After announcing in bold print that "Purchases for the Season Already Exceed $140,000" (Witcher supplied wholesale goods by the wagonload to stores up to 150 miles away), the ad pointed out that "our present stock is larger, we think, than all the stocks in Lampasas combined. We have already paid out this season over $110,000 for wool, cotton and grain. Considering the magnitude of our business, is it unreasonable for us to sell goods for considerably less than the little fellows that bark at us?"[29]

C. N. Witcher built the Texas Trading Company into Lampasas' largest and most far-reaching business (until it was surpassed by the Stokes Bros. enterprises of his nephews). —Courtesy KSM

By the time he was in his forties, Charlie Witcher had been in Lampasas for two decades and he had built the town's largest and most far-reaching business. His right-hand man in the Texas Trading Company was his nephew, Melmoth Young Stokes. Young's brother, Charlie Stokes, also had joined the firm. Learning business from a master, the Stokes brothers would go on to exceed their uncle's impressive entrepreneurial achievements.

The Stokes brothers led the second wave of Lampasas entrepreneurs. Like their uncle, M. Y. and Charlie Stokes were born and raised in Georgia. Their mother, Nancy Elizabeth Witcher Stokes, was Charlie Witcher's sister. Their father, Tom Stokes, was elected to the Georgia State Senate before the Civil War. Tom and Elizabeth bought a farm just east of Atlanta to be near the state capitol. But during the war their house was burned and their livestock confiscated by General William T. Sherman's army. Their sons, M. Y. and Charlie, were born during this difficult time, in 1862 and 1865 respectively. After the war the family lived in a log cabin on their farm while Tom tried in vain to rebuild their fortune. He suffered a fatal stroke, and Elizabeth contracted tuberculosis.[30]

Charlie Witcher wrote Elizabeth a series of letters urging her to move to Lampasas. He promised employment for her sons and extolled the curative powers of the mineral springs. The sale of the Stokes's farm to an Atlanta rail yard paid off their debts with a little cash left over. The family journeyed by train to Round Rock, where they took a stagecoach to Lampasas. Eighteen-year-old M. Y. Stokes was hired as bookkeeper for the Texas Trading Company. But at fifteen Charlie Stokes could not resist the great adventure of the day. Big for his age, Charlie hired out as a cowboy. Twice he helped trail cattle herds to Kansas, and at Big Spring Charlie rode with a Texas Ranger posse. An outgoing young man with a hearty sense of humor, Charlie honed his talent as a natural storyteller in bunkhouses and around campfires. He became comfortable in the company of cowboys and cattle ranchers and, later, sheep ranchers. Charlie's easy familiarity with men of the land would be an invaluable asset when he finally settled down to a business career with his brother.[31]

While Charlie was riding the range, M. Y. Stokes was becoming an expert businessman. Bright and hungry for knowledge, he learned a great deal from his uncle, while building a large personal library. Dressed every day in a business suit, he worked long hours. As a bookkeeper, his value to the Texas Trading Company was affirmed by the astronomical salary of $200 per month. He saved his money and aggressively sought opportunities for investment, and while still in his twenties he amassed a capital of $10,000.[32]

Charlie Stokes married in 1886, and he and Katie had the first of their two children the next year. Although only in his twenties, family responsibilities exerted a maturing effect, and Charlie embraced his brother's offer of a business partnership. M. Y. Stokes and Brother, a produce firm, opened for business in Goldthwaite, the seat of recently organized Mills County. Goldthwaite proved to be too small for their purposes, but the brothers worked well as a team.

In 1889 M. Y. Stokes agreed to become treasurer of a new firm, Yates, Beall & Stokes, Inc. But he wanted a permanent business arrangement with his brother, and he withdrew from Yates, Beall & Stokes in 1893. Thanks to the legal efforts of Judge William B. Abney, Stokes received a profitable settlement. Abney was an urban pioneer who rode horseback into Lampasas in 1875 at the age of nineteen. He read law in a local office, was quickly admitted to the bar, and in 1876 he was appointed to serve as district judge during the illness of Judge W. A. Blackburn. Judge Abney thereafter served as a judge only in special cases, preferring to concentrate on the practice of civil law, and his services would prove highly beneficial to the Stokes brothers.[33]

M. Y. Stokes had married in 1891, and he and Mary raised three children. They established their family home just east of Uncle Charlie Witcher's house. When Charlie Stokes built his permanent home, he bought a plot of land from Uncle Charlie and erected a splendid residence on a ridge in the western edge of Lampasas.[34] The proximity of these three homes, with two highly successful nephews choosing to live adjacent to the uncle who welcomed them to Lampasas, and who had nurtured their entrepreneurial gifts, was a physical expression of three pre-eminent businessmen. Elizabeth Stokes died two years after reaching Lampasas, and the Stokes brothers already had lost their father, but Uncle Charlie Witcher provided a strong measure of parental guidance.

Stanley Walker knew the Stokes brothers during the prime of their careers. The grandson of Lampasas County pioneers, he spent a quarter of a century as a noted journalist in New York City before returning home to Lampasas County. In his insightful book, *Home to Texas*, Walker reflected upon the Stokes brothers. "They were an unusual pair: C. D. was a man of the world, expansive, impulsive, with the touch of the born

The business district extended west of the square for three blocks along Third Street, as evidenced by these commercial buildings on the north side of Third. —Courtesy KSM

gambler in his make-up; M. Y. was religious, abstemious, and something of a scholar—for years he was the only man in Lampasas who could, and did, sing the songs of Gilbert and Sullivan."[35]

Stokes Brothers & Company was organized in 1893, when M. Y. Stokes was thirty-one and Charlie was twenty-eight. They were youthful, energetic, ambitious, full of ideas and brimming with confidence. They launched their partnership during an ideal time for capitalists. There was no income tax, so businessmen kept every dollar of their profits, and smart businessmen reinvested most of their profits during the explosive economic expansion of the late nineteenth century. There was little federal regulation to slow expansion; indeed, the federal government aided American businesses with high import tariffs and with policies that encouraged the growth of the nation's largest industry, railroads.

In this atmosphere the Stokes brothers of Lampasas, in the underdeveloped Hill Country of Texas, enjoyed the freedom to grow the local and area economy as rapidly and widely as they dared. Following the example of their uncle's Texas Trading Company, the Stokes brothers intended to benefit their customers, primarily farmers and ranchers, as well as the firm. The firm would buy anything their customers produced; then find a market. Multiple lines of business should be developed, and all lines should enhance the profitability of other lines.[36]

Stokes Brothers dealt in wholesale groceries, shipping anywhere, especially into West Texas, utilizing railroads and wagons. The firm bought—then sold—cotton and wool and pecans, from the pecan trees that grew naturally along the Colorado River and the Lampasas River and its tributaries. They bought chickens and eggs and turkeys. Charlie Stokes was a gifted salesman, and he traveled far and wide to buy wool and mohair. Charlie especially sought woolgrowers in the south part of the Hill Country, where there were two clips of wool annually, as opposed to one clip per year north of Lampasas and in the San Angelo area to the west.[37]

Within two years, in 1895, Stokes Brothers opened a private bank to facilitate their transactions. The producers of cotton, wool, pecans, and all other products purchased by the firm were encouraged to do their banking and borrowing from Stokes Bros. Bank. While making large wool purchases in West Texas, Charlie Stokes could draw time drafts on the bank in Lampasas, then cover them with drafts from banks in New York City and Boston, where the firm had accounts.[38]

A two-story building was erected on the northwest corner of the town square to house the Stokes Bros. Bank. Other Stokes Brothers buildings were adjacent on the north side of the square, and the retail store was on the west side. Eventually more than twenty buildings in Lampasas were used for wool and mohair storage by the firm.

The teenaged Stokes brothers who came to Lampasas from Georgia in 1880 became the town's largest employers. With vision and remarkable business skills, they expanded and impacted the economy of Lampasas and the surrounding region for half a century. M. Y. and Charlie Stokes were the most successful entrepreneurs in Lampasas history.

CHAPTER FIVE

Lampasas and the Cattle Frontier

"I believe I would know an old cowboy in hell with his hide burnt off. It's the way they stand and walk and talk."
—E. C. "Teddy Blue" Abbott,
We Pointed Them North

The most colorful and unforgettable chapter of America's last West was the cattle frontier. The cowboy, galloping across an open range with boots, spurs, bandana, lariat, leather chaps, and big hat, was destined to become the world's most popular folk hero. "Say *Texas* anywhere, and people answer *cowboy*," stated Texas historian T. R. Fehrenbach. Longhorn cattle, cowboys, ranches, and long cattle drives evolved in Texas, then "exploded . . . a new way of life, across the entire North American West." In Fehrenbach's ringing prose, the range cattle industry "burned its image like a smoking cattle brand into the consciousness of not only North America but the whole world."[1]

From pre-Civil War years through the spectacular explosion of the cowboy culture and of the range cattle industry, Lampasas played an eventful role in this unique frontier enterprise. Among the earliest settlers of Lampasas were stock raisers who brought cattle to the county's open ranges. After the Civil War cattle ranches were established throughout the county, including several spreads near Lampasas whose owners lived in town. By the 1870s cowboys, with their distinctive dress and swagger, were a common sight in the streets and saloons of Lampasas. Most notable was the involvement of Lampasas County in the most picturesque adventure of the range cattle business, the long and dangerous trail drives to faraway cowtowns and other markets.

In 1854, when Richard King was beginning to stock his new ranch in South Texas with Mexican longhorns, Perry Townsen started a modest cattle operation in the rocky wilderness about twenty-five miles north of Lampasas Springs. A native of Tennessee, Townsen was a twenty-eight-year-old bachelor when he pioneered the northern apex of what would become, two years later, Lampasas County. In 1855 Perry persuaded his twenty-two-year-old nephew, Jasper Townsen, to join him. Perry and Jasper formed a partnership, calling their spread the Townsen Cove Ranch. In 1856 Perry and Jasper diversified, building a grist mill on the Lampasas River three miles east of their wilderness headquarters. During the next few years they were joined by many more members of the Townsen clan.[2]

Although the isolated Townsen Cove Ranch was vulnerable to Comanche raids, the herd multiplied amid the rugged thickets of northern Lampasas County. In the spring of 1864, Perry and Jasper and various family members moved their livestock to better range, more than 150 miles to the west. The Townsen herd was settled around the deserted rock buildings of Fort Chadbourne, which was established in 1852 but abandoned when Texas seceded from the Union. In December 1864 Jasper returned to the Townsen Cove Ranch long enough to marry Mary Ann Stanley, and the first of their four children was born in 1866.

That year Texas cattlemen Charles Goodnight and Oliver Loving blazed the Goodnight–Loving Trail, which angled southwestward from Fort Belknap, passing near Fort Chadbourne through a long waterless stretch to the Pecos River. The trail then followed the Pecos River north into New Mexico Territory, and soon it would stretch farther north into Colorado and beyond. In 1866 Perry Townsen led a drive along the new trail to Fort Sumner, where slaughter animals were being bought to feed 8,500 reservation Indians. There was another drive in 1867, then in 1868 Perry trailed one of the first herds to Cheyenne, which soon would become known as the "Holy City of the Cow." For his 1868 crew, Townsen enlisted several relatives and in-laws—John and Bill Townsen, Tom Stanley, Bob Mitchell—as well as his seventeen-year-old neighbor in Lampasas County, Pink Higgins.[3]

Following this drive, Perry and Jasper decided to reunite their family and move back to Lampasas County. They disposed of the Townsen Cove Ranch and relocated south, about sixteen miles north of Lampasas.

Perry and Jasper put in another mill, and later a cotton gin. But they also brought back to Lampasas County the experience of conducting long cattle drives, knowledge of the techniques and tactics required to push herds hundreds of miles to market, and a cadre of drovers who also had been up the trails. The cattle drive business was entering its heyday, and trail bosses and drovers from Lampasas County would help their home town and county to participate actively in the most captivating adventure of the range cattle industry.

While the Townsens were developing their cattle herd and learning the trail driving business, other men were bringing cattle onto their own spreads near Lampasas. Brothers Mark, William, and Tilford "Snap" Bean, like the Townsens, established small cattle ranches before Lampasas County was organized.[4]

The Bean brothers had been bequeathed a couple of slaves each, and Thomas Huling also owned slaves. In 1855 Huling disposed of his East Texas plantation and moved to Lampasas Springs with his family, equipment, livestock, and twenty-one slaves. (The Census of 1860 listed only 153 slaves and thirty-two slave owners in Lampasas County.) The Huling wagon train was commanded by freedman Morgan Jordan, who, at six-feet-eight-inches, was the tallest man in Lampasas County. Thomas Huling built a rock house that still stands five miles west of Lampasas. His oldest daughter, Bell, married Mark Bean in Lampasas in 1859. Both Huling and son-in-law Mark Bean died in 1865, but the widowed Bell Huling Bean soon married Snap Bean, and the rock ranch house was their family home for more than half a century.[5]

J. J. Greenwood began raising cattle in Lampasas County in the 1850s. After the Civil War, now in his early thirties, he took a twenty-year-old bride from Belton named Georgiana. She was pleased to find that her ranch house "was made of lumber" instead of logs, and she did not mind that the furniture was "crude and rough" and that there was no glass in the windows, only shutters.

"We cooked on an open fire in huge iron ovens and a woman needed no rouge in those days to render her complexion a Carmen shade," she quipped. "Our lights were candles manufactured at home by first killing a beef to obtain the tallow, then rendering it and molding it, and even spinning the wicks. My mold held only six candles, which necessitated making candles very often. To make the tallow hard we used our own manufactured beeswax. . . . Our soap was made at home from lye which we procured from wood ashes and though it did not improve our hands, it made the clothes snowy white. At that time cotton was scarce and few people could afford pure cotton beds, so we mixed it with [corn] shucks which . . . was both a noisy and uncomfortable bed."[6]

Georgiana Greenwood operated her household like almost every other ranch wife in the county during this pioneer period. She felt no sense of privation: "We had no luxuries at that time, but we did not want for the necessities as fat beef, butter, milk, honey and vegetables were plentiful. . . ." Echoing the spirit of Lampasas residents as well as country people, she emphasized that "we were all like one family, a neighbor was a real friend, and whatever we had we were willing to share with those less fortunate."[7]

Another experience that was common to the pioneer ranch wives of Lampasas County was the dread of Comanche attack. Mary Richardson lived with her family on a small ranch in the northernmost section of the county. In the fall of 1858 Mary wrote to her brother, General H. L. Burkitt of Tennessee, about a raid against her isolated home:

Dear Brother,

On the 4th of September last the Indians came in among us, and after doing some mischief, they paid me a visit. My husband was away from home on business, and I was alone with my five little children, two miles from any other house. I had sent my two oldest, Mary and John, to drive up the cows, and did not suspect that the Indians were lurking near. They espied the children about three hundred yards from the house and chased them toward the home, where they fled for protection, and little was the protection that I, alone, a timid woman was able to give against eight savages, thirsting for blood and plunder. Mary, the oldest, made good in her retreat; but Oh! Imagine my feelings when I saw them overhaul little John and begin to stab him with a lance! I was much frightened and expected nothing but to be massacred, together with my children. I thought of my gun at that critical moment. I took it down and fired, and kept firing until assistance came to my relief. The Indians (as I suppose) thought there were men in the house prepared to receive them, and fled and left my child alive, but stabbed in the back, through the arm, and in the right side. He has recovered from his wounds.

Your sister,
Mary H. Richardson[8]

John, who was six when he was attacked (Mary was ten), married and raised a family on a farm near Adamsville.

Alex Northington, a leading Lampasas entrepreneur since his arrival in 1868, was drawn to the profits possible from selling four-dollar-a-head Texas longhorns for thirty or forty dollars or more at a distant market. Alex, in partnership with the Townsens, invested in a herd of 2,200 longhorns. With the help of the Townsens, Alex put a crew together and trailed the herd to Sidney, Nebraska. A buyer in Sidney requested delivery in Cheyenne, so the drive extended another one hundred miles westward to the Wyoming Territorial capital. Now committed to the cattleman's lifestyle, Northington established a ranch. In 1881 he traded 400 head of cattle for a 4,000-acre spread just a few miles east of Lampasas. He moved his family from the house he had built on South Live Oak Street to a three-room log cabin on the ranch. Soon he built a ranch house four miles from town. Throughout his lifetime Northington remained active in business in Lampasas, and he held important public offices, but when he died in 1905, he was in his beloved ranch home.[9]

Alex Northington's 4,000-acre ranch was large by the standards of Lampasas County. But no Lampasas County ranch could compare with the largest cattle kingdoms of Texas. The first great cattle operation, the King Ranch of South Texas, ran 75,000 head of cattle on 1,150,000 acres. Other enormous ranches sprawled across the vast grasslands of West Texas and the Panhandle. Charles Goodnight ran 100,000 cattle on

The ranch home of Alex Northington was built four miles east of Lampasas. Northington owned 4,000 acres of land. —Courtesy KSM

the 1,335,000 acres of his JAs Ranch. The West's largest ranch, the XIT, held title to 3,050,000 acres of Texas Panhandle range, and 150,000 head of cattle. Numerous other Texas ranches encompassed hundreds of thousands of acres. But in Lampasas County ranches were measured in the thousands or even hundreds of acres. Such ranches could support only small herds, a few dozen head or perhaps a few hundred. Lampasas County would not produce a cattle king (except for John Sparks, who would build his ranching empire in Nevada) such as Charles Goodnight or Shanghai Pierce or Richard King. Alex Northington was prosperous, but his ranch was only part of his entrepreneurial package. Most small ranchers of Lampasas County struggled for subsistence on their little spreads.

Large ranches such as the XIT or the JAs or the Four Sixes could send multiple herds up the trail each spring and summer. The optimal size of a trail herd was 2,500 to 3,000 cattle. Such a herd required a trail crew of at least ten or twelve men, including the trail boss. The remuda of eight to ten mounts per drover required a horse wrangler. The mule-drawn chuck wagon, a Charles Goodnight invention, was driven by the cook. A trail crew of such numbers usually could not be drawn from a ranch bunkhouse. Many small ranches had no permanent employees, just a father and his sons. Even large ranches that employed several year-round cowboys could not staff a trail crew, and if they did their ranch would be stripped of employees. Besides, a majority of trail herds were made up of cattle from many smaller ranches.

Therefore a professional trailing contractor would be employed to form a crew and drive a herd to market, either from a large ranch or from multiple smaller ranches. The trailing contractor charged a flat fee, usually $1.00 or $1.50 per head delivered, in return for providing drovers, chuck wagon, and provisions. Often the contractor served as trail boss, and he and his drovers would work two drives per season. But a dozen or so major trailing contractors handled many herds a year, employing numerous trail bosses and crews—and earning large profits. Jimmy M. Skaggs, the pre-eminent authority of the cattle-trailing industry, termed the contractors "hip pocket" business men. Even the largest of these contractors "kept few business files, if any." The western cattle business was famous for deals sealed with a handshake, and contractors and their trail bosses worked in haste while putting together herds from multiple owners. When crossing from Texas into Indian Territory a bill of sale was required. Such documents were brief, often only a paragraph, and if the herd was made up from multiple owners, the bill of sale customarily added a list of owner brands. The paper trail for cattle drives was meager. While lamenting the lack of documentation, Skaggs concluded that "few records were needed" by contractors and trail bosses and ranchers. This lack of documentation certainly pertained to the trail driving business in Lampasas County.[10]

The most famous of all cattle trails was the Chisholm Trail, opened in 1867. A network of feeder trails led from South Texas most of the way north to the Red River. The main trail crossed the Brazos River at Waco, which became known as "Six-Shooter Depot." The Chisholm Trail led through Fort Worth, then into Indian Territory at Red River Station. The long trek finally ended at Abilene, first of the Kansas railheads. After five years the railroad built south, first to Newton, then to Wichita, and finally Caldwell on the Kansas border. In 1869 350,000 head of Texas longhorns were shipped out of the Abilene stockyards, and in 1871 a record total of more than 600,000 cattle were driven up the Chisholm Trail.

One of the feeder trails of this busy thoroughfare passed through Lampasas, which became a stopping point. "The trail drivers made a practice of stopping at Lampasas for a day or so, resting their herds on the grass just outside of town, and taking a breathing spell for themselves," wrote Stanley Walker, who heard the stories from his grandparents. "Some of them sampled the mineral water, but most of them preferred something a little stronger," which they found in several Lampasas saloons.[11]

The imagination of America was captured by the long cattle drives, which would be romanticized by countless Western novels and motion pictures. The West long had attracted adventurous youngsters, and now adolescents and young men eagerly signed up to become a cowboy on a trail drive—just as New England farm boys once sought adventure before the mast. With trail herds stopping at Lampasas, then angling through the county, local youths who were aspiring cowboys had opportunities to hook on with a trail crew. Furthermore, small ranchers in the area could provide cattle to make up trail herds that would start from Lampasas County.

When the Townsens moved back to Lampasas County, after engineering three long drives from Fort Chadbourne, cattle drives began to be organized within the county. These herds and crews were dominated by Lampasas County cattle and drovers. Jasper Townsen, his cousin Bob

Mitchell, and Pink Higgins drove a small herd about ninety miles east to a buyer in Calvert in 1870. In 1872 Jasper Townsen and Bob Mitchell put together a herd of beef steers, then gathered a crew for a drive eastward across Texas to Shreveport, Louisiana.[12]

Pink Higgins provided information about a group which, in 1871, bought 900 head of yearling steers at fifty cents per head. In 1872 Pink and the others purchased 1,700 more yearling steers at one dollar per head. The next year Pink, Jasper Townsen, and Bob, Ben and Alonzo Mitchell, among others, drove this herd up the newly opened Western Trail, past Fort Griffin and Fort Belknap to Doan's Store on the Red River. After crossing the Red, the trail led north through western Oklahoma, then into western Kansas. This large herd was more than four months on the trail, allowing ample time for the cattle to graze and gain weight. En route there were "some thrilling experiences with the Indians." It was late July before the herd finally reached Dodge City.[13]

The Kansas market was strong in 1873, and there were ready buyers in Dodge City when the big Lampasas County herd arrived. The two-year-olds sold for eight dollars apiece. Pink Higgins was only twenty-two, but this was the greatest success he would ever enjoy in the range cattle business. Higgins next drove a herd to the Kansas City stockyards, heading east from Lampasas County until intersecting the Chisholm Trail. At Fort Worth the herd left the Chisholm Trail, moving northeast to the old Shawnee Trail. After crossing the Red River the Shawnee Trail angled northeast across eastern Oklahoma to Baxter Springs in the southeastern corner of Kansas. From Baxter Springs the trail stretched north another 170 miles to Kansas City.[14]

Now a successful trail boss, Pink Higgins would be employed in the future to lead other drives. While not on the trail, Pink spent a great deal of time in the saddle, buying and selling and trading cattle. The Higgins ranch was in northeastern Lampasas County, only a few miles from the Townsens and the Mitchells. The ranch house was beside Higgins Mountain and near another "mountain" (actually both were rocky hills) which formed Higgins Gap. On the first day of 1875 Pink married a neighbor, Betty Mitchell May, a young widow with a little daughter. Pink and Betty became the parents of three children, and his parents helped with the growing family and the ranch while he was absent on trail drives.

Long cattle drives bristled with hazards, particularly treacherous river crossings and stampedes, which usually erupted at night. "Chain lightning caused more stampedes than anything else, and next came lobo wolves—the smell of them," related veteran drover Alonzo Mitchell, who rode for Pink Higgins and other Lampasas County trail bosses. "After we got them up into Indian Territory, we could depend upon nearly all the

Trail boss Pink Higgins, seated at right, poses with a crew of drovers. Front row, from left: Felix Castello, Jess Standard, Bob Mitchell, Pink Higgins. Back row: Powell Woods, unknown, Buck Allen, fun-loving Alonzo "Lonce" Mitchell (Lonce and Bob Mitchell were Pink's brothers-in-law). —Author's collection

storms coming from the northwest. We and the cattle both generally got warnings out of the sky, but the storm nearly always broke with great suddenness and fury."[15]

The flamboyant combination of dangerous frontier journeys and brave, colorful cowboys created a romantic adventure that captivated the American public. The exciting climax to that adventure was the arrival of the herds and crews in Abilene or Dodge City or other railhead towns. These towns, with their saloons and dance halls and red light districts, became part of the cowboy legend. Lampasas County drovers rollicked their way through the dives of these raucous towns. During the open range era, cowboying was largely seasonal work, and many drovers were employed only during round-ups and trail drives. Some young cowboys, looking to revisit the hilarity of end-of-the-drive sprees in Dodge or Abilene or Wichita, liked to loaf around the saloons of Lampasas. When they drank too much fights broke out, with fists and, all too often, with sixguns.

An inescapable element of the cattle frontier was the theft of livestock, horses as well as cattle. As soon as settlers began to move into Lampasas County, Comanches helped themselves to their horses. Comanches were the most successful horse thieves the county—and much of Texas—would ever see. No matter what precautions were taken, Comanches could steal horses almost within reach of the owners. More horses were stolen in Lampasas County than in almost any other county. After Comancheros found a market for cattle in New Mexico and Arizona, raiders began to steal cattle as well as horses. Year after year, livestock was taken from the pastures and stables of Lampasas County.

In the absence of nearby military protection, Lampasas settlers resorted to pursuit posses. Comanche raiders often were intercepted, especially if they were driving large herds of stolen animals. Sometimes there were running fights, but more often Comanches would abandon stolen livestock and gallop away to safety. Many stolen animals were recovered, therefore, but many more were driven out of the county, never to return.

By the time Comanche raiders disappeared from Lampasas County, Anglo rustlers had been stealing horses and cattle for years. Lampasas County was open range country, and it was relatively easy to steal cattle as well as horses. Every issue of Lampasas newspapers listed missing horses under a small headline: "ESTRAY NOTICE" or "STRAYED" or "$50 REWARD." A description of the horse would follow: "a fine sorrel Mare—black mane and tail—about 6 years old—branded on the shoulder J-T connected together—a white spot on the neck." The date and place of disappearance was mentioned, along with the amount of reward offered. Many ads began, "STRAYED OR STOLEN," and some ads even stated the name and description of the suspected rustler. The first Lampasas newspaper, the *Chronicle* of October 1, 1859, listed five stray notices. The next newspaper was the *Lampasas Dispatch* of 1871, and thereafter newspaper after newspaper listed strays, through the 1880s and into the 1890s. Of course, most of the "strays" had not strayed— they had been taken by thieves.[16]

If pursuit posses were effective against Comanche raiders in the absence of the military, they could just as readily be utilized against rustlers in the absence of inadequate legal authority in Lampasas County. Such posses were extralegal, but extralegal action in America traced back to the 1760s and 1770s, when British authority began to break down in the face of scores of colonial riots, most famously the Boston Massacre (1770) and Boston Tea Party (1773). In this atmosphere of unsanctioned violence, an outbreak of frontier crime in South Carolina triggered an extralegal response by angry citizens. From 1767 through 1769, respectable citizens organized themselves as "Regulators" and tried troublemakers, flogging and expelling many undesirables. One outlaw gang was cornered, and sixteen members were slain.[17]

This successful Regulator movement inspired hundreds of similar actions during the remainder of the eighteenth century, throughout the nineteenth century, and into the twentieth century. For a century these extralegal groups usually were called "Regulators," but by the late 1800s the customary term had become "vigilante." Another term common to extralegal experiences was provided by Colonel Charles Lynch, a prominent citizen of Bedford County, Virginia (the town of Lynchburg was named for Colonel Lynch). By 1780, with the American Revolution still raging, Bedford County had become a hotbed of outlawry. Leading citizens formed a court with Colonel Lynch sitting as presiding judge. Regular—if illegal—trials were held, with flogging as the common punishment. This court thereby dispensed "Lynch Law," although in time this term came to mean a far more lethal form of law than flogging. Indeed, during the eighteenth, nineteenth, and twentieth centuries, more than 6,000 men and a few women were executed by vigilante activities.[18]

Vigilantism flourished on the frontier in the 1800s. The westward movement regularly outraced the establishment of courts, law officers, and even jails. Extralegal action was quicker and cheaper than any system of courts, judges, juries, attorneys, trials, appeals, and institutional punishment.

Such conditions long prevailed in Lampasas County. The county did not have enough money to build a proper courthouse. The small, rattle-trap jail on the south side of the square could not be relied upon to hold prisoners determined to escape. The sheriff, chief law enforcement officer of the county, was paid so poorly that no one was willing to serve for long. The first sheriff, H. B. Dobbins, left his post within seven months. His successor served less than a year, while the third sheriff lasted only three months. The fourth sheriff was in office a little more than eight months. Sheriff Tom Hardy was the first to serve a full term, August 1858 to August 1860. Not until S. T. Denson, December 1869 to December 1873, did a sheriff serve consecutive terms.[19]

With scant legal apparatus in Lampasas County, it was natural for posses that pursued Comanches for horse theft to pursue rustlers for the same offense. Aside from hot pursuit there was little deterrence to stock thieves. A measure of organization was provided by the Law and Order League, which grew up across Texas somewhat after the fashion of the Ku Klux Klan elsewhere in the state. Like the KKK, the Law and Order League readily employed lynching. Also like the KKK, secret methods of communication were practiced by members. When encountering a stranger at night, for example, a Law and Order man would inquire, "Who comes?" If the moon was up, the correct reply was, "Moon down," and if the moon was down, the response was, "Moon up." A daytime encounter would begin with, "How may I know you?"—to which a fellow Law and Order man would say, "I'll word it with you." Then the two men would alternately call out the letters, "D, N, R, S."[20]

While still a teenager, Pink Higgins joined the Law and Order League, pursuing rustlers as zealously as he pursued Comanche raiders. When he was eighteen, Pink and several other Law and Order men gave chase to a horse thief, doggedly following their prey for two days and two nights. Along the way, Law and Order supporters provided fresh mounts. When the rustler finally was overtaken, the tired pursuers decided to apply summary justice. A rope was thrown over the limb of a hackberry tree, and Pink adjusted the noose around the captive's neck. Given an opportunity to speak, the rustler gamely allowed that he was going to hell, and that he wanted to arrive in time to find a partner for the first dance. Then he kicked his horse out from under himself and commenced his final journey.[21]

A decade later a horse was stolen from a ranch near Lometa. A pursuit posse trailed the rustler to a ranch near Adamsville. The horse thief was seized and hanged, and the corpse swayed from the hanging tree for three days. "The local people decided they ought to bury the body," said Charles Van Trease, whose ranch was the site of the burial, "so they did somewhere in the woods where the earth wasn't all rock and the earth easy to dig in."[22]

The most notorious cattle rustlers in Lampasas County were the Horrell brothers. The Horrell clan came to Lampasas in 1857, but twice left the county to move west. When the Horrells returned to Lampasas from New Mexico the first time, in 1869, their father and oldest brother had been killed, and they had lost their cattle herd. "They had nothing but their teams and wagon with them," remembered a neighbor, John Nichols.[23] Five years later, following another violent stay in New Mexico, the surviving brothers again returned with almost nothing. The Horrell herds were rebuilt at least partially by rustling. Pink Higgins was one of their victims in the 1870s. Predictably he responded with violence, and—triggered by cattle rustling—a murderous blood feud exploded in the streets of Lampasas.

A cowboy named George Potter was widely suspected of stealing cattle in Williamson County to the south. In the summer of 1882 Potter was noticed riding near a herd in Townsen country—and he had no credentials as a cattle inspector. On August 2 Potter was taken into custody by an armed "party of unknown men." These men escorted Potter from the herd near Townsen's Mill to a secluded location beside a creek. Potter was shot to death—lynched by gunfire—and his corpse was left near the stream.[24]

Both livestock theft and cattle ranching in Lampasas County were affected by a transformative invention of the 1870s. Fencing was needed by farmers to keep cattle out of their cultivated fields, and by ranchers to enclose pastures and water sources. Smooth wire was tried in western country, but hungry cattle could break through such harmless fencing and ravage a cornfield. Thorny shrubs were tried in South Texas, but rugged longhorn steers were able to eat their way through this ineffective barrier. Wire with barbs proved to be an impassable obstacle to animals, but early versions had barbs that were large enough to cut a plug from the hides of horses and cows, and this fencing was too expensive to manufacture and market profitably. Open range remained open.

During the decade after the Civil War, 122 patents were registered for new types of fencing, most of which proved impractical. But near DeKalb, Illinois, Joseph Glidden struggled with an inexpensive method of enclosing his 600-acre farm. By 1874, he had devised a way to twist together two strands of wire so that they could hold pointed wire barbs. Glidden patented the wire, rented a small factory in DeKalb, and began manufacturing. Sales were so brisk that within a few months steam machinery was installed, increasing production to five tons a day. Annual sales jumped from three million pounds of barb wire fence in 1876 to 12 million pounds the next year, 50 million pounds in 1879, and 80 million in 1880. Production on such a scale dropped the prices from $20 per 100 pounds in 1870 to $10 in 1880 to less than $4 a decade later. Competitors enjoyed success with similar models of barbed wire, which further reduced prices.[25]

By the 1880s barbed wire was being sold by Lampasas merchants, and the county soon was crisscrossed by "bobwire" fences. During the fall of 1888, for example, the *Lampasas Leader* regularly ran barbed wire ads for two stores. S. T. Singletary & Co., a farm machinery firm, included "Glidden Barbed Wire" in its large ad. A smaller ad headlined: "Barbed Wire! Barbed Wire!," emphasizing that "W. E. Gilbert is selling for cash the cheapest and best barb wire made."[26]

The long cattle drives ended during the mid-1880s, just as barbed wire closed the open range of Lampasas County. Instead of round-ups and trail drives to distant cattle towns, cowboys now mended fences and produced winter feed and performed other work that seemed more like farm chores than cow work.

No matter. The cowboy culture already was as permanently ingrained in Lampasas as in most of the rest of cow country. In 1888, even though long drives were a thing of the past, J. M. Coleman, a dealer in saddles and harness on the north side of the square, stressed in his advertising: "RANCHMEN'S OUTFITS A SPECIALTY."[27] Cattle country clothing still could be worn, and men continued to ride horseback.

Pink Higgins led trail drives as long as possible. In 1882 he advertised:

CATTLE WANTED
I want to purchase any number of good cattle,
For which I will pay the highest cash price. Call
on our address.   PINK HIGGINS
Lampasas, Texas[28]

Will Standard, son of Lampasas County trail driver Jess Standard, was born in 1879. As a teenager Will followed his father into cowboying, posing with a gun rig and chaps—and tie. But Will married at twenty-four, and he quit the range to find steady work in Lampasas, although he trained horses the rest of his life. —Author's collection

"Our address" was the meat market he had opened in Lampasas and which served as an outlet for the cattle he raised at Higgins Gap. His 1882 ad helped produce a herd of 1,600 cattle, which he drove up the Western Trail to Dodge City.[29]

During this period Higgins was in business with a cattleman named Al Shanklin, who was backed by his family. In 1881 Higgins and Shanklin sent 10,000 head of cattle in five herds to Colorado. Bob Fudge was a strapping cowboy who rode with the last of the 1881 herds, and he reminisced that his crew consisted of eight cowboys, a horse wrangler, and a cook. This crew departed in May and delivered their herd in August to Hugo, on the plains of east-central Colorado. According to Fudge, Higgins and Shanklin went broke on the 10,000 cattle they contracted for that year, but "Shanklin's people were very wealthy and staked him again." Fudge hired on with Higgins and Shanklin once more in 1884, helping to drive cows and calves to Charles Goodnight in the Texas Panhandle.[30]

Pink Higgins had become Lampasas County's most active and prominent trail contractor. But the trail drive era soon ended. In middle age Pink followed the old ways to West Texas, becoming a stock detective—a highly intimidating stock detective—for the 570,000-acre Spur Ranch. As a seventeen-year-old cowboy, Pink Higgins helped drive a herd of longhorns 1,100 miles to Cheyenne. For the remaining forty-five years of his life, in one capacity or another, Pink lived as a cowman.[31]

Jess Standard, one of Pink's drovers in the 1870s and 1880s, had to leave a wife and three little boys behind in Lampasas County when he was on a trail drive. During the 1880s his young wife died, the trail drives ended, and he remarried. His new wife owned a small spread outside Tuscola, south of Abilene. Jess moved to Tuscola, worked the spread, which was more farm than ranch, and on the side plied the carpenter's trade. But to the end of his long life, the old trail driver wore a Texas ten-gallon hat, uncreased. His son, Will Standard, stayed in Lampasas, found work as a cowboy, and fell in love with horses. After he married he took steady employment in town, but he trained horses on the side, and he always wore cowboy boots and a Stetson. Will's son, Ted Standard, became a master saddlemaker, competed in rodeos into middle age, and wore boots and jeans and cowboy hats all his life.[32]

Today many Lampasans still wear boots and jeans and cowboy hats. By the 1870s the culture of "long-horned steers, cow-ponies and six shooters"[33] had become imbedded in the culture of Lampasas, and today many elements of the old-time cowboy life remain an inextricable part of the Lampasas identity.

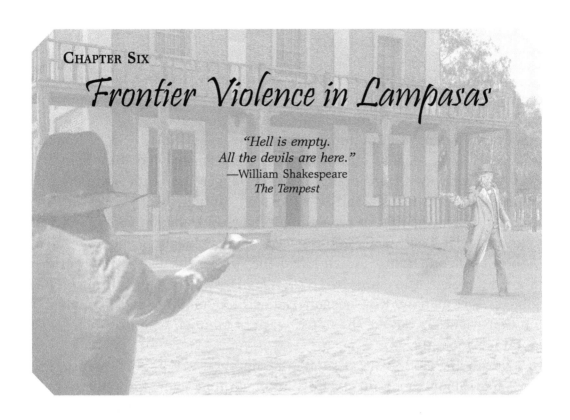

CHAPTER SIX

Frontier Violence in Lampasas

"Hell is empty.
All the devils are here."
—William Shakespeare
The Tempest

Texas was the gunfighter capital of the West. In the 1840s Texas Rangers began using the newly invented, small-caliber, five-shot Paterson Colt revolver during horseback fights against Comanche warriors. Texans quickly refined and popularized the revolver, and by the 1850s they were blazing away at each other in gunfights with large-caliber six-shooters. The era of the Western gunfighter had begun.

After the cowboy, the most colorful and romanticized frontier figure is the gunfighter. Western novels and movies distorted both the cowboy and the gunfighter, but whatever the reality, Texas had more cowboys and gunmen than any other frontier state or territory. A survey of 256 Western gunfighters and 589 shootouts in which they participated reveals that Texas dominated the tally sheet of frontier shootists. More of these gunfights—nearly 160—occurred in Texas than in any other state or territory. Most western states or territories saw widespread gunplay for only a brief number of years before law and order prevailed: Kansas, for example during the cattle town era; New Mexico during the bloody Lincoln County War; and Oklahoma during its lawless heyday as an outlaw refuge. But gunfighters first opened fire in Texas during the 1850s and continued their life and death encounters until past the turn of the century.[1]

More frontier gunfighters were born in Texas than in any other state or territory, and more died in Texas. Texas produced many prominent gunfighters, from the psychopathic John Wesley Hardin to the West's premier assassin, Killin' Jim Miller. There was famed Texas Ranger John R. Hughes, deadly outlaw-lawman King Fisher, and John Selman, who numbered Wes Hardin and ex-Texas Ranger Baz Outlaw among his victims. Eleven of Ben Thompson's fourteen gunfights were in Texas. Doc Holliday fought the first of his eight gunfights in Dallas in 1875, and the following year Bat Masterson engaged in his inaugural shootout in a Mobeetie saloon. Henry Brown killed the first of his five career victims in a Panhandle cattle camp in 1876. Wes Hardin, Ben Thompson, John Selman, Baz Outlaw, King Fisher, Dallas Stoudenmire, and "Longhair" Jim Courtright are among the noted western gunmen who lost their lives in Texas shootouts.

During the 1880s at least ten fatal gunfights erupted in Tascosa, including a saloon shootout in 1886 in which four men were killed—one more than the legendary gunfight at Tombstone's OK Corral in 1881. Other Texas towns which proved to be hotbeds of gunfighter action included San Antonio, El Paso, Fort Worth—and Lampasas. A spectacular saloon fight in Lampasas in 1873 resulted in the deaths of four officers of the Texas State Police, which created a startling infamy for Lampasas in the annals of saloon gunplay. Furthermore, Lampasas produced a gunfighter of the front rank, Pink Higgins, who used his guns against Comanche warriors, stock thieves, and personal adversaries from the time he was a teenager until he claimed his last victim in a *mano a mano* rifle duel when he was in his fifties.

The Lampasas heyday of homicidal saloon fights and street shootouts was the decade of the 1870s, but the first fatal gunfight occurred in the summer of 1855, when the new townsite was surveyed and lots sold. At Hancock Springs, where hundreds of people were camped, Bob Willis fatally wounded a man named Nixon. Instead of settling in town, Willis made his home on School Creek, north of Lampasas. On October 1, 1872, Willis was slain at his home by an assassin who was never identified. The motivation could have been anything, because by the 1870s Lampasas County was wracked by violence. But revenge for the Nixon killing cannot be discounted, even though seventeen years had passed. Memories of the killing of a loved one were long on the frontier, and in seventeen years a Nixon son could have grown up enough to satisfy family honor.[2]

During the 1860s the principal frontier violence in Lampasas County involved clashes with Comanche raiders. During this long conflict a number of Lampasans were brutally slain and mutilated, while in retribution many warriors were killed without mercy. This protracted and nearby warfare hardened the citizens of Lampasas County to bloodshed. When gunfights replaced Comanche skirmishes during the 1870s, Lampasans were not squeamish or fearful.

Furthermore, during the 1870s a significant development in weaponry took place. The old cap-and-ball revolving pistols, tedious and slow to reload, were made obsolete by cartridge revolvers. In 1873 the Colt .45 Peacemaker, a classic weapon of the frontier, was introduced to immediate popularity. Also in 1873 Winchester Arms introduced the Model 1873, which utilized a .44-caliber center fire cartridge. Lever-action, repeating rifles had been available since 1860, but the Winchester '73 became the best-selling rifle in the West. The Winchester '73 was so popular that in 1878 Colt chambered its single-action Peacemaker for the same .44 cartridge so that a man could use interchangeable ammunition in his revolver and his shoulder gun. During the gunfighting era in Lampasas and vicinity, these were the weapons most commonly used by shootists.

"At this time Lampasas was a frontier town and wide open as far as saloons and gambling were concerned," reported Texas Ranger Jim Gillett. "The Horrells, like most cattlemen of the period, loved to congregate in town, go to the saloons and have a good time, perhaps drink too much, and sometimes at night shoot up the town for fun, as they termed it." The door of a law office on the southeast corner of the square absorbed twenty or more bullets, while roisterers shot out the windows of the *Lampasas Dispatch* building.[3]

A rowdy midday saloon celebration resulted in the shooting of Sheriff S. T. Denson. Shadrick "Shade" Denson was born in Mississippi in 1833, and he married Elizabeth Sparks, daughter of Lampasas County pioneer Samuel Sparks. Shade and Elizabeth moved near the Sparks home east of Lampasas before the Civil War. Elizabeth died in 1861, shortly after giving birth to their fourth child. Shade volunteered to serve in the Lampasas company of R.T.P. Allen's Infantry Regiment, and when the Civil War ended he was a captain. Captain Denson remarried, and Shade and Adeline had nine children. He was in his second term as sheriff when he almost lost his life in a Lampasas saloon.[4]

Jerry Scott, a crony of the Horrell brothers, recently had opened "a first class DRINKING SALOON on the N.W. corner of the Public Square."[5] On Tuesday, January 14, 1872, court was in session in the frame building on the south side of the square that served as a court-house. During the noon recess Sheriff Denson heard a loud disturbance from across the square. The trouble spot was Jerry Scott's saloon, where the Short brothers, Mark and Wash, had been drinking since morning. John Nichols was a neighbor of the Horrells and knew the brothers and their pals. "Mark Short was a wild man who tried to paint the town up," related Nichols.[6]

Sheriff Denson entered the saloon, tried to make an arrest, then found himself locked in a scuffle with the Short brothers. Denson shouted for help, but Mark shot him in the side. Tom Sparks, Denson's brother-in-law, and several other citizens hurried to offer help. But Tom, Mart, and Ben Horrell blocked their path so that the Short brothers—fel-low saloon denizens—could escape. Sparks quickly mounted a posse, but the Horrells already had jumped on their horses. The Horrell brothers again blocked the pursuers long enough for Mark and Wash Short to

Saloons were part of the life of frontier Lampasas, but during the 1870s a series of deadly shootings erupted in the town's whisky mills. —Courtesy KSM

gallop into the countryside. Sheriff Denson recovered from his wound and served the rest of his term, leaving office in December 1873, but he carried Mark Short's bullet the rest of his life.[7]

Sam Denson, Shade's oldest son, was seventeen when Mark Short shot his father. In 1876, when Sam was twenty-one, Short was apprehended in another county, and he was returned to Lampasas in September, posting bond to stand trial in district court. Texas courts were notoriously lenient regarding gunfights, particularly when no one was killed, and Sam Denson wanted revenge. Finding his father's attacker in a saloon, Denson proclaimed: "Mark Short, you are my meat!" Denson killed Short with three revolver bullets, then escaped on horseback to Montana. Changing his name, he worked as a cowboy, eventually serving as foreman of one of his Uncle John Sparks' Nevada ranches. In 1892, when his father died at the age of fifty-nine, Sam returned to Lampasas and won a not guilty verdict from a friendly jury.[8]

Meanwhile, the Horrell brothers continued to cause trouble, as they had since they were youngsters in Lampasas County. Sam Horrell moved his family from Arkansas in 1857, when he was thirty-seven and his wife Elizabeth was three years younger. Sam and Elizabeth were the parents of seven boys and an infant daughter: Bill, eighteen; John, sixteen; Sam Jr., fourteen; Mart, eleven; Tom, nine; Ben, six; Merritt, three; and baby Sally. John Nichols described the brothers as "very clannish." Although the boys sometimes scrapped with each other, they learned to rally to any family member with fists or guns. "Well," observed Elizabeth Horrell with the pride of a frontier mother, "I raised my boys to be fighters."[9]

Her oldest son, Bill Horrell, went off to fight in the Civil War, but he died of illness while in Confederate service. Sam Horrell, who had enlisted in the Lampasas Guards during the Comanche alarms of 1859, also served in home guard units during the Civil War, and so did his next oldest sons, John and Sam Jr.

Also during the war the boys began to marry. John, Mart, and Ben wed Grizzell sisters. When the wives of Sam and Mart had a falling out, "Mart was going to whip Sam over it," related John Nichols. "Mart was rather surly at times. When a quarrel started he did not want to waste any words but wanted to go straight to business." When he went straight at his brother, though, Sam clubbed him with his revolver, and Sam Sr. intervened to settle down the feisty Mart. Mart's feistiness would translate into raw courage when bullets were flying.[10]

In 1868 the family decided to move to California. But in New

Mexico they sold their cattle herd, forty-eight-year-old Sam was killed in an Apache attack, and twenty-eight-year-old John was shot to death by a drover who claimed he had not been paid. With both the patriarch and the now-oldest son dead, and with no cattle to drive, the surviving Horrells returned to Lampasas County. The two widows settled at Lampasas: Elizabeth found a house near the town square, while young Sallie Ann Horrell moved onto property owned by John near one of the springs, eking out a living by renting space to health-seeking campers. Tom established a small ranch on Mesquite Creek ten miles east of town. At sixteen, Ben married a fifteen-year-old, and Merritt married when he was nineteen.[11]

Although slightly cross-eyed, Tom "was the smartest of them all," stated John Nichols. The "general" of the brothers, Tom "was a natural diplomat, suave, polite, gushing and talkative when he met you." Fair-haired with a florid complexion, like all of the brothers, Tom was five-feet-nine-inches and weighed about 165 pounds. The pugnacious Mart was the same size, while Merritt was smaller, no more than 140 pounds. "All of them were a little better than average shots," pointed out Nichols. They were fond of carousing in Lampasas saloons. "They drank considerable," said Nichols, adding ominously that "they were always loaded for bear, drunk or sober."[12]

Tom, Mart, and Ben Horrell probably had been drinking, and certainly they were "loaded for bear" when Sheriff S. T. Denson was wounded while trying to arrest Mark and Wash Short in Jerry Scott's saloon. The three Horrell brothers helped the Short brothers escape. Frustrated by the wounding of their sheriff, by the flagrant support of the Shorts by the Horrells, and by the general lawlessness, county officials sent a request for help to Governor E. J. Davis.

Davis was a Republican and a former Union officer who was handed the governorship by Reconstruction officials through the scandalously fraudulent election of 1869. Among the controversial actions of Governor Davis was the creation of a State Police force. The authorized strength was 257 men, but the number of officers never exceeded 200. The force was active in arresting criminals, but their authority was resented, especially since more than one-fifth of the officers were former slaves. But Sergeant J. M. Redmon and a detail of the State Police responded to the Lampasas request for assistance, intending to make numerous arrests. Sergeant Redmon posted a proclamation from the governor prohibiting the wearing of sidearms. Two years earlier Lampasas

County and twenty other counties, because of Comanche raids, were exempted from an act regulating "the keeping and bearing" of firearms. Lampasans responded to the new prohibition by discharging firearms during the middle of the night to defy the detested State Police. After several days, Sergeant Redmon led his men back to Austin, empty-handed.[13]

Sheriff Denson immediately wrote to Adjutant General and Chief of the State Police F. L. Britton, asking for a return of state officers. Within a few weeks Captain T. W. Williams was dispatched with a squad of men to ban the use of firearms in Lampasas and to make key arrests. On the road from Austin to Lampasas, Captain Williams, who had been drinking, remarked to a passerby that he intended "to clean up those damned Horrell boys."[14]

Williams led his men into Lampasas on Friday afternoon, March 14, 1873. As the policemen tied their horses to live oak trees clustered in the town square, Williams saw a man who was wearing a revolver enter a saloon. The armed man was Bill Bowen, and the saloon he entered was the favorite haunt of the Horrell brothers and their friends. Jerry Scott's saloon was on the west side of the square, the second door from the northwest corner. Williams left a black officer and two other men with the horses, taking three policemen with him into the saloon.

Mart, Tom, and Merritt Horrell, along with brothers-in-law Bill Bowen, Ben Turner and Jim Grizzell, the Short brothers, and several cowboys, were lounging inside the saloon. A game of billiards was under way and in one corner a fiddle and a banjo provided music, but all eyes suspiciously shifted to the lawmen as they entered.

Williams approached the bar, ordered drinks, and then boldly addressed Bowen. "I believe you have a six-shooter," he said, nodding at Bowen's holstered revolver. "I arrest you."[15]

"Bill," snapped the pugnacious Mart Horrell, "you have done nothing and need not be arrested if you don't want to."

In the face of open defiance, Captain Williams whipped out a six-gun and pumped a slug into Mart. Immediately Tom, Merritt, Jerry Scott, Bill Bowen, and several others produced weapons. The narrow room quickly became hazy with acrid white smoke, but the saloon men found their targets.

Captain Williams and Private T. M. Daniels slumped to the floor, mortally wounded. Privates William Cherry and Andrew Melville bolted for the door, but Cherry was killed as he stepped outside and Melville was hit as he sprinted away. Melville managed to stagger to the Huling Hotel, where he died four weeks later. On the square the black officer watching the horses vaulted onto a mount and galloped toward Austin, while the other two policemen followed close behind.

Tom and Merritt Horrell carried their wounded brother to their mother's house nearby, then joined their fellow gunmen in heading for the open range. Adjutant General Britton promptly led a dozen members of the State Police to Lampasas, where he arrested Jerry Scott, the bedridden Mart Horrell, Jim Grizzell, and cowboy Allen Whitecroft. These prisoners were taken to Austin, then transferred to Georgetown, not quite thirty miles north of Austin.

The three deceased officers were buried in Lampasas the day after the shooting, but at state expense the bodies soon were moved to the State Cemetery in Austin. The mortally wounded Andrew Melville, still hopeful of recovery, gave his account to officials and reporters. He felt that Bill Bowen was "a decoy" who lured Captain Williams into the saloon. Melville also said that Williams simply "attempted to wrest" Bowen's gun from him, when he was shot in the back of the head, where-upon "at least eight or ten men" opened fire (and one of them would have hit Mart Horrell with friendly fire). A coroner's jury, which in-cluded Alex Northington, concluded that the men responsible for the killings were Tom, Merritt and Mart Horrell, Bill Bowen, Jerry Scott, Ben Turner, James Grizzell, Allen Whitecroft, Bill Gray, and Joe Bolden. The state offered a $500 reward for each of these men who remained at large. When Adjutant General Britton returned to Austin, ten officers were stationed in Lampasas.[16]

But on April 22, 1873—over a month after the shootout, and nearly two weeks after Private Melville died—the legislature disbanded the police force. In just under three years of existence, ten state policemen were shot to death in the line of duty, and the last four died in Lampasas.

The Horrells laid plans to free their incarcerated comrades. Artemisa Grizzell Horrell, Mart's wife, was permitted to nurse the wounded man in his cell. After more than two months Artemesia finally sent word that Mart was well enough to travel. About an hour before midnight on Friday, May 2, the four Horrell brothers sallied into Georgetown at the head of a large party of armed men and rode boldly to the jail.

While the others stood guard with rifles, Bill Bowen dismounted and assaulted the door with a sledgehammer. Aroused townspeople rushed toward the jail and both parties began firing. Bowen ignored a bullet which drew blood and kept swinging until the door shattered. When A. S. Fisher, a local lawyer who advertised in the *Lampasas Dispatch* ("Will practice in all the counties of the 32nd Judicial District, and in the Supreme Courts at Austin."), was shot in the leg and side, the citizens retreated. Now unchallenged, the Horrell party thundered triumphantly out of town.[17]

The wanted men remained at large in the Lampasas County countryside. Although there seemed to be little enthusiasm for trying to arrest such lethal desperadoes, the Horrell brothers wisely decided to move west out of Texas jurisdiction. Livestock was rounded up, wagons were packed, and other preparations were made for the exodus from Lampasas County. The Horrell clan, including Bill Bowen and Ben Turner, along with several other cowboy-gunmen, comprised such a formidable force that they went unchallenged by authorities. The Horrells even informed Sheriff S. T. Denson of their exit route, brazenly confident that they would not be molested.

"I had dinner in camp with the outlaws, who made no effort to hide from the authorities," reminisced James Gillett who, as a sixteen-year-old cowboy, helped deliver a herd of cattle to the Horrells in Coleman County, en route to New Mexico. "I remember they sat about the camp with Winchesters in their laps."[18]

Unhurriedly the Horrells ventured back into New Mexico Territory—where once again they would become embroiled in homicidal conflict. The Horrells leased range in Lincoln County, at 27,000 square miles the largest county in the United States. Comprising the entire southeastern quarter of New Mexico, Lincoln County was inadequately policed by one sheriff and a handful of deputies. In this lawless area the Horrells soon went to their guns. Twenty-two-year-old Ben Horrell was killed in a shootout in Lincoln. The constable who was trying to arrest him also was killed, and so were two of Ben's drinking companions.

Blood called to blood. The Horrells launched a vendetta that erupted into the "Horrell War," a violent preview of the far more famous Lincoln County War that would gain notoriety for Billy the Kid a few years later. The Horrell War produced nearly thirty fatalities, including Ben Turner and two Horrell gunmen. With the countryside mobilizing against them, the Texans suddenly ended the Horrell War by pulling out in February 1874. They had to fight their way past various adversaries, but by early March they were back in the Lampasas area.[19]

News of the violent trek from New Mexico to Texas preceded their return. Albertus Sweet, recently elected sheriff of Lampasas County, led a search for the fugitives. On March 5, 1874, a large posse jumped part of the Horrell faction, wounding Jerry Scott and another partisan and capturing a third man. Merritt Horrell also was nicked, but he escaped, along with Mart and Tom, who rode up during the fight, then spurred away under fire into the brush.[20]

By this time Governor E. J. Davis had left office, following a resounding defeat by Democrat Richard Coke. Also in 1874 the Frontier Battalion of Texas Rangers was authorized and formed, under the leadership of the redoubtable Major John B. Jones. With Davis out of office and his despised State Police disbanded, the Horrell brothers, hiding out in the wilderness, were advised "by the best citizens of Lampasas County" that the time was favorable to clear up the charges relating to the slaying of four unlamented state policemen. Released under bond, the Horrells were not tried until October 1876, when a sympathetic jury acquitted Mart, Merritt, and Tom—without leaving the jury box.[21]

After returning from New Mexico, the Horrell brothers prudently kept a low profile before their trial. But their inclination for trouble, their willingness to go to their guns, would not be stifled for very long after their acquittal. Two brothers already had been shot to death, and three more soon would die by gunfire. Between 1868 and 1878 five Horrell brothers were killed by gunplay, but they left a bloody casualty list behind.

The Horrells were prominent among numerous sets of gunfighting brothers across the West. Frontier families learned early to stick together for sheer survival, and brothers often backed each other with guns. The most famous gunfighting brother duos were Frank and Jesse James, Texans Ben and Billy Thompson, and Arizona's Ike and Billy Clanton and Frank and Tom McClaury (all four Arizonans were killed in shootouts, including three at the OK Corral). Bat, Ed, and Jim Masterson wore badges in various frontier towns, and Ed was killed while marshal of Dodge City. Wyatt, Virgil, Morgan, and Warren Earp also were generally on the side of the law, and Morgan and Virgil were shot in Arizona. Frank Dalton was killed while serving as a deputy U.S. marshal, but his brothers Bob, Emmett, Grat, and Bill went bad, and all but Emmett were gunned down. Also on the wrong side of the law were the Younger brothers: John was killed in a shootout with Pinkerton detectives, while the other three were badly wounded during an abortive bank robbery.

The oldest Horrell brother, Bill, fell to illness while wearing a Confederate uniform. The other six brothers shot it out with Indians and lawmen and assorted other opponents. They engaged in saloon shootouts and street battles and running fights—they even killed four men while shooting up a Mexican wedding dance in Lincoln. They fought for vengeance and for survival and, sometimes, because they were drinking too much. They went to war in a Lampasas County blood feud, and in New Mexico they had a war named after them. And during their decade as almost compulsive shootists, five Horrell brothers were shot to death. By any measure—number and variety of shootouts, number of wounded or dead victims, number of dead brothers—the Horrells of Lampasas County rank at the top of any list of gunfighting brothers.

If the Horrells were instrumental in maintaining the atmosphere of

This cell is part of a cell block from the 1870 Lampasas county jail, which housed a succession of troublemakers and criminals during the wild years of Lampasas. This cell block now stands behind the Keystone Square Museum. —Photo by the author

frontier violence in Lampasas County, other men were emboldened to go to their guns. On December 10, 1874, for example, two cowboys settled a dispute with gunplay in the countryside north of Lampasas. Charlie Boyd and Stumpy Watson badly wounded each other, and they were carried to the cabin of pioneers Pleasant and Martha Jane Cox. Martha Jane cared for them, but they both died twelve days later. On August 13, 1875, Charles Keith killed William Britnal. Keith was arrested, tried in October 1876, and convicted of second degree murder. Sentenced to ten years in the state penitentiary in Huntsville, Keith was temporarily jailed in Burnet County. One of his jail mates was Horrell brother-in-law Bill Bowen. In December 1876, before his delivery to Huntsville, Keith escaped jail, along with Bowen and another prisoner.[22]

Two months after Charles Keith shot William Britnal, Dr. J. W. Hudson was killed just outside town. Like the dentist Doc Holliday, Dr. Hudson left the practice of medicine to become a gambler. Dr. Hudson was operating a gambling house in Lampasas in November 1875 when he was summoned by a grand jury for questioning. When Dr. Hudson failed to report, Deputy Sheriff W. S. Douglass was directed to bring him under arrest to the grand jury. Rounding up a small posse, Douglass found Hudson about two miles outside town. But as the party rode back into Lampasas, Hudson broke off and spurred away from the posse. Douglass shouted for him to stop, but Hudson drew a pistol. Douglass pulled out his Winchester, there was an exchange of gunfire, and Hudson was shot off his horse. Taken into town, he died the next day.[23]

Deputy Douglass had married Sally Horrell, sister of the gunfighting brothers. But Douglass was wanted for murder in Virginia, and in 1878 Sheriff Albertus Sweet was notified of an $1,100 reward for the former deputy. Sheriff Sweet and Deputy Doolittle "found out where Douglas [*sic*] was hiding," according to John Nichols. "Doolittle crawled into a thicket where he was, jumped on Douglas, and Douglas almost bit his finger off; but they took him, sent him back to Virginia, and got a liberal reward."[24]

In 1876 Sheriff Sweet was asked to provide custody for two notorious gunmen of the murderous Mason County War, Scott Cooley and John Ringo. In February 1876 Cooley and Ringo were indicted in Burnet County for "seriously threatening to take the life" of the county sheriff and one of his deputies. There was a change of venue to Lampasas County, and Cooley and Ringo were transferred to the jail south of the Lampasas public square. Like most county jails in the area, including Burnet's, the Lampasas lockup was vulnerable to escape attempts. Sheriff Sweet took the precaution of posting around-the-clock guards.[25]

But the night guard was seized by four friends of Cooley and Ringo early on the morning of May 1, 1876. The guard was tied to a fence while two men tried to cut through the wall of the jail. Unsuccessful, they rode west out of town, taking the guard about two miles before releasing him. Four days later, on May 5, allies of the prisoners returned in force. First riding to Sheriff Sweet's home, the gang of fifteen armed men threatened to kill the sheriff and his family if he did not turn over the jail keys. Sweet complied, and the gang proceeded to the jail, catching the two guards outside. The outnumbered guards did not put up a fight, and Cooley and Ringo were delivered from their cell. They had been "hobbled," but the hobbles were placed across a log and cut with an axe. Now freed, Cooley and Ringo rode to Llano County with their rescuers.[26] The deadly Cooley soon died of illness, while Ringo made his way to Arizona. There his lethal reputation exceeded his deeds, and he was killed in 1882.

Sheriff Sweet and the county commissioners belatedly decided to strengthen the jail with a protective wall. "The barricade around the jail is nearly completed," reported the *Dispatch*, "and although an eyesore to our people, we hope [it] may be of service in keeping more securely the prisoners in jail."[27]

In the same month, September 1876, that Sam Denson killed Mark Short in a Lampasas saloon, County Attorney B. F. Hamilton was called an "S.O.B." by Newton Cook. Responding to the insult in a manner not befitting his office, Hamilton confronted Cook in front of a saloon. Producing a derringer, Hamilton managed only to shoot himself in the hand. Cook angrily pulled a revolver and triggered a shot at Hamilton,

About to depart, this stagecoach stands in front of a Lampasas hotel. Stagecoach travel in and out of Lampasas was heavy—a temptation to frontier highwaymen. —Courtesy KSM

who fled to the live oak trees around the public square. An inebriated Constable Elwood Bean brandished his own revolver and pursued Cook. Bystanders Tom and Merritt Horrell, acting in the unfamiliar role of peacemakers, averted bloodshed by disarming Hamilton and Bean, respectively. Hamilton and Bean were charged with assault with intent to kill, and Hamilton resigned as county attorney.[28]

On Friday, September 21, 1877, Lampasans had the opportunity to see the deadliest gunfighter in Texas. Preacher's son John Wesley Hardin killed his first man at the age of fifteen. He drank and gambled and pulled his revolvers at the slightest provocation. Among his victims were several lawmen, including state policemen. After killing Deputy Sheriff Charles Webb in Comanche in 1874, Hardin fled the state with his wife and children. Texas Rangers captured him in Florida in August 1877, and he was hauled back to Texas and incarcerated in Austin's Travis County jail. Within a few weeks arrangements were made to try Hardin for killing Deputy Sheriff Webb, and "a strong party of Rangers" escorted him to Comanche. When the notorious killer and his guards passed through Lampasas, gawkers turned out in large numbers. "More people rushed to see him than if he had been a rhinoceros," reported the *Dispatch*, "and he seemed not to be displeased with the eager attention shown him."[29]

Of course, 1877 was the year of the Horrell–Higgins Feud, which included a gunbattle on the square and other shootouts, and which will be addressed in a separate chapter. The next year, 1878, featured a downtown gunfight between

When John Wesley Hardin passed through Lampasas in the custody of Texas Rangers, Lampasans gathered in large numbers to view the notorious mankiller. —Author's collection

bartender Newt Cook, who was wounded, and a newcomer to town named Walter Coffee Harcrow. (This fight was described in the chapter on Watering Seasons.) The following month James McMasters was killed by a shotgun-wielding assassin at his spread seven miles east of town. For several nights he had slept outside to keep his cattle away from his wheat stacks. About midnight he was blasted with nine buckshot while he slept in his blanket; his body was found at dawn by his wife.[30]

A week later Walter Coffee Harcrow was murdered in a deserted house in East Lampasas. In his early twenties, with dark hair and moustache, Harcrow rode into Lampasas in the spring of 1878. He habitually wore a revolver, and early in June he shot Newt Cook in the right thigh. On Sunday night, July 21, Harcrow and a companion ventured into East Lampasas. The men split up, and about ten minutes later six gunshots exploded in the night air. Harcrow, unarmed for once, was found dead, hit at point-blank range in the head, stomach, and wrist. A coroner's jury questioned more than fifty individuals, but like the McMasters assassin, the killer remained unknown.[31]

A classic form of frontier lawlessness was the robbery of banks and stagecoaches. Frontier Lampasas had no banks to rob, but early in its existence the town enjoyed thrice-weekly stagecoach runs to Austin. By the 1870s stagecoaches came or left town daily and in various directions. Even after the railroad reached Lampasas in 1882, stagecoaches continued to run to the west, carrying passengers and mail. In October 1882 a solitary robber held up a stagecoach several miles northwest of Lampasas. The bandit went through the mail pouches and robbed the passengers. Driver Jack Martin lost a gold watch and chain with a distinctive charm. But soon the lone bandit, wearing the stolen charm, was apprehended at a small post office north of the robbery site. A year later three Barker brothers held up the stagecoach, again northwest of Lampasas. The brothers were caught, tried in Austin, and sentenced to the penitentiary.[32]

Stagecoach robberies, saloon fights, street shootouts, murders— Lampasas ran the gamut of frontier lawlessness. Lampasas County produced a gunfighter of top rating, as well as a set of gunfighting brothers who proved themselves as dangerous as any set of brothers in the West. All that was lacking to complete the Lampasas totality of frontier violence was a blood feud, and the Horrell brothers and Pink Higgins, plus their gunslinging relatives and friends, provided the murderous Horrell–Higgins Feud.

There were two stagecoach robberies near Senterfitt, a thriving village fifteen miles northwest of Lampasas. The livery stable, where stagecoaches changed teams, still stands. —Photo by the author

Rear view of Senterfitt's hotel, where stagecoach passengers ate and sometimes stayed. The ghost town is on the ranch of Robert Oliver, who maintains the few remaining buildings. —Photo by the author

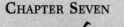

CHAPTER SEVEN

The Horrell-Higgins Feud

"Mr. Horrell, this is to settle some cow business."
—Pink Higgins to Merritt Horrell,
just before shooting him

The first blood feud in Texas was the Regulator–Moderator War, from 1840-1844. Thirty-one men were killed, including a district judge, the sheriff of Harrison County, the founder of Marshall, and a Republic of Texas senator who had signed the Texas Declaration of Independence. The backwoods warriors of frontier East Texas established for future feudists an imposing standard of murderous violence, as well as for deeds of heroism, endurance, and sheer physical courage.

During the next three-quarters of a century, Texas shootists aggressively engaged in blood feuds. Indeed, there were more feuds in Texas than in any other state or territory. The poisonous atmosphere of Reconstruction spawned the Early–Hasley Feud of 1865-1869 and the vicious Lee–Peacock Feud, 1867-1871, each conflict pitting former Confederates against Union supporters.

The widespread Sutton–Taylor Feud produced numerous victims during the 1860s and the 1870s. In the 1870s Texas was rife with lawlessness and feuding was at its height. Lynching feuds in Shackleford County and in Bastrop County featured vigilante hangings triggered by cattle rustling, highway robberies, and retributions. In Hood County the Mitchell and Truitt families feuded in 1874 over a land dispute, with members of each clan dying by gunfire or hanging. Near to Lampasas, the Mason County War, or Hoo-Doo War, was a violent clash between Anglo- and German-Americans, with the murderous conflict aggravated by cattle theft.

Accounts of the various shootouts, lynchings, slaying of law officers, and other violent events of these feuds were spread by the state's newspapers, as well as by word of mouth. Lampasans were keenly aware of the blood feuds that swirled through Texas counties, and—after years of Comanche raids and saloon shootings—there could have been little surprise when a slam-bang feud exploded in Lampasas during several bloody months of 1877.

Although there would be feudist gunplay in the countryside of Lampasas County, the first killing, as well as a major gunbattle, would take place in downtown Lampasas. On Monday morning, May 12, 1876, Pink Higgins rode into Lampasas and spotted one of his yearlings tied to a live oak tree on the public square. Jim Grizzell owned a meat market on the square, where the courthouse now stands. When queried by Pink, Grizzell admitted that he had bought the yearling from his brother-in-law, Merritt Horrell.

Pink angrily retrieved his property, then swore out a warrant for Merritt's arrest. In court it was proven that the yearling was Pink's property "and that Horrell had no claim whatsoever to the animal . . . ." But juries across the cattle frontier were notoriously reluctant to convict rustlers, and the Lampasas jury delivered a not guilty ver-

Pink Higgins battled stock thieves from the time he was a teenager, and he did not hesitate to take up arms against the Horrell brothers. —Courtesy Betty L. Giddens

dict. Disgusted over this failure of the legal system, Pink grimly warned Merritt "that he would never bother the law with him again, but he would settle the matter himself with a Winchester rifle."[1]

Although Pink was only twenty-five, he had battled stock thieves for more than a decade. Since his teenage years he had ridden with pursuit parties against Comanche raiders and against rustlers. Twice he had been wounded in running fights, and once he had placed a noose around the neck of a rustler just before an impromptu hanging. Since boyhood Pink Higgins had dealt harshly with stock thieves, and his warning to Merritt Horrell throbbed with deadly intent.

But with suicidal arrogance Merritt underestimated the deadly seriousness of Pink's threat. On Saturday, January 20, 1877, Merritt drove a small herd into Lampasas to settle a debt to cattle dealer Alex Northington. Several of the bunch belonged to Pink Higgins, and Northington prudently notified him. Pink promptly rode into town, cut out his cattle, drove them home and penned them. He sent word to Merritt Horrell that if he had a better claim to the cattle, "to come and get them." Wisely Merritt did not come.[2]

But Pink did not drop the matter. On Monday, January 22, "a cold, drizzly, gloomy day," Pink armed himself and rode into Lampasas, accompanied by brother-in-law Bob Mitchell and a few other riders. Carrying his Winchester, Pink stalked into "the old deadfall saloon," Merritt's favorite haunt and the site where the Horrell faction gunned down four state policemen in 1873. Merritt was warming himself at the fireplace along the rear wall of the room.

"Mr. Horrell," announced Higgins, "this is to settle some cow business."[3]

Higgins abruptly triggered a Winchester round into Horrell. The impact knocked Merritt off his feet, but he rose shakily and leaned on the shoulder of James Ervin. Higgins fired again, and once more Merritt was slammed to the floor. Pink walked over to the prone figure and cold-bloodedly fired two more slugs into Merritt, who died on the spot.[4]

Eager for more confrontation, Pink led several allies out of town east on the Belton road, in the direction of the Horrell ranch on Mesquite Creek. Tom Horrell, riding into town from the north, was told about the killing by someone, who added that Higgins and his men were headed toward Mesquite Creek. Tom immediately decided to ride crosscountry and try to reach the ranch before the Higgins party could arrive.

"He was in his shirt sleeves and unarmed," related John Nichols. "But the party turned off and he met them . . . and was immediately covered by their guns." Some of Pink's men wanted to kill Tom. "It will be just another Horrell less," explained one hard-bitten partisan with deadly logic, "and we had better kill him now as we will have to sooner or later."[5]

But big Bob Mitchell would not condone killing an unarmed and out-numbered man. "Keep your hand off that gun, Pink," he insisted.[6]

Tom was released, and Higgins and Mitchell headed north, soon disappearing into the rugged countryside. A posse, which was joined by Tom and Mart Horrell, arrested four peripheral Higgins allies. Jailed in Lampasas, three men posted bonds and one was released for lack of evidence. Pink remained at large, perhaps because lawmen did not conduct much of a search for the killer of a rustler and chronic troublemaker. "The old timers say now that Pink never left the county and did pretty much as he pleased, staying most of the time at the home of one of his friends."[7]

Hoping to avoid an outbreak of violence after the killing of Merritt Horrell, Sheriff Albertus Sweet requested assistance from the Texas Rangers. Rangers had been inactive during the Civil War and Reconstruction, but the force was reorganized in 1874 as the Frontier Battalion, commanded by Major John B. Jones. There were six companies in the Frontier Battalion, and at this point Company C was headquartered in San Saba, about thirty-five miles northwest of Lampasas. Captain John Sparks led sixteen Rangers to Lampasas, camping in the shady grove near Hancock Springs. Sheriff Sweet seemed intimidated by the remaining Horrell brothers and their confederates. "These men have never been arrested," the sheriff told Sergeant N. O. Reynolds, "and it is my honest opinion they cannot be."[8]

But the surviving Horrells were sobered by the violent death of another brother, and they maintained a low profile for the next couple of months. While the Horrells refrained from retaliation, Pink Higgins again seized the initiative. Having opened the bloodletting by killing cattle thief Merritt Horrell, Pink aggressively decided once more to carry the fight to the Horrells.

Tom and Mart Horrell were scheduled to appear in district court before Judge W. A. Blackburn on Monday, March 26, 1877. On the appointed day a squad of Rangers rode into town in case of trouble. Their anticipation of violence proved correct, but Higgins outguessed the

Rangers—and the Horrells—regarding location. Pink Higgins, Bill Wren, Bill Tinker, and a couple of other men set an ambush four miles east of town at the crossing of a stream soon to be christened "Battle Branch." When Tom and Mart reached the creek about ten in the morning, they stopped to water their horses. Without warning, the concealed gunmen opened fire.

Tom was knocked out of the saddle with a bullet in the hip, while his horse was mortally wounded. Mart suffered a flesh wound in his neck and his horse bolted, but he controlled the animal and turned back to his immobile brother. Unsheathing his Winchester from its saddle scabbard, Mart jumped off his skittish mount and began firing his lever-action rifle. Consumed with battle lust, Mart executed a one-man charge which routed the bushwhackers. Had he been wearing a military uniform, Mart would have earned a combat medal for this coura-

geous exploit. While Pink and his men scrambled for their horses, Mart managed to carry Tom to the nearby house of John Tinnin.[9]

While Mart galloped into town for help, Higgins and his men rode hard to the northwest, splitting into two groups after five miles. The Rangers came out to the ambush site, then followed the trail without overtaking any suspects. Bill Tinker soon was taken into custody, but he provided an alibi and was released. Hoping for similar leniency, Bill Wren turned himself in on Monday, April 2, a week after the ambush, and soon was discharged from custody. The presence of Texas Rangers probably dissuaded other shootouts between the feudists.[10]

The author holds a single-shot Ward-Burton breechloading rifle which belonged to the Horrells. The 1871 Ward-Burton was America's first military bolt-action rifle, but it did not achieve widespread acceptance. This historic weapon is on display at the Keystone Square Museum, and Bob Gantt took this photo.

Three weeks after Wren submitted to authorities, and three months to the day after the death of Merritt Horrell—on April 22, 1877—Pink Higgins and Bob Mitchell surrendered to the Rangers. Higgins and Mitchell, who surely had no intention of being confined inside the crackerbox Lampasas jail, were held at the Ranger camp. Soon they each were granted a $10,000 bond, and after posting surety, Higgins and Mitchell again were on the loose.[11]

Sensing that he was being stalked, Higgins would not allow a light in his house after dark, and even when "he stepped into the woodpile his Winchester went along." He said that he engaged a spy, "who posed as a gunman from Mexico, and got into their employ," then tipped off Pink about Horrell movements by placing "unsigned letters in an old hollow tree." Long after the feud, Pink claimed that two black men were paid by the Horrells to report on the movements of the Higgins faction. Supposedly, Pink and three of his men played a game of Seven-Up to determine who would put these informers "out of the way," after which Higgins "got both of them himself."[12]

There is no record of the deaths of two additional men, black or white, although it is possible that the disappearance of two former slaves might have been ignored by authorities of that era. But there may have been a tipoff by some sort of spy or informer. On Thursday, May 31, a party of Horrell riders ventured into the Higgins-Mitchell neighborhood. When they reached School Creek, Higgins riders appeared on the opposite bank. There was a sudden exchange of shots, then the Horrell party broke off the skirmish. The Higgins party pressed forward, collecting "a field glass, a saddle and other plunder from their adversaries."[13]

This encounter was the first clash since the ambush at Battle Branch, more than two months earlier. But the pace of feud activity suddenly accelerated. A number of cases pertaining to the feud were pending in district court in Lampasas. On Monday night, June 4, just four days after the skirmish at School Creek, unknown parties broke into the flimsy court building and stole all district court records, including cases unrelated to the feud. These records presumably were burned, because no documents survived. Governor Richard Hubbard, scheduled to speak at the Lampasas County Fair later in the summer, offered a $500 reward for the identity of the culprits. No one stepped forward; such a revelation would have been extremely dangerous to the informant.[14]

Only three days after the court records were stolen, on Thursday, June 7, the Horrell–Higgins Feud suddenly and unexpectedly climaxed in a wild shootout in downtown Lampasas. The Horrell brothers and several allies came to town Thursday morning. Mart Horrell entered the store of Alex Northington, "to be paid for some hogs delivered to my dad a few days previously," recalled Mott Northington, a young eyewitness to the day's events.[15] Meanwhile, Pink Higgins and Bob Mitchell learned of the theft of legal documents and decided to ride into Lampasas to reaffirm their bonded status. Although not expecting the Horrells to be in town, they took the precaution of bringing a dozen men or so as an armed escort. Riding in from the north, several of the party dropped off a couple of miles outside town. While Alonzo and Bill Mitchell, Newt Higgins, John Cox, and other riders waited, Pink and Bob Mitchell proceeded on into town, accompanied by Bill Wren and Ben Terry.[16]

Wren and Mitchell rode beside each other and in front of Higgins and Terry. About ten o'clock the four men turned into town on Second Street, riding west a block north of the square. Wren and Mitchell, in the lead, reined their horses left, to ride one block down Live Oak Street to the public square.

A public well was shaded by live oak trees in the northwest portion of the square. Lounging around the well were Tom, Mart, and Sam Horrell, along with Bob McGee, a few other friends, and a gunman known as Jim Buck Miller (alias Jim Buck Palmer and Buck Waldrop), who had just signed on with the Horrells. Tom Horrell was the first to sight Bob Mitchell and Bill Wren riding in his direction.

"Over yonder comes the Higginses," shouted Tom. Without hesitation, Tom and his brother Sam pulled their guns and ran toward their adversaries, taking cover behind a load of wire in front of Mellon's Store, on the northwest corner of the square. Mart Horrell and Jim Buck Miller seized their Winchesters and darted across Live Oak Street to Townsen's Store west of the well.[17]

Gunfire suddenly broke out, and Wren and Mitchell hastily dismounted to find cover on opposite sides of Live Oak Street. Wren ducked behind a hackberry tree in a wagon yard, while Mitchell headed for the alley to the west, slipping behind a picket fence as bullets began to fly. Tom Horrell peered around the corner of the limestone store building, hoping to fire at Mitchell. But Mitchell fired first, triggering a round each time Tom's head came into view. Mitchell squeezed off three shots, each time coming so close that the bullet knocked rock dust into Tom's eyes. Tom "would jerk his head back and wipe the dust out before shooting again," according to an eyewitness, while Tom's bullets hit the fence near Bob's head.[18]

Thursday, June 7, 1877

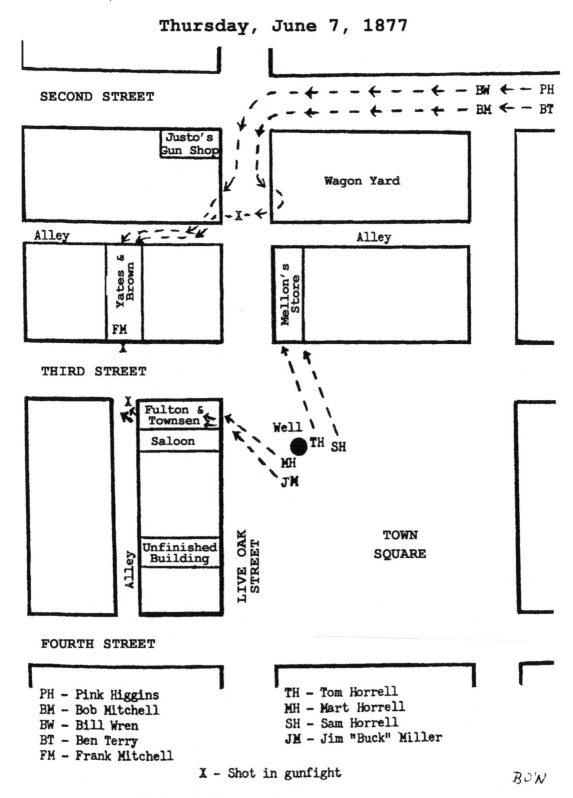

PH – Pink Higgins
BM – Bob Mitchell
BW – Bill Wren
BT – Ben Terry
FM – Frank Mitchell

TH – Tom Horrell
MH – Mart Horrell
SH – Sam Horrell
JM – Jim "Buck" Miller

X – Shot in gunfight

Battle on the Lampasas Square —Diagram by the author

Bill Wren could not find a good target, so with boldness—and fool-hardiness—he decided to sprint across the street to join Bob Mitchell. "Get back there or they will get you!" cautioned Mitchell.

"I can't see anybody to shoot at," fumed Wren.[19]

Wren tried to run across the street, but a bullet caught him in the thigh. Wren hobbled over to Mitchell's position, then Bob helped his wounded comrade up the alley. They entered the rear of a two-story building which housed the Yates & Brown Store on the ground floor, then they struggled upstairs to the law office of Judge J. A. Abney. Within moments they were joined by Bob's younger brother, Frank Mitchell, who had been unloading flour from a wagon at the Yates & Brown Store when the firing broke out.

"Honest, industrious, and inoffensive,"[20] Frank was a thirty-four-year-old family man who had taken no part in the feud. By tragic coincidence, Frank and his father were in town on business, and when he saw his brother under fire, blood called to blood. Although Frank was unarmed, he borrowed a revolver from Bill Wren and went downstairs to find a target. Carefully Frank slipped out of the front door to peer down Third Street toward the square.

Hoping to flank Bill Wren and Bob Mitchell, Mart Horrell and Jim Buck Miller hurried through Fulton & Townsen's Store and exited the back door into the alley. They were spotted by Frank Mitchell, who fired one shot and drilled Jim Buck Miller in the chest. Jim Buck and Mart instantly returned fire, and a Winchester slug slammed into Frank Mitchell. The stricken man staggered back inside, then collapsed behind a store counter and died. Although both Mart and Jim Buck had snapped off rifle rounds at Frank, "Mart claimed he was the one that shot Mitchell," related John Nichols knowingly, "as he wanted the credit."[21]

Mart helped the wounded Jim Buck Miller down the alley to an unfinished rock building that faced the square. There they were joined by Tom and Sam Horrell, along with a few other allies, and the Horrell party forted up inside the rock structure. "A regiment of men could not have driven them out."[22]

While Bill Wren and the Mitchell brothers were battling the Horrell faction, Pink Higgins galloped back to collect the other men. By the time these reinforcements thundered into town, citizens had locked the doors of their buildings, or fled downtown for parts of Lampasas that were out of range. "Dad quickly slammed the door and barred it," related Mott Northington.[23]

With Frank Mitchell dead and the redoubtable Bill Wren wounded, no one had the stomach to charge the Horrell stronghold. The "Battle of the Square" soon became a sniping duel. The feudists recognized that the current fight had become a standoff, and they were receptive to peace overtures. Summer campers were beginning to arrive in Lampasas, and civic leaders were horrified that a pitched battle on the square, that continuing violence, would severely curtail tourist traffic. "Through the influence and work of several prominent citizens—Alex Northington and others—an armistice was patched up, both parties were disarmed and the Horrells were placed under arrest."[24]

The confiscated weapons were placed in Alex Northington's building on the square. "My dad carried all the Winchesters to his storeroom upstairs," said Mott Northington. "I sneaked up the back stairway and tried to count the stacked rifles through the keyhole."[25] There were twenty-four rifles; apparently the combatants kept their handguns. Pink Higgins led his men out of town about noon, after two hours of hostilities. The Horrells submitted to "arrest," but after dark they were released from protective custody and allowed to ride to their homes.

Jim Buck Miller died on Tuesday, and the Horrells had to bury yet another man. Attended by his grieving family and friends, Frank Mitchell was interred in the Townsen Cemetery, near his rural home, a sobering loss for the Higgins–Mitchell faction.

Apparently helpless to halt outbreaks of feudist warfare, Sheriff Albertus Sweet again requested assistance from Major John B. Jones of the Texas Rangers. Major Jones gathered a detail of fifteen men and rode into Lampasas on Monday, June 14, a week after the two-hour shootout in town. The Rangers camped at Hancock Springs and during the next several days were active in helping Sheriff Sweet and other area officers to round up fugitives.

None of the arrests were members of the Horrell or Higgins factions. Pink Higgins and his allies stayed on good behavior, while the Horrell brothers left the county after the gunbattle in town and did not return for almost four weeks. After the Horrells reentered the county early in July, Major Jones reported that he had begun diplomatic efforts "to intercede and endeavor to reconcile the difficulty and thus terminate this long continued feud. I am on good terms with both parties and hope to effect something towards the desired object in a few days."[26]

Within two weeks, however, the Horrells were the chief suspects in the death of Elihu Graham, a Higgins–Mitchell partisan. Graham was gunned down by unknown parties near Townsen's Mill on Tuesday, July 24. Major Jones and four Rangers rode north to investigate the killing, but found nothing except rumors about the Horrells.

But at sunset on July 27, Bob and Alonzo Mitchell and Bill Wren rode into the Ranger camp at Hancock Springs, informing Major Jones that a Horrell party had been seen ten miles north of town. Major Jones immediately dispatched Sgt. N. O. Reynolds and six privates to the trouble spot, with the Mitchell brothers and Wren acting as guides for the night ride. But at some point during their dark journey, the Rangers were informed that the Horrells had moved on to their ranch on Mesquite Creek.

Accordingly, "I changed the direction of the scout," stated Sergeant Reynolds. His guides led the Rangers to the Mesquite Creek ranch, but by the time of their approach, about five o'clock, a hard rain was falling. Reynolds did not want Wren and the Mitchells as part of the arrest party, and they stayed with the horses while the seven Rangers quietly surrounded the house. Eleven men slept inside, along with a few women and children, on pallets and beds.[27]

Sgt. N. O. Reynolds of the Texas Rangers was instrumental in halting the Horrell–Higgins Feud. Reynolds liked Lampasas and moved his family to the town. He served as city marshal, county sheriff—and saloon owner. —Courtesy Chuck Parsons

The officers crept inside, cocked rifles at the ready, and Sergeant Reynolds loudly announced the presence of Texas Rangers. "The Horrells thus rudely aroused, and confused as to the character of their early visitors, sprang to their weapons," reported Reynolds. For a horrible moment the Horrell men seemed to believe that their enemies were in the house. Mart mumbled that they could not surrender, and Tom defiantly snarled that they might as well die fighting as submit to mobs in Lampasas. Sam grabbed for the sergeant's Winchester, but in the ensuing scuffle the gun discharged, igniting a mattress but quieting the room.

Reynolds shouted assurances that his men were Texas Rangers. He pledged his word that prisoners would be under Ranger protection, and that only Tom, Mart, and Sam need submit to arrest. Four armed Horrell riders would accompany the party as "guards" on the journey to the Ranger camp.

"Boys, this seems reasonable," said Mart, eyeing the cocked Winchesters. "I believe these Rangers can be relied on to protect us. Besides this fight has been thrust on us. If we can get a hearing we can give bond."[28]

The brothers were taken to the Ranger camp, then placed in the little court building under protection of the Rangers, who moved their camp to the square. Major Jones promptly employed his considerable skills as a negotiator, and within two days produced a conciliatory document signed by the Horrells.

Lampasas Texas
July 30th 1877

Messrs Pink Higgins, Robert Mitchell and William Wrenn.
Gentlemen:

From this standpoint, looking back over the past with its terrible experiences both to ourselves and to you, and to the suffering which has been entailed upon both of our families and our friends by the quarrel in which we have been involved with its repeated fatal consequences, and looking to a termination of the same, and a peaceful, honorable and happy adjustment of our difficulties which shall leave both ourselves and you, all our self respect and sense of unimpaired honor, we have determined to take the initiatory in a move for reconciliation. Therefore we present this paper in which we hold ourselves in honor bound to lay down our arms and to end the strife in which we have been engaged against you and exert our utmost efforts to entirely eradicate all enmity from the minds of our friends who have taken sides with us in the feud hereinbefore alluded to.

And we promise furthermore to abstain from insulting or injuring you and your friends, to bury the bitter past forever, and join with you as good citizens in undoing the evil which had resulted from our quarrel, and to leave nothing undone which we can effect to bring about a complete consummation of the purpose to which we have herein committed ourselves.

Provided:

That you shall on your part take upon yourselves a similar ob-

ligation as respects our friends and us, and shall address a paper
to us with your signatures thereupon, such a paper as this which
we freely offer you. Hoping that this may bring about the happy
result which it aims at we remain

Yours respectfully,
Thos. L. Horrell
S. W. Horrell
C.O.M. Horrell

Witness
Jno. B. Jones
Maj. Frontier Battalion

The Horrell brothers, who had almost no education, could not have
written such a letter. This document, and the one which followed, almost
certainly came from the pen of Major Jones. The forty-two-year-old Jones
was a native of South Carolina; he had enjoyed a formal education and
had risen to the rank of major during the Civil War. Steeped in the
traditions of the South, Jones understood the art of negotiating a peaceful solution between potential duelists. Dueling was commonplace in
the South, but once a challenge was issued, friends and "seconds" of
the antagonists made every effort to arrive at some sort of apology or re-
traction that would satisfy honor short of conducting the proposed duel.
Carefully worded notes and letters often averted violence, and Jones
clearly was a master of the peacemaker's language.

On Tuesday, July 31, the day after the Horrells signed their letter of
conciliation, Major Jones arrested Pink Higgins, Bob Mitchell, and Bill
Wren. They quickly posted bond and were released, but Jones showed
them the Horrell letter, emphasizing that the brothers had initiated a
pledge, "to abstain from insulting or injuring you and your friends, to
bury the bitter past forever. . . ." Now the honor of the Higgins faction
demanded "a similar obligation."

The following day, August 1, while Major Jones crafted a suitable response, the Horrell brothers were released after posting bond. Mart tear-
fully wrung the hand of Sergeant Reynolds and announced, "You are undoubtedly the bravest man in the world today."[29]

On Thursday, the day after the Horrells were released, Pink, Bob
Mitchell, and Bill Wren signed a letter of reply. Pink had no more education than the Horrells, and the language is the same as in the first document. Thus Jones had artfully answered his own letter:

Lampasas Texas
Aug 2nd 1877

Mess. Mart. Tom and Sam Horrell
Gentlemen

Your favor dated the 30th ult. was handed to us by Maj. Jones. We have carefully noted its contents and approve most sincerely the spirit of the communication. It would be difficult for us to express in words the mental disturbance to ourselves which the sad quarrel with its fatal consequences, alluded to in your letter occasioned. And now with passions cooled we look back with you sorrowfully to the past, and promise with you to commence at once and instantly the task of repairing the injuries resulting from the difficulty as far as our power extends to do.

Certainly we will make every effort to restore good feeling with those who armed themselves in our quarrel, and on our part we lay down our weapons with the honest purpose to regard the feud which had existed between you and us as a by gone thing to be remembered only to bewail.

Furthermore as you say we will abstain from offering insult or injury to you or yours and will seek to bring all our friends to a complete conformity with the agreements herein expressed by us.

As we hope for future peace and happiness for ourselves and for those who look to us for guidance and protection and as we desire to take position as good law-abiding citizens and pre-servers of peace and order we subscribe ourselves.

Respectfully & C.
J. P. Higgins
R. A. Mitchell
W. R. Wren

Witness
Jno. B. Jones
Maj. Frontier Battalion

The two letters, plus a detailed report from Sergeant Reynolds in the form of a letter to the editor, were published in the *Lampasas Dispatch* on August 9, 1877. A headline proclaimed:

PEACE RESTORED IN LAMPASAS!
THE HIGGINS AND HORRELL PARTIES
HAVE LAID DOWN THEIR ARMS!!

Peace prevailed throughout the rest of the summer, which was a banner year for campers and tourists at the springs and at the Lampasas County Fair of 1877. In March 1878 court hearings related to the feud were held in Lampasas. The former combatants rode into town armed to the teeth, but a squad of Texas Rangers was on the scene to preserve the peace.

Although Lampasas seemed tame, the Horrells soon found trouble elsewhere. On May 28, 1878, a Bosque County storekeeper named J. F. Vaughn was murdered by a gang of horsemen who stole $3,000 from his safe. As the desperadoes galloped into the night, witnesses sent a hail of gunfire after them, and a horse was wounded. A detective from Waco followed the getaway trail south to Mart Horrell's ranch and discovered that the wounded animal belonged to Bill Crabtree, a longtime Horrell ally. The detective apprehended the twenty-five-year-old Crabtree and brought him to Meridian, where he implicated Mart and Tom Horrell.

In September a large posse, including Texas Rangers and the sheriff of Bosque County, surrounded Mart's house and arrested the two brothers. John Nichols insisted "that none of the Horrells were in this robbery, just some of their gang," but that the Horrells planned the holdup. "They had a good alibi in this," pointed out Nichols, "but they had no chance to use it."[30]

Bill Crabtree was shotgunned by concealed gunmen on the outskirts of Meridian, where he was buried in a pauper's grave. Judge W. A. Blackburn requested that Mart and Tom Horrell be returned to Lampasas to answer charges related to the feud. The judge in Bosque County declined to release them, remarking that feelings were so strong in Meridian that it would be unsafe for the Horrells outside the stone jail. It also proved unsafe for them inside the jail.

On Sunday evening, December 15, 1878, a mob of more than one hundred masked men converged on the Bosque County jail. Lynch mobs rarely found it difficult to gain access to jails, because outnumbered jailors were not inclined to fight to the death against friends and neighbors on behalf of criminals. About fifty vigilantes crowded around the cell and committed lynching by gunfire, riddling Mart and Tom with bullets. Mart Horrell, the hero of Battle Branch, rattled the cage and cursed his attackers until he collapsed—from twenty-three bullet wounds. The brothers were taken back to Lampasas for burial in the new City Cemetery on a hill northwest of town.[31]

With all six of his brothers dead, Sam Horrell decided not to make it unanimous. He moved west, eventually settling in California, where he died peacefully in his nineties.

In September 1878, while Mart and Tom Horrell were behind bars in Meridian, Pink Higgins was tried and found not guilty of the murder of Merritt.[32] Three months later, when news arrived of the lynching of Mart and Tom Horrell, Higgins certainly felt no remorse. For Pink the death of any enemy was good riddance, and he must have believed that Mart and Tom had received their just desserts. Indeed, it was not long before more harsh justice was meted out to surviving members of the Horrell faction.

"'Vengeance is Mine!' saith the Lord. But in and out of Texas he has always had plenty of help." Dr. C. L. Sonnichsen, an avid "feud collector" of Texas blood conflicts, became convinced that vengeance was a key element of any feud. He defined a feud as: "any prolonged quarrel involving blood vengeance between families or factions." The Horrell and Higgins family-factions of the 1870s certainly fit the Sonnichsen definition. Sonnichsen reflected upon "the instinct for getting even" and upon "the oldest code known to man—the law of private vengeance."[33]

This grave marker is located in Block #1 of the Oak Hill Cemetery in Lampasas. It has been conjectured that Mart and Tom Horrell were interred here after being lynched in Meridian, and Merritt, killed by Pink Higgins, also may be buried nearby.
—Photo by the author

The lust for vengeance seems to have led to a post-feud vendetta. Such retribution was common in the wake of a feud, and with the Horrell brothers gone, their one-time allies seemed particularly vulnerable. On April 3, 1879, a dozen night riders approached the home of James Collier, who lived on Mesquite Creek near the former ranch of Mart Horrell. Collier had been a friend of Mart, and unwisely he left his family to go with the riders. The next day he was found hanging from a tree. Pinned to his clothing was a note written by someone with only a rudimentary education:

FAIR WARNING—EVERY HARBERER—
THAT HARBERS—THEAVES AND MURDURES—
WILL BE SERVED—THE SAME—WAY[34]

Four nights later, on April 7, a party of riders entered the camp of Bill, Thomas, and Jesse Vanwinkle north of Lampasas. One of the riders claimed to be a sheriff and ordered Bill Vanwinkle, who had been sought by Texas Rangers two years earlier, to come with the posse. Thomas and Jesse Vanwinkle remained in camp, and within half an hour they heard gunfire. The next day they found Bill's bullet-riddled body.

On the night of July 28, 1879, a quartet of riders approached the house of Alex Campbell, located near Higgins Gap. Campbell was the stepfather of Gus and William Kinchelo, whose mother was Sam Horrell's sister-in-law. Gus and William were suspected rustlers, and when the night riders asked them to come outside, the brothers made a dash for safety. William was shot to death in the yard. Gus was hit in the wrist, but he managed to escape into the darkness.

None of the night riders were ever identified, and no charges were filed in any of these three killings. Because the victims could be connected with rustling or the Horrells or both, it might have been easy to speculate that the night riders were members of the Higgins faction. But such speculation also might have been unsafe, and no accusations were made public.

With his most dangerous enemies dead or gone from Lampasas County, Pink Higgins was free to resume his normal activities as a rancher and trail driver. As a stockman, Higgins was away from home a great deal, buying or selling or delivering animals, trading cattle and horses, hiring drovers, rounding up herds, and leading drives that lasted for months. Pink's frequent absences from home contributed to serious stress on his marriage to Betty. By 1881 she had entered into an adulterous affair with Dunk Harris, who recently moved with his parents and brothers to Lampasas, where he worked in the family mercantile business.

A woman who lived on a ranch could not long conceal an illicit romance with a man who lived in a small town. When Pink found out, he packed Betty and her personal belongings into a buggy, permitting her to take only Ida May, the daughter from her first marriage, as she left Higgins Gap.[35] Somewhat surprisingly, Pink did not shoot Dunk Harris. Perhaps thinking of his three small children, Pink avoided the legal difficulties that a killing would have created. Perhaps, too, Pink sometimes had strayed from wedding vows at the end of trail drives.

Pink initiated divorce proceedings and agreed to pay the modest legal costs. The divorce was finalized on May 24, 1882,[36] while Pink was leading a trail drive to Dodge City. Six-year-old Cullen, four-year-old Malinda, and two-year-old Tom stayed at home with their grandparents, John and Hester Higgins, who played an important role in raising the children while Pink was gone.

Partly because he so often was an absentee father, Pink recognized that his children needed a stepmother. He soon found a new wife in pretty Lena Rivers Sweet, daughter of Albertus Sweet, a Confederate veteran who was the sheriff of Lampasas County from 1874 to 1878. In 1881, while serving as deputy marshal of Belton, Sweet was fatally wounded during an attempted arrest. Only thirty-eight when he died, Sweet was brought back to Lampasas for burial. Born on February 9, 1868, Lena was only thirteen when her father was killed.[37]

Pink and Lena married on June 8, 1883. He was thirty-two and she was fifteen, but her mother Lavina had been just thirteen when she wed eighteen-year-old Albertus Sweet. Pink towered over his pretty, blue-eyed bride, who brought a sweet and loving temperament to the marriage. Not surprisingly, she was deferential to her older husband, and she earned the devotion of her stepchildren. Lena and Pink would have six children of their own, five girls and a boy.[38]

After the Horrell–Higgins Feud ended, there were no more Horrell brothers to be lightning rods for trouble, while Pink Higgins focused on his family and work as a rancher and trail boss. The final vestige of the feud—the apparent vendetta in 1879 by night riders—climaxed the homicidal disorder of the 1870s in and around Lampasas. The 1870s had witnessed exceptional violence: Comanche raids, saloon fights, street shootouts, a blood feud. But the end of the feud at the close of the decade seemed to signal a marked reduction in frontier mayhem, and the subsequent absence of frequent and sometimes startling violence allowed Lampasans at last to expand their little town to unprecedented levels during the 1880s.

CHAPTER EIGHT

Sheep on the Range

"Lampasas has no rival as a wool market in the State."
—*Lampasas Leader*, May 11, 1889

Lampasas was the service center for many small cattle ranchers. During the 1870s and 1880s trail drives were put together in Lampasas County, and local cowboys rode out as drovers on one of the great adventures of the Old West. Many cattle buyers headquartered in Lampasas, and cowboys with big hats, boots, and spurs were constantly sighted around town.

But for all of the dominance—then and now—of the cowboy culture in Lampasas, the town was destined to become the hub of a sheep-raising region. An article written for the *Texas Almanac* in 1858, when Lampasas Springs was only three years old, pointed out that the surrounding terrain "is very broken," then stated that "this county is best suited to the raising of horses and sheep. . . ." Following further explanation, the *Almanac* reporter observed emphatically: "the day, no doubt, is not far distant, when this county will export more wool than any county in this State."[1] This early prediction was borne out by the 1880s and 1890s.

But the presence of sheep in cattle country triggered a vicious conflict across the West. During half a century, from the 1870s until the 1920s, in nine western states or territories there were at least 128 raids and skirmishes between cattlemen and sheepherders, producing more than fifty human casualties and the slaughter of at least 53,254 sheep. Throughout the West sheep were shot, clubbed, knifed, poisoned, dynamited, and rimrocked. In 1875 Texas raiders destroyed almost 500 sheep by driving them into quicksand. Sometimes a herd of horses would be stampeded through a flock, cruelly trampling sheep underfoot. Sheep usually were penned at night, and raiders occasionally threw flaming torches to set the fleece aflame on live animals. Twenty-eight sheep ranchers or herders are known to have been killed across the West, and others were injured. Sixteen cattle ranchers or cowboys were slain, including two in Texas—one of those near Lampasas after he opened fire on an area sheep rancher.[2]

Hostilities began in Texas during the 1870s. Spanish *pastores* first drove sheep north into Texas in the 1600s and began grappling with danger. Native American warriors attacked exposed flocks, and Mexican desperadoes crossed the Rio Grande to raid Texas livestock. Herders were slain and sheep were stolen, scattered, butchered, drowned, or shot by Comanches, Kiowas, Apaches, Tonkawas, Wacos, Mexicans, and occasionally even the French. So when cattle ranchers and cowboys began challenging sheepmen over rights to the range, it was only another chapter in the difficulties faced by woolgrowers.

Cowboys were contemptuous of bleating woollies and the men who tended them, and this scorn was reflected in the language of the range. Regarding sheepherders, Ramon Adams pointed out: "The cowman never called him a *shepherd*. Since Christ was a shepherd, that word sounded too pastoral and honored, and the cowman had anything but Christ-like feelings toward the sheepman. As one cowman said, 'There ain't nothing dumber than sheep except the man who herds 'em.'"[3]

Cowmen derisively referred to sheepmen as "mutton punchers," "lamb lickers," and "snoozers" (cowboys felt that sheepherders did little besides sleep). Western cowmen who despised sheep were merely carrying out an ancient tradition. The prophet Ezekiel (34:18, LB) recorded Biblical annoyance: "Is it a small thing to you, O evil shepherds, that you not only keep the best of the pastures for yourselves, but trample down the rest?" Cowboys cursed sheep as "hoofed locusts," "stinkers," "stubble jumpers," "maggots," and "baa-a-ahs." ("If you want to start a fight," declared Adams, "just blat this at a cowboy.") A cowboy's name for rotgut whiskey was "sheepherder's delight." A sheepherder in Del Rio was told with a hint of menace: "Young men in Del Rio never heard of a sheepman, since the customary title for them was damn sheepman. Sheepmen were little better than a pelon dog."[4]

During more than a decade and a half of conflict in Texas, there were at least twenty-nine violent incidents between cattlemen and sheepherders. A total of 3,215 sheep were killed, along with four sheepmen and two cowboys. There may have been more sheepherders who were homicide victims. The West's premier assassin, Killin' Jim Miller, was reputed to have murdered "a dozen" sheepherders. According to his biographer, he was hired by Texas cattlemen at $150 per killing. With typical disdain for sheepmen, he confided to a Fort Worth acquaintance: "I have killed eleven men that I know about; I have lost my notch stick on sheepherders I've killed out on the border."[5]

The violence stretched across western Texas from the Panhandle to the Rio Grande, and incidents erupted near Lampasas. During a two-month period beginning in December 1879, there were half a dozen raids against sheep camps in San Saba County, adjacent to Lampasas County on the west. The worst depredation came on the night of January 12, 1880, when raiders entered two pens and cut the throats of more than two hundred and forty sheep. In Hamilton County, just north of Lampasas County, one band of sheep was destroyed by raiders, other flocks were scattered, and sheepmen were forced out of the region. Reacting to such incidents, the editor of *Texas Wool* grumbled: "In almost every case the aggressors have been the cattlemen. As a class, the sheepmen of Texas are quiet, law abiding, and industrious. . . ."[6]

A great deal of violence was associated with the Texas fence-cutting wars, which climaxed in 1883. As barbed wire restricted open range throughout the West, fences were cut in many states, and often the violence was between homesteaders and cattlemen, or even between open range cattlemen and cattle ranchers who had fenced their range. Half of the counties in Texas reported fence-cutting, but there were many instances which did not involve sheepmen. Nevertheless, in Texas barbed wire seemed to bring to a head the bitter antagonisms between sheepmen and cattle ranchers.

The first primitive wire fences were put up in Texas in the 1860s, and by the 1880s fencing bees had helped to close off open range across the state. By 1883 the "Knights of the Knippers" had cut fence in half of the state's counties. A Central Texas sheep rancher wrote to the editor of *Texas Wool* that if sheep ranchers in his area used any materials other than rock, the fence would be cut or burned within the year. Hundreds of miles of barbed wire and fence posts were destroyed.[7]

These fence-cutting wars reduced tax evaluations in Texas by millions of dollars, and state legislators were deluged with petitions and letters protesting the lawless depredations. Because "fences are being continuously destroyed in many parts of the state by Lawless persons," lawmakers suspended the usual legislative process and hurried to make fence-cutting punishable by one to five years in prison. Furthermore, it was made a misdemeanor knowingly to fence public lands or lands belonging to others without the owner's consent. Anyone who had built such fences was given six months to take them down, and any rancher who built fences across public roads was required to place a gate every six miles.[8]

It was in this turbulent atmosphere that Lampasas County became a major sheep-raising district. Early Lampasas pioneers sometimes brought with them a few sheep, not for commercial purposes but for household use. Sometimes the family ate mutton, but usually the sheep were shorn for the wool. Each sheep generally yielded about five pounds of wool, which would be manually carded, then spun into wool yarn on the fam-

Low rock fences were built to hold sheep. This fence still stands, in disrepair, near the stone ranch house begun by Thomas Huling in 1855 a few miles west of Lampasas. —Photo by the author

ily spinning wheel. The fuzzy yarn then could be knitted into socks, mittens, or clothing items for small children. While many pioneer households had a spinning wheel, a loom took up a lot of space. But if a loom was available, yarn could be woven into blankets or homespun fabric, which would be fashioned into clothing. This rough material could be dyed with roots, berries, or tree bark. "I made my husband an entire suit of clothes which I wove, half wool and half cotton, made entirely by hand, as I had no sewing machine," reminisced Georgiana Greenwood of her years as a new bride just after the Civil War.[9] For two decades most of the wool produced in and around Lampasas was consumed at home.

During that period sheep thrived on the rocky ranges of Lampasas County; their small mouths could consume vegetation that cattle could not reach. One Lampasas observer pointed out that "there are a great number of . . . plants which are eaten by sheep and goats, of which 'buffalo clover' . . . and an endless variety of daisies . . . are the most abundant. Indeed the great profusion of varieties and species of plants found in this section of Texas render ours a peculiarly fine one for sheep and goat raising."[10]

By the 1870s sheep ranching began to spread through the Hill Country as economic reality lent growing appeal to this sometimes controversial enterprise. One great advantage of raising sheep was that the sheepmen had two products to sell, wool and mutton, while the cattleman marketed just beef. Cattle prices fluctuated wildly from season to season, while wool and mutton, even though also subject to great fluctuation, remained dependably profitable throughout the late 1800s. And in Lampasas County a wool clip would be harvested both in the spring and in the fall. Furthermore, a sheep raiser could enter business with a smaller initial investment than that required of a cattle rancher. There was a measure of truth in the Old Texas adage: "You raise cattle for prestige, you raise sheep for money."

"Certain sections of this county cannot be excelled for sheep raising," pointed out a Lampasas reporter in 1878, while lamenting that "very few persons have as yet embarked in sheep husbandry." That same year Lampasas merchant D. W. Phillips added his evaluation. "Our range is the finest I have ever seen and stock of every description do well." And Phillips had witnessed the beginnings of this promising venture: "Sheep are a perfect success here."[11]

The greatest boost to Lampasas County's fledgling sheep industry was the arrival of German immigrant William Mark Wittenburg. Born in 1825, young Wittenburg worked as a "lamb boy" for one of Germany's most successful sheep masters. Before migrating to the United States in his early twenties, Wittenburg earned a sheep master's license. Soon he moved to Texas, married, served in the Texas State Troops during the Civil War, lost his wife, remarried, and sired several children. All the while he built a flock of quality sheep. In 1879, when he was fifty-four, Wittenburg brought his flock, his family, and a few head of cattle to a homestead in western Lampasas County.[12]

The presence of a large, quality flock and an expert flockmaster almost immediately animated the county's small sheep ranchers to a higher level. The Census of 1880 recorded the presence of 8,814 sheep in Lampasas County. Two years later the railroad reached Lampasas, making it possible to transport almost limitless quantities of wool and sheep. Within five years the county's sheep population soared to 47,294 (en route to a peak of nearly 138,000 in 1940). In that year of 1887, there were 32,618 Lampasas County sheep sheared, with a wool clip totaling 284,990 pounds at a value of $33,280. Also in 1887, 1,443

In 1879 William Mark Wittenburg brought a large flock of sheep to Lampasas County. Wittenburg and his wife Julianna developed the Providence Ranch. The presence of an experienced flockmaster and quality sheep was instrumental in advancing sheep ranching in the county. — Courtesy KSM

sheep died on the range in Lampasas County (often by predators), while 466 were slaughtered for mutton.[13]

One Lampasas sheepman built a shearing machine. The *Texas Live Stock Journal*, in its San Antonio letter, reported: "G. Richardson, of Lampasas, is here with his sheep shearing machine, which is the result of several years' practical experiment and the many sheep men who see it are favorably [impressed] with its practicability."[14]

A description of the Lampasas County sheep industry in 1889 stated the number of sheep owned by county ranchers, then proudly emphasized that "the wool clip of some 300,000 sheep from ten or twelve other counties find its way here, the result being that Lampasas has no rival as a wool market in the State." Lampasas wool commission merchant W. A. Patterson "has already handled 800,000 pounds of wool," even though it was only May and early in the season. Because so many sheep were brought to Lampasas from other counties, "all the supplies needed by these sheepmen are purchased here, thus circulating a very large sum of money every year." The effect on Lampasas, with its population of 2,750, was pronounced. "To accommodate the large trade coming from the surrounding counties, our merchants are obliged to carry an enormous stock of goods. . . ."[15]

The rapid proliferation of sheep raising in Lampasas during the 1880s came at a time when the conflict between Texas cattlemen and sheepherders was at its height. In nearby counties there were vicious raids on sheep camps, as well as destructive fence-cutting episodes.

There were no raids on sheep flocks within Lampasas County, but in the fall of 1883 an epidemic of fence-cutting broke out, along with a double murder related to fence cutting. In the north part of the county Tom Snipes saw three men cutting fence, and on September 19 he was mysteriously hanged, "and when dead, the body was cut down and thrown into a thicket." One of the suspects, J. J. Watson, soon disappeared, and five months later his badly decomposed corpse was found. "There were evidences of five gunshot wounds in his body."[16]

Also in September 1883 dry grass in a pasture on the Colorado River was burned, and three hundred yards of wire fencing was snipped every few yards. A few miles away was the large sheep operation of Arthur North. A native of England, North arrived in Lampasas in 1876 as an ambitious, thirty-four-year-old bachelor. He purchased 1,280 acres for one dollar an acre, then added substantially to his property with a series of land transactions. North's ranch was above Senterfitt, encircling the future townsite of Lometa. He raised quality sheep and began fencing his growing range. But on Tuesday night, October 9, 1883, fence-cutters destroyed almost all of his fencing, although only one-eighth of his ranch was enclosed.[17]

Later in the month another fence-cutting assault was launched against a 2,500-acre pasture on the Colorado River. "About 2 miles of the fence of Brooks and Standifer's pasture near Red Bluff on the Colorado, was cut the other night," reported the *Galveston Daily News*. "The posts were pulled up and a portion of them burned. One post was hung to the limb of a tree with the picture of a coffin tacked to it, as a warning to the owners as to what they may expect if it is rebuilt."[18]

On Friday night, December 9, a town meeting was held at the new Lampasas courthouse. The principal speakers were two leading citizens from Brown County, the site of severe fence-cutting incidents. The Brown County men urged everyone to abide by the laws, even though there was considerable sympathy for the fence-cutters, because favorable legislation was on the way. But within a few weeks, on Sunday night, December 30, half a mile of fence was cut about twelve miles from Lampasas.[19]

All of these incidents were reported in the *Galveston Daily News*. Prominent Galvestonians were investing heavily in Lampasas, and there had to be apprehension that Lampasans might return to the homicidal violence of the 1870s. In March 1884 the *Daily News* reported with guarded relief about Lampasas: "Fence-cutting has subsided, but whether it is the legislation, or for lack of material to operate upon, is a question. There are but few pastures left here to cut, and none are being rebuilt."[20]

But Lampasas now was entering an exciting new era as the Saratoga of the South. The promise of unprecedented prosperity was everywhere, and sheep ranching now was a significant and profitable element of the county's economy. Fencing of the open range around Lampasas continued, including low rock fences good enough for confining sheep. But barbed wire went up everywhere—and there was one final fence-cutting episode.

In 1886 fencing began to be cut on a large ranch in the north part of Lampasas County. Reacting promptly to stamp out this latest outbreak of fence-cutting, Adjutant General W. H. King summoned to Austin Sergeant Ira Aten from Camp Leona, a Texas Ranger encampment near Uvalde. Sergeant Aten, twenty-two, was a crack shot and an energetic law officer. General King outlined the situation and assigned Aten to special duty. "After our conference the General ordered me to proceed to Lampasas County to catch the fence cutters who had been destroying wire fences on a large ranch there."[21]

In Lampasas Sergeant Aten conferred with Sheriff N. O. Reynolds, a former Ranger who had decided to make Lampasas his home and had been elected to the first of two consecutive terms in 1886. Investigation soon indicated that the culprits were two teenaged boys who "were rather proud that their fence-cutting job had created such a stir in the county." Working undercover, Aten quickly won their confidence. "They readily accepted me as one of their gang when I told them some wild stories of what a bad man I was."

When the next fence-cutting expedition was planned Aten tipped off Sheriff Reynolds. "One moonlight night the three of us were leading our

In 1886 Texas Ranger Ira Aten worked undercover to halt fence-cutters in Lampasas County.
—Author's collection

horses and cutting the fence wire twice between each post when a command came out of the thicket nearby: 'Hands up or we will shoot!'"

The boys wanted to run, but Aten played his role to the hilt. "No,
don't run," he snapped, dropping his nippers and throwing up his hands.
"They will shoot us." The boys raised their hands slowly, and Sheriff
Reynolds and a posse stepped forward to make the arrests.

Later, while Aten was testifying for the state in the new Lampasas
County Courthouse, the defense attorney asked: "Did you tell a lot of lies
while you were trying to catch these boys?" Aten admitted that he had,
then was asked if he were still telling lies. The Ranger shook his fist and
in his reply growled the word "damn," whereupon the judge ordered a
fine of fifty dollars. "He said I was an officer of the court and therefore
such language could not be overlooked."

By this time the era of long cattle drives had ended, and as sheep
came to dominate the ranges of the Hill Country, many cowboys had to
move to West Texas to find work. To be displaced by woollies exacer-
bated the resentment harbored by some cowboys against sheep and
sheepmen. Even though the troubles between cattlemen and sheepherders in Texas had abated by the mid-1880s, the potential for sudden
violence still lurked not far below the surface.

In 1889 an unemployed cowboy sought a job from sheep rancher
Andy Feild. Feild's ranch was a few miles south of Lampasas, and he
needed a herder. The neighborhood remained largely unfenced, making
it necessary for a herder to guard the flock during the daytime, then pen
the defenseless animals for the night. The cowboy had a revolver
strapped around his waist and he voiced a willingness to tend sheep.

Feild showed the newcomer where he wanted his flock to graze during the next few days, carefully indicating the boundary of his neighbor
Taylor's range. But soon Taylor came to Feild complaining that the sheep
were grazing on his land.

Assuming that the new man had misunderstood the boundary mark-
ings, Feild rode out with his hired hand to indicate the range limits
again. A day or two later, Taylor returned with the same complaint. It
was obvious that the cowboy was ignoring the flock. That evening, after
the sheep were penned, Feild described Taylor's second visit, then told
the cowboy he was fired. Feild added that he could stay the night in his
shed room off the kitchen, but ordered him to leave the ranch following
breakfast. The discharged hand took the news with ominous silence.

The next morning Feild was dressing when his wife came to tell him of sounds, like the clicking of a revolver, that she had heard coming from the shed room while she prepared the morning meal. As a precaution, Feild pulled out a .41-caliber Colt he rarely used, stuck it into his waistband, then went to the pen to mend harness before breakfast. His nine-year-old son, Albert, tagged along.

The disgruntled cowboy wolfed down his food, then rode his horse to the pen. He dismounted and tossed his reins over the low fence.

"You son-of-a-bitch," he spat out, "you've fired your last man!"

He palmed his revolver and snapped off a shot. The bullet missed, and Feild whirled around, gun in hand. Feild charged, firing rapidly, and hit the cowboy in the elbow and chest. The man fled on foot, already in shock from his wounds and surprised that Feild was armed. As he looked back over his shoulder to see if his pursuer was gaining, Feild triggered another slug which caught him between the eyes and hurled him to the ground.

After Feild calmed his family, he saddled a horse and rode to town to the sheriff's office. The Feild sheepdog went to the fallen figure and

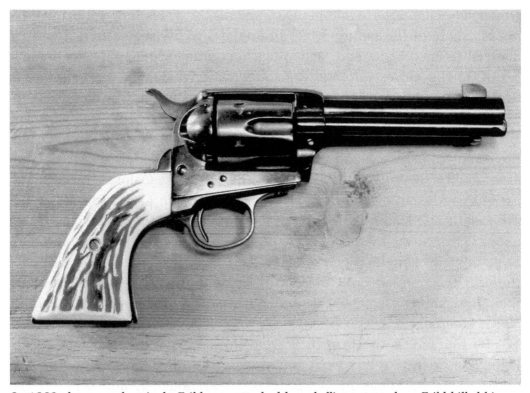

In 1889 sheep rancher Andy Feild was attacked by a belligerent cowboy. Feild killed his assailant with a .41 caliber Colt revolver. More than sixty years after the shooting Andy's grandson, Mark Field, placed staghorn grips on the gun. —Photo by the author

began to lick at the wounds. Suddenly the "corpse" moaned and began to move.

Mrs. Feild and Albert loaded the cowboy into a wagon and took him to the house of a neighbor named Murphy. Dr. Marcus Feild, father of Andy, was summoned, and the wounded man lingered through the day and night. But the cowboy died at dawn and was buried in a solitary grave.[22]

Such incidents soon ended in Texas, although cattlemen-sheepherder violence continued elsewhere well into the twentieth century, especially in Wyoming, Arizona, and Colorado. By the 1880s Texas was the leading wool-producing state in the Union, with eight million sheep on the vast ranges of the Lone Star State. With its railroad connection Lampasas now was an important wool market, and the county boasted sheep ranches large and small.

Sadly, Arthur North could not complete the sheep empire he had begun in Lampasas County. Late in 1884, while working on his ranch, North was accidentally cut with a hatchet. Blood poisoning set in, and North died at forty-three on December 11, 1884. He was buried at Senterfitt Cemetery. He had made out a will the previous year, bequeathing his share of the family estate in England to his sister. To a friend in Senterfitt, merchant and schoolteacher Frank McKean, North left $1,000. His closest friend was a fellow Englishman, merchant and Senterfitt postmaster Frank Longfield, who had arrived in Lampasas in 1880. North named him his chief beneficiary.[23]

With the unexpected death of Arthur North, Longfield inherited thousands of acres of land and improvements, as well as large bands of high quality sheep. Within a few months the Gulf, Colorado and Santa Fe Railroad began extending their tracks west from Lampasas. With the proposed route leading through the former North property, Longfield donated right-of-way, then sold two hundred acres for the townsite that became Lometa. Longfield had married Kate Hoy in 1882, and in 1885—the year the railroad built through their new property—the couple had their first child, a son. Frank and Kate named their baby boy Arthur North Longfield.[24]

By the 1890s the firm of Stokes Brothers was ranging far outside Lampasas County to buy wool and mohair. In time Stokes Brothers used twenty-three buildings in Lampasas for warehousing, and other firms had additional warehouses. Lampasas long was a bastion of the "Texas triumvirate": cattle, sheep, and goats.

CHAPTER NINE

That Old-Time Religion

*"Our city is strong! We are surrounded by
the walls of his salvation!"*
—Isaiah 26:1 (LB)

L ampasas was founded barely two decades after Texas won its independence from Mexico, thereby ending Catholicism's official domination of spiritual life. Texas now was open to Protestant denominations, although Baptist, Methodist, and Presbyterian missionaries already had penetrated Anglo Texas, conducting sporadic preaching services and camp meetings for years prior to the revolution against Mexico.

The Methodist Episcopal Church was gathered for its annual general conference in Cincinnati in May 1836 when word came of the spectacular Texan victory at San Jacinto. Texas offered a mission field of rich opportunity. Three Methodist missionaries promptly answered the call to the Texas field, and other denominations soon sent their own missionaries.

Methodists maintained their head start in Texas by founding churches, organizing circuits, and forming Sunday schools. By 1860 there were more than 30,000 Methodist members, over 400 congregations, and 224 "circuit riders." On Sundays these traveling preachers customarily held services at perhaps three churches, often riding horseback forty or fifty miles.

In 1860 Baptists boasted more than 500 congregations, including one in Lampasas, which was organized in 1856, as described in Chapter

Three. There were only seventeen members of the Lampasas Baptist Church, and for nearly two decades the little congregation had no building. Indeed, in 1860 Texas Baptists lagged well behind Methodists, both in numbers of church buildings and in total membership.

Presbyterians had seventy-two churches and more than 2,300 members in 1860, while there were nineteen Episcopal church buildings in Texas. The Disciples of Christ had only five buildings in 1850, but there were thirty-nine by 1860. With their long presence in Spanish and Mexican Texas, Catholics had thirty-three buildings by 1860, ministering primarily to German- and Mexican-Texans.[1]

All denominations suffered during the Civil War. With over 60,000 Texans in military service, the total of churchgoing men was drastically reduced, along with the number of available preachers. Between 1861 and 1864 Texans paid $37,486,854 to the Confederate government in taxes, and almost no resources were left over for churches, as well as for schools or roads. The *Texas Baptist*, a denominational journal launched in 1855, ceased publication because paper was unavailable during the war.[2]

After the war church growth was rapid in Texas. By 1870 there were 843 churches of all denominations and a total of 200,000 members. While Methodists still had the largest denomination, Baptists were gaining rapidly. By the end of the century Baptists comprised one-third of all Texas church members, with Methodists substantial in second place with twenty-seven percent. Together Baptists and Methodists provided three-fifths of Texan churchgoers, exerting a growing influence over Texas life and politics. Baptists and Methodists of the nineteenth century were fundamentalist and emotionalistic, with preachers thundering from their pulpits against evil and the devil. But the Methodist denomination was hierarchical, while Baptists recognized only the authority of the local congregation. Every member of a Baptist congregation, no matter what age, could vote on every matter, and the majority ruled. It was democracy in purest form, which had strong appeal to frontiersmen. Individualistic and democratic by nature, Texans gravitated in growing numbers to Baptist churches. It was fitting of the times that in the frontier village of Lampasas, the first congregation to organize was Baptist.

Texas frontiersmen, whether or not they were churchgoers, had an Old Testament orientation. "The land they lived in had many parallels with the land of Canaan, and they themselves with the children of Israel," explained Texas historian T. R. Fehrenbach. "They were beset with dangerous heathen enemies. The land was scourged by ravaging insects and burning drouth; the imagery of the Israelite deserts struck home in the Texan heart. . . . The Old Testament had a relevance it would have for no later American generations."[3]

A special element of religion in Lampasas was the annual summer watering season. As described in the chapter on watering seasons, preachers often came to Lampasas during summer months to conduct services among the campers, who could provide far larger crowds than usual for itinerant ministers. In the summer of 1856, a Southern Baptist missionary, Richard Howard, who headquartered in Burnet, came to Lampasas Springs to preach and to organize a Baptist congregation. The organizational meeting and service was held at the White Sulphur Springs Hotel, so the congregation called itself the White Sulphur Springs Baptist Church. Appropriately, the name soon was changed to Lampasas Baptist Church, and later, when the town grew, to First Baptist Church of Lampasas.

Within a year Reverend Howard had baptized two new Christians, and there were seventeen members of the Lampasas Baptist congregation. Howard also was busy with other churches, and in 1861 W. O. Spencer took responsibility for Lampasas Baptist Church. During the Civil War and afterward Spencer did his best under difficult conditions, but in 1868 there were only fifteen members. There were three other pastors after the Civil War, but none stayed in Lampasas for more than two or three years.[4]

From 1872-1877, however, Rev. H. M. Burroughs brought Lampasas Baptist Church a sustained pastorate for nearly six years. A capable and devoted minister, Burroughs baptized three dozen new Baptists, including ten in his final year. There were twenty-two members when Burroughs arrived in 1872. Membership rose to thirty-four the next year, to forty-two in 1874, and to sixty-five during his final year, 1877. An exceptional event of that year was an eleven-day brush arbor meeting conducted by Maj. W. E. Penn, a Confederate veteran and lawyer from Jefferson who became the first fulltime traveling evangelist in Texas. Major Penn spoke with dramatic fervor, and he converted thousands during his ministry. One night in the Lampasas brush arbor an overturned oil lamp blazed suddenly, fatally burning two women. Following a night of prayer, Major Penn resumed the revival and converted 300 sinners.

A major reason for the notable growth of the Lampasas congregation was the erection of a house of worship. Burroughs pushed for a church building from the beginning of his pastorate, and in 1874 Lampasas Baptist Church opened its doors. Located at the northeast corner of Fourth and Main, the simple frame structure seated nearly three hundred and was the town's first church building. Other denominations were organizing during this period, and sometimes the Baptist church was rented out to one congregation or another.

On December 21, 1874, Reverend Burroughs baptized an unassuming Lampasas cowboy named L. R. Millican—destined to become famous as the "Cowboy Preacher." Leander Randon Millican was born in 1853, the fifth of seven children whose parents were among Stephen F. Austin's "Old Three Hundred" colonists. The legendary Sam Houston sometimes visited in the Millican home.[5]

"Although I was only seven or eight years old I remember [one] visit well," recalled L. R. Millican. "My father had just died and Sam Houston called me to him and talked to me . . . 'Remember, my boy, if you are good and obedient you may become Governor when you grow up. And whatever you do—never touch liquor.'"

Houston's admonition was taken to heart by young Millican. "Sam Houston had been a heavy drinker and the Indians had called him 'Big Drunk.' I took his advice on liquor. I never drank any except for medicinal purposes and then I didn't like it."[6]

Begun in 1886, the impressive First Baptist Church was dedicated in 1890, serving the congregation until it burned in 1937. —Courtesy KSM

At the age of fourteen, in 1867, the orphaned boy came to Lampasas to the home of his Aunt Amanda, wife of county tax assessor-collector L. D. Nichols. Although Amanda and L. D. had eight children of their own, she "took me to her heart" in an effort to replace her sister in his life, "but I had been a great mother's boy and for a long time was disconsolate and downcast."[7]

But the wolf-howl community of 1860s Lampasas appealed to the rough sense of adventure of the teenaged Millican. "Lampasas was then a typical frontier town with a flotsam and jetsam element seldom found in such proportions elsewhere . . .," he reminisced with relish. "Society must have its fling even in the wild and stormy life of the west and dances and funfests were everyday occurrences. It also had its midnight revelers and two-gun men aplenty—a wild, unruly set. . . . Outlaws were common, gambling and drinking red liquor the order of the day. If these were insufficient excitement, the Comanches were on the warpath, and raids and killings by bands of them . . . occurred regularly in the light of the moon."[8]

Millican gravitated to the "wild, unruly set." He rarely attended church, but enjoyed hanging out in the saloons of Lampasas, even though he did not drink. "I was an expert shot, but held aloof from quarrels, nor did I side with any gang or make any gun plays. This probably was because I remained sober."[9]

He knew the Horrell brothers and all of the other cowboys who enjoyed saloon life in Lampasas. When he was fifteen and sixteen he rode the mail route between Lampasas and Austin, once eluding a Comanche war party. In 1870 Millican landed a job cowboying on the ranch of John Sparks, east of Lampasas. "Bunking with a real outfit, rounding up, cutting, branding and marking calves in the spring was new, and I fell my full length for it. Did I like it? Well, I will say I did, so well that I stayed with Mr. Sparks two years."[10]

When he was twenty, in the summer of 1874, the cowboy found religion at a Methodist camp meeting in San Saba County. Millican felt compelled to preach, and in December 1874 he joined the First Baptist Church of Lampasas. He enrolled for a time in Baylor University at Independence, engaging in "a close and prayerful study of the New Testament, to know my duty and what and how to preach." He began preaching the Gospel at every opportunity, and on February 4, 1878, Millican was ordained to the ministry at Lampasas Baptist Church, with pastor H. M. Burroughs conducting the examination."[11]

While he was a young, unordained preacher, Millican lost a horse to the Horrell brothers, and he angrily retrieved his mount from the notorious rustlers. In January 1877 the Horrells asked Millican to conduct graveside services for brother Merritt, who had been killed after stealing cattle from Pink Higgins. Millican used the occasion to admonish the surviving brothers to look to their souls.[12]

Reverend Millican continued to live in Lampasas for several years. He married Georgia Katherine Saunders in 1878 and the couple began raising their children in Lampasas. Reverend Millican preached once a month in Burnet, then he founded a church in Llano, while becoming active in affairs of the Texas Baptist Convention. He was instrumental in organizing the famous Paisano Baptist Encampment near Alpine, conducted among cowboys and ranchers for decades by the legendary George W. Truett, whose first revival was in Lampasas, and who pastored First Baptist Church of Dallas for forty-seven years.

Reverend Millican's work eventually took him to West Texas, where he pastored—and often founded—Baptist churches in San Angelo, Midland, Pecos, Big Spring, El Paso, Fort Davis, Toyah, Van Horn, Odessa, Sierra Blanca, Clint, Fort Hancock, Presidio, and other communities. Reverend Millican ranged to the far corners of West Texas to distribute Bibles and Baptist literature. "In the early part of my ministry I went always on horseback, sometimes breaking in a bronc for its use in my work, making many long trips over the plains and through the mountains, sometimes with nothing but my saddle blanket for a bed, saddle for a pillow and the heavens for a covering. Have worn out several pairs of saddle bags during my early ministry carrying good books and tracts to give away or loan."[13] The long, remarkable career of the Cowboy Preacher began at Lampasas Baptist Church.

When he was a young man, L. R. Millican cowboyed around Lampasas and was good with a gun. But he was converted at a camp meeting, joined the Lampasas Baptist Church, and became a West Texas missionary renowned as the "Cowboy Preacher."
—Courtesy First Baptist Church, Lampasas

Rev. Abram Weaver succeeded H. M. Burroughs in 1878. The new pastor led the congregation in forming a church choir. On Thursday evening, June 6, 1878, a "number of ladies and gentlemen" gathered at the Baptist church. "It was apparent from the first hour's practice that we have a sufficient amount of musical talent in our midst to form an excellent choir, which would add no little to the attractions of public worship." The choir began to meet regularly for practice on Sunday afternoons.[14]

Reverend Weaver maintained a Sunday School, and attendance continued to rise. He advertised his sermon titles ("The Righteousness of God's Moral Government"), and in these ads he urged everyone to come ("Visitors, strangers and the public generally invited. Seats free." Or: "Seats free. Visitors invited. The poor welcome.")[15]

In 1882 the railroad reached Lampasas, and so did Rev. J. M. Carroll, D.D. Dr. Carroll was one of the most important Texas Baptist leaders of the era, often working fulltime as a denominational executive or as the founder and president of Baptist colleges. But early in his career, and sometimes later, he served as pastor of several Baptist churches. Carroll's tenure at Lampasas, 1882-1887, is regarded as his most successful pastorate.

James Milton Carroll was born in 1852 in Arkansas. One of twelve children of a Baptist preacher, J. M. moved with his family to Texas in 1858. An older brother fought in the Civil War and became a giant among Texas Baptists, and J. M. eventually wrote his biography: *B. H. Carroll, Colossus of Baptist History*. J. M. married at the age of eighteen; his bride, Sudie Eliza Womble, was sixteen. The couple would have three children, but two died in infancy. A daughter grew to maturity, and so did an adopted son.[16]

J. M. started married life as a farmer, but when he felt a call to preach, he moved to Independence and began studies at Baylor, while his wife enrolled in Baylor Female College. In five years at Baylor he won every academic medal the school awarded. Three pastorates followed, along with increasing involvement in denominational work. At twenty-nine, already highly regarded in Baptist circles, J. M. Carroll assumed pastoral duties at the First Baptist Church of Lampasas.

Lampasas was booming when Reverend Carroll moved to town in 1882. By year's end there were 164 members, a number which jumped to 235 in 1883, when Carroll baptized twenty-one new believers. By 1886 membership rose to 330, and in 1887 there were thirty baptisms.

When Carroll arrived there were no trained deacons, the choir had disbanded, and there was no organist. Reverend Carroll personally trained deacons and Sunday School teachers. He organized a Ladies' Society and a mission band, and re-organized the choir. A mission church was formed in "Depot Town" in northeast Lampasas. Carroll persuaded his congregation that a larger and more imposing building was needed, and in May 1886 construction began at the southwest corner of Third Street and Key Avenue.[17]

In 1885 Carroll used his denominational influence to bring to Lampasas the annual Texas Baptist State Convention. A number of statewide meetings were held at the "Saratoga of the South" during this period, but in the religious annals of Lampasas this gathering of Baptists from across the Lone Star State was a landmark event.

Rev. J. M. Carroll served as pastor of the First Baptist Church from 1882-1887. He more than doubled membership, brought the annual Texas Baptist Convention to Lampasas, and launched construction of a handsome new sanctuary. Later, while working as a denominational leader, Carroll maintained his family home in Lampasas for several years. —Courtesy First Baptist Church, Lampasas

At this meeting the Texas Baptist Convention formed a Board of Relief for Disabled Ministers. Former Lampasas pastor H. M. Burroughs agreed to serve as Corresponding Secretary of the organization, soon called the Ministers Relief Board. Within two years Reverend Burroughs reported that the convention was aiding twenty-six destitute ministers, six ministers' widows, and a number of orphaned children. In 1892 the Ministers Relief Board established "an old Minister's home and Sanitarium" in a fifteen-room house in Lampasas. Three elderly couples moved into the comfortable facility, but they quickly became unhappy.

No one visited them, they were unable to go anywhere, and they yearned to see old friends. "All six who were in the 'Home' finally signed a petition asking that they might be returned to their old communities," reported J. M. Carroll. In 1893 the well-intended Minister's Home in Lampasas was discontinued.[18]

By that time the Lampasas congregation was enjoying a handsome new stone house of worship. Although the cornerstone was laid in 1886, church membership declined by about fifty after J. M. Carroll departed in 1887. The Lampasas boom also tapered off during this period, and when funds dried up construction halted with the church half-completed. The new pastor, Rev. J. C. Midyett, baptized thirty new converts in his second year, 1889, and boosted membership to 282. Early in June 1889 Reverend Midyett spoke at commencement exercises at Baylor University, now relocated to Waco. But in September the Midyetts' oldest child, Bessie, died at home, and by the end of the year the family left town.[19]

But by the time of the Midyett departure, construction had resumed on the uncompleted church. A total of $5,000 was spent on the four-year project. The stately stone sanctuary, featuring a soaring steeple tower, opened in 1890 and served the First Baptist congregation for nearly half a century.[20]

In 1866, eleven years after Baptists formed a congregation in Lampasas, Methodists organized the Lampasas District. Methodism was well-structured in Texas, and in April 1866 the Methodist General Conference, meeting in New Orleans, turned their attention to the steadily-expanding West Texas Conference. Four new districts were established: the Waco District, Lampasas District, Waxahachie District, and Springfield District. On Wednesday, September 26, 1866, the 24th session of the West Texas Conference met in Waxahachie. With Bishop E. M. Marvin presiding, the Lampasas District was organized, and James M. Johnson was appointed Presiding Elder. "Lampasas Circuit to be supplied," read the minutes, which meant that Methodist circuit riders would provide sermons on a periodic basis.[21]

William F. Cummins was the first circuit rider of record in the Lampasas District, serving in 1867 and 1868. Almost all of his successors also preached for two years in the Lampasas District before being reassigned. J.W.B. Allen preached in 1875 and 1876, then returned two years later for a three-year stint, 1877-1879. During this time "Lampasas District" was changed to "Lampasas Station," suggesting that a preacher was assigned to Lampasas fulltime. In that case he would have served the Lampasas Methodist Church, College Church just north of town, and Northington Church, which met in the little frame school built by Alex Northington on his ranch three miles east of Lampasas.

By 1880 the growing Lampasas congregation erected a church building in the 700 block of East Fourth Street. The frame structure was the second church building in town, and served Lampasas Methodist Church for two decades. In 1884, when College Church was organized to serve students at newly-opened Centenary College, thirty-four members of the older congregation transferred to the new congregation.[22]

Centenary College of Lampasas was a singular Methodist accomplishment of the late nineteenth century in Texas. The first "college" in Texas was Rutersville College, a Methodist institution (closer to a secondary than a college curriculum) established in 1840 in Fayette County. In subsequent years three more Methodist colleges merged into Texas University, located in Georgetown. Several years later, when a state university was planned, the Methodist institution of higher learning changed its name to Southwestern University.

Methodist officials decided, in 1883, to locate a new denominational college in Lampasas, which was enjoying the sudden growth of its rail-

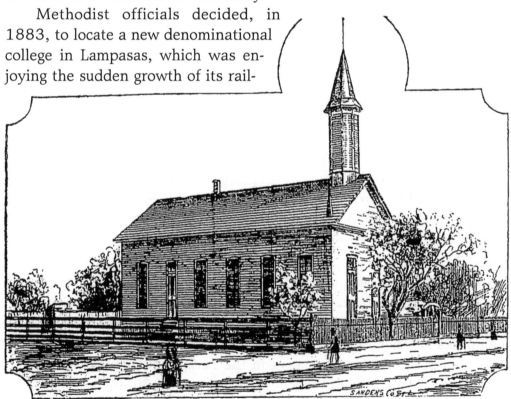

Methodists built their first church building in 1870, on East Fourth Street.
—*Lampasas Leader,* May 13, 1891

road boom. A site was secured on a hill one mile north of Lampasas. Two frame three-story buildings were erected on "College Hill." The Girls' Dormitory featured a parlor and a dining hall on the lower floor, as well as an apartment for the president and his family; the upper two floors were comprised of dorm rooms. The Boys' Dormitory had classrooms and a dining hall on the lower floor, with dorm rooms on the top two floors. Marshall McIlhaney was employed at $150 per month as President and Professor of Mathematics. G. S. Bruce was paid $80 monthly as Professor of Ancient Languages and chaperone of the Boys' Dormitory. There were three other male professors, along with three females who taught the "preparatory school;" these six teachers were paid $65 per month.[23]

During the first term, in the spring of 1884, a total of 174 students enrolled in the college and preparatory school, more than the dorms could accommodate. A number of students had to board in town, while there were many "day pupils" whose homes were in Lampasas. Prima Baker Moses reminisced that for students who lived in town, "free transportation was furnished in the 'College Hack,' which made the trip daily out to the end of Third Street and back down Second Street picking up students, then returning them in the afternoon, 'always in charge of reliable drivers.'"[24]

Among the five students who received degrees in May 1892 was French Ames, who then was added to the faculty. In 1889 the music professor was a Miss Tatum, who had studied at the Cincinnati Conservatory. Professor Tatum combined her talents and those of her students with the choir of the First Baptist Church to present a musical program to a standing-room-only crowd in the courtroom of the new courthouse in February 1889. Four years later Miss Mary Wright joined Centenary College as Dean of the Fine Arts Department and teacher of piano. A gifted performer and inspiring teacher, Mary Wright remained in Lampasas for eleven years, instructing aspiring pupils and enriching the community's musical scene.[25]

The Methodist college permitted little contact between the two sexes, "except when the rules were suspended once a month and a party given in the girls' dormitory," recounted Centenary student Ettie Aurelia Adkins. In her first week at Centenary College, the daughter of Dr. J. N. Adkins was given a demerit for talking with a male student who had been a playmate since childhood. "The President and authoritative body in Centenary College had an established law unto themselves," she

The two principal buildings of Centenary College were three-story structures with Mansard roofs. The college stood atop a hill just north of Lampasas. After Centenary closed, one building burned, but the surviving structure later housed St. Dominic's Villa, a Catholic institution.
—Courtesy KSM

fumed. But the Board of Trustees, which included the pastor of Lampasas Methodist Church, along with J. A. Abney, and M. Y. and C. D. Stokes, supported the straitlaced Victorian morals of the era. More than two dozen rules strictly prohibited drinking, smoking, gambling, profanity, ostentatious dress—and communication between young men and women.[26]

Through Centenary College, Methodists provided Lampasas with an institution of higher learning for a dozen years. In 1894 the president and board accepted a financially beneficial offer to move the college across town to a larger facility, but within a year this attractive opportunity would bring disaster to Centenary College.

Baptists and Methodists formed the first two congregations in Lampasas and erected the first two houses of worship. Even as other denominations organized, the Baptist and Methodist churches remained the largest in town, and there was a friendly rivalry, as embodied by a prominent Lampasas couple. Business and civic leader J. R. Key was a devout Baptist. During the 1880s and later J. R. and his brother, Harry Newton Key, engaged in the drug and grocery and banking businesses. J. R. and Lula Key had five children, and following Lula's death J. R. married Emily Lois Cook, who was a staunch Methodist. On Sundays J. R., a deacon, attended services at the First Baptist Church, while Emily went to the First Methodist Church. Back at home, J. R. invariably said, "Mrs.

Key," in the formal address of the era, "we had fine attendance today. And how many did you have?" After attendance totals were exchanged, J. R. then insisted on comparing amounts from their respective collection plates. This amicable Baptist-Methodist competition was conducted every Sunday after church.[27]

Baptists and Methodists were joined in Lampasas by an Episcopalian congregation in 1873. The first Bishop of Texas, The Rt. Rev. Alexander Gregg, became aware that there were several Episcopalian families in frontier Lampasas. Bishop Gregg asked Dr. Thomas S. Denny to become a layreader and organize a mission in Lampasas. Dr. Denny, an Austin physician and former vestryman at St. David's Episcopal Church, accepted the charge. Dr. Denny arrived late in 1872 and soon reported that there were eight Episcopalian families in Lampasas, as well as three single adults of the Episcopal faith. In 1873 Bishop Gregg licensed Dr. Denny as a layreader. Rev. J. T. Hutcheson came to Lampasas in June 1873, during the watering season, and officiated at services on four Sundays. In July Rev. T.R.B. Trader visited Lampasas and officiated six times: "four times in the morning in town and twice in the afternoon out at the springs campground." Bishop Gregg made the first of several trips to Lampasas on October 8, 1873.[28]

Early in 1873 two saloon shootouts resulted in the wounding of the Lampasas County sheriff and the deaths of four members of the State Police, and late in the year a catastrophic flood swept through Lampasas. But Dr. Denny was conscientious in his labors, and in 1875, the Episcopalian mission at Lampasas Springs was formally recognized by the Diocese of Texas (the mission would not achieve parish status until 1952).

St. Mary's congregation met variously in the First Baptist Church, the courthouse, and the First Presbyterian Church. In 1882 a site for a church was purchased at the southeast corner of Chestnut and Fourth. The cornerstone and foundation were laid in 1884, but funds became scarce and construction halted. A former Methodist minister, J. A. Duncan, became layreader in charge at St. Mary's, and he was aided in pushing construction by progressive businessman W. T. Campbell and other church leaders. In 1884 St. Mary's received its first priest in residence, Rev. F. W. Wey.

Local contractor Pat Gallagher, a master stonemason, supervised the cutting and hauling of building stones from Casbeer's Quarry, three miles north of town. The edifice was built in a Victorian Gothic architectural

St. Mary's Episcopal Church was completed in 1890. St. Mary's continues to serve the parish today, and it is the oldest church building in Lampasas. —Courtesy Jane McMillin

The Lampasas Christian Church was dedicated in March 1883 on Fourth Street. —*Lampasas Leader*, May 13, 1891

style and reportedly modeled on an Anglican parish church in Rugby, England, boyhood home of W. T. Campbell. The handsome building opened in 1890, and still serves the parish today. St. Mary's Episcopal Church is the oldest church building in Lampasas, an impressive, tangible architectural link with the past.

Professor A. P. Aten, who founded Aten College, was an ordained minister in the Disciples of Christ Church. He opened the two-story Aten College to Disciples of Christ adherents. "There is a small congregation of Disciples in Lampasas who are bravely struggling . . . that they may take their position in the community . . .," reported Professor Aten in the *Christian Standard* of August 9, 1879. "Judge Abney and Dr. Adkins, one in the practice of law, the other in medicine, are both able and acceptable preachers of the work and work harmoniously together in the congregation."[29]

With three prominent men to lead in preaching and ministry, the Disciples of Christ congregation grew rapidly, and in 1880 work began on a frame sanctuary on Fourth Street, between Elm and Hackberry. But funding failed to materialize, and after two years, in March 1882, a special meeting was called to determine how to complete the church building. V. R. Stapp agreed to become the first fulltime pastor, and a building committee was appointed to raise funds and finish the sanctuary. A large crowd gathered on Sunday, March 25, 1883, for dedication services of the Lampasas Christian Church.

The Presbyterian Church opened in 1883 on the southeast corner of Fifth and Walnut streets. A later expansion added a steeple and bell. —Lampasas Leader, May 13, 1891

That same year the Presbyterian Church was

opened on the northeast corner of Fifth and Walnut streets. In 1881 Rev. D. H. Dodson, a missionary of the Presbyterian Church of U.S.A., requested the Austin Presbytery to appoint a committee to organize a church in Lampasas. The First Presbyterian Church U.S.A. of Lampasas was formed on October 28, 1881. The congregation met in the homes of members and in the Methodist Church, on Sundays when the Methodists did not hold services.[30]

The first pastor was Rev. J. Griffin, who began his pastorate on September 29, 1882. The railroad had reached Lampasas, and Rev. Griffin immediately launched a building project. Within a month the new trustees obtained a lot from the Lampasas Springs Company, a development firm, for one dollar. Rev. Griffin applied to the Presbyterian Church Erection Board for a $500 loan. Built within several months, the solid frame structure was twenty-four feet wide and forty-four feet deep, and a later expansion added a steeple with a bell.

There always were a few Catholic families in Lampasas, primarily Hispanics, but they were too few in number to support a church. With the railroad boom, Bishop Nicholas Gallagher decided to build a church in Lampasas. Aware that the Santa Fe Railroad employed many Irish-Catholic laborers, Bishop Gallagher personally went up and down the line soliciting donations. St. Mary's Church opened in 1885, and Father F. J. Smith conducted the first Mass, although services were not held regularly until 1892. That year Father Pius Lennertz was appointed St. Mary's first rector, traveling weekly from Temple.[31]

Like the Methodists, the Catholics made a memorable contribution to Lampasas education, even utilizing the same facility as the former Centenary College. In 1900 Dominican Sisters from Galveston traveled to Lampasas to escape malaria and humidity during the summer months. They rented the big Girl's Dormitory built for Centenary (the Boy's Dormitory had been razed). Early in September 1900 Galveston was devastated by a hurricane which killed 6,000 and damaged or destroyed every building in the port city of 36,000. The Dominican Sisters decided to move their Galveston boarding school to Lampasas. The Sisters purchased forty acres and the dorm building from a man named Harding, who had bought the Centenary College property. By the second year seventy girls were enrolled at St. Dominic's Villa. After a quarter of a century the school was closed, and the Sisters moved out in 1929.[32]

"I was a pupil at St. Dominic's," reminisced Sister M. Sabine. "After my years of training for the Sisterhood, I was sent there as a teacher. The beautiful and genial spirit of both pupils and teachers can never be forgotten. Anyone who had the good fortune of living at the Villa regrets that the dear old Villa, as it was called, is now only a pleasant memory."[33]

Frontier Lampasas and the Saratoga of the South witnessed the organization of six congregations, the construction of seven houses of worship, and the founding of a Methodist college. Within a thirty-year period congregations were formed by Baptists (1855), Methodists (1866), Episcopalians (1873), Disciples of Christ (1879), Presbyterians (1881), and Catholics (1885). During a period of eighteen years, seven church sanctuaries were built by Baptists (1872 and 1890), Methodists (1880), Disciples of Christ (1883), Presbyterians (1883), Catholics (1885), and Episcopalians (1890). Methodists operated Centenary College in Lampasas for twelve years (1884-1895).

From the beginnings of Lampasas through its heyday as the Saratoga of the South, there was a strong and influential religious presence in the community. Frontier wives and mothers always wanted churches, to satisfy their own spiritual and social needs, and for the moral instruction of their children. There were women and children in frontier Lampasas from the founding days of the community, along with a number of men—generally husbands and fathers—who also supported churches. By the 1880s Lampasas churchgoers could choose from half a dozen different types of worship. From time to time notable men of God—bishops, legendary Baptist preachers, the first fulltime evangelist in Texas—conducted services in Lampasas. Lampasas churches greatly enriched the community's social life, with ladies' meetings and Christmas tree parties and church socials, as well as the town's cultural life, particularly music, with church choirs and pianos and organs—and the quality musical instruction available at Centenary College.

Lampasas had more than its share of gunfighting and drinking and rustling. But throughout its wild years the outlaw influence was balanced to some degree by churches and churchgoers. And as Lampasas matured, the atmosphere of morality disseminated by churches throughout the community, the values reinforced by a growing number of churchgoers, would help propel Lampasas into a new century as a decent and increasingly virtuous town in which to work and live.

CHAPTER TEN

Railroad Boom

*"Horses had been unhitched from all vehicles as a safety precaution,
as very few, if any, of these animals had ever seen a train."*
—Ettie Aurelia Adkins

"T he crowd was so dense they could not get near the depot," remembered Ettie Aurelia Adkins. "Every tree, as far as one could see, was full of boys, and they were also standing on the roof of the station."[1]

Tuesday, May 16, 1882, was a gala occasion in Lampasas, a landmark date in the twenty-seven-year history of the frontier town. Railroad tracks at long last had reached Lampasas, and the first passenger train was scheduled to pull into town. "The train was due at 10 A.M.," wrote Miss Adkins, "but people from the surrounding counties began arriving the day before." The Adkins home had been crowded for days with visitors who had come to attend the great event.[2]

The respected Dr. Adkins was part of a committee appointed to greet officials of the Gulf, Colorado and Santa Fe Railroad when the train arrived. He wore his best suit and a tall stovepipe hat. A barbeque was planned for the railroad dignitaries. Women were to bring pies and cakes, and men would provide the meat. Of course there would be speeches and other activities, all at Hancock Park.

The train was late, and the crowd became restless. There was speculation that the train might have jumped the track. Hours passed, but

146

periodically someone would say hopefully, "Listen, I think I hear it coming!" At last, hours later, the train whistle sounded and "rippling smoke" was sighted down the tracks.[3]

A few families had taken picnic baskets to the Sulphur Creek bridge east of town "to watch the train come in," recounted Effie Osburn Greenwood. These families picnicked "amid much merriment and anticipation of the special train." When the overdue train finally passed before them, "We cheered wildly and waved hands, handkerchiefs, and baskets frantically."[4]

Because the tracks ended in Lampasas, there was a turnaround on the approach to the depot, and the train backed into the station. Sheriff George Wolf and a squad of special deputies kept the crowd at bay while the dignitaries boarded several buggies and led a procession to the park. A glorious event finally was launched, and frontier Lampasas would never be the same.

In 1860, when Lampasas was a five-year-old village, there were 31,000 miles of railroad track in the United States, but there were barely 400 miles in Texas—a state that eventually would lead the nation in railroad mileage. After the Civil War, railroad construction exploded across the nation, especially in the western states and territories. Railroads became America's greatest industry, dominating the economy and politics of the era. Tens of thousands of men were employed by railroad companies. Five transcontinental railroads were completed by 1893, with construction stimulated by federal loans and land grants. A network of branch lines tied into major trunk lines. Towns that were bypassed by railroads soon faded way, but a railway connection seemed to assure a community's prosperity.

Texas, with its vast size, along with almost limitless agricultural and commercial potential, was the site of feverish railroad construction. Entry of the Texas Republic into the Union as a state was unique, and unlike any other state, Texas retained its public lands, rather than turning them over to the federal government. Therefore Texas was able to emulate the U.S. government in offering vacant lands as an inducement to promising railroad companies. Texas gave a staggering 32,150,000 acres to railroads. But by 1889 there were 8,486 miles of track in Texas, an important factor in a population that soared from 818,579 in 1870 to 2,235,527 in 1890.

The Gulf, Colorado, and Santa Fe Railway Company was chartered on May 28, 1873, with an authorized capital stock of $2,000,000.

Offices of the GC&SF were located in Galveston, and a great deal of the stock was subscribed by local investors. The projected route was to construct a line northwestward across Texas, without going through rival city Houston, while eventually reaching Santa Fe and connecting with the Denver and Rio Grande Railroad. Although construction began on May 1, 1875, it was 1879 before the line reached Richmond; in four years merely sixty-three miles of track had been laid.[5]

The GC&SF was financially shaky. For example, even though the GC&SF eventually received certificates for 3,554,560 acres of vacant state lands, sales of these lands netted the company only $211,168. In 1879 trustee and treasurer George Sealy of Galveston reorganized the GC&SF, and construction resumed early in 1880. By late in 1881 the line had been extended another 291 miles, from Richmond to Fort Worth. Several branch lines also were built, including a forty-eight mile line from Belton to Lampasas.

Construction methods were perfected during the building of the first transcontinental railroad, from 1864 until the Golden Spike was driven in 1869 at Promontory Point, Utah. Two railroad companies built toward each other: the Central Pacific, from California toward the north, and the Union Pacific, from Nebraska toward the west. Each company employed 10,000 men, the largest work forces yet assembled by the American economy.

A great many employees of the Central Pacific were Chinese workers, but with the close of the Civil War, Union veterans signed on with the Union Pacific in large numbers. Work force, financing, materials, equipment—all reached unprecedented scale. Gen. Grenville Dodge, who surveyed 60,000 railroad miles in a career interrupted by the Civil War, explained that "material for a mile of track required forty cars, besides the necessary cars for supplies and for the population that was along the side of the road." Logistical problems were enormous, but men who had dealt with vast logistical demands during the war were available. Former army officers handled railroad logistics and were in charge of other divisions, and former non-coms served as crew foremen.[6]

Such men were readily drilled onto laying track in a rapid, precision assembly line. "The whole organization of the force engaged in the construction of the road is, in fact, semi-military," observed surveyor William A. Bell. "Track-laying on the Union Pacific is a science," he stated, describing the process in detail:

Less than thirty seconds to a rail for each gang, and so four rails go down the minute!. . . . The moment the car is empty it is tipped over on the side of the track to let the next loaded car pass it; and then it is a sight to see it go flying back for another load, propelled by a young Jehu, who drives furiously. Close behind the first gang come the gangers, spikers, and bolters, and a lively time they made of it. It is a Grand Arrival Chorus that these sturdy sledges are playing across the plains. It is in triple time, three strokes to a spike. There are ten spikes to a rail, four hundred rails to a mile, eighteen hundred miles to San Francisco.[7]

Techniques thus developed in the 1860s were utilized by later transcontinental railroads, as well as by lines of lesser scale. Gen. Braxton Bragg, a Union combat commander, was the chief engineer of the Gulf, Colorado and Santa Fe Railway. When the GC&SF began building west, out of Belton, construction methods were standardized. But many of the workmen on the forty-eight-mile line to Lampasas were convicts, leased by the state prison system to railroad construction foremen, as well as to planters and other large-scale employers. The inmates were guarded while working and bunked on convict trains with barred dormitory cars. (The next year, in May 1883, a gang of convicts were working at the rock quarry north of town, and three inmates—including E. J. Vaughn of Lampasas—managed to escape into the countryside.)[8]

The chief surveyor for the GC&SF was H. L. Higdon, brother of enterprising Lampasas businessman John Higdon. H. L. Higdon hiked long miles through the rugged terrain to survey a feasible route to Lampasas. After the line was surveyed, grading crews and bridge crews went out in advance of the tracklayers. Numerous small bridges were built across creeks and rocky depressions, while the largest bridge spanned the Lampasas River about ten miles east of Lampasas. East of town bridges twice crossed Sulphur Creek. Meanwhile, tracks ascended the Balcones Escarpment west of Belton and advanced directly toward Lampasas.

A telegraph line already had been built to Lampasas, and a journalistic correspondent was engaged to wire Lampasas news items to the *Galveston Daily News*. On March 15 the correspondent reported that GC&SF tracks were within twenty-six miles of Lampasas. Twenty days later tracklayers reached the Lampasas River, but there was a delay of a few days while the bridge was completed. By Thursday, April 14, news came that the "Santa Fe Railway is seven and one-half miles from town tonight." Three weeks later, "A delegation of railroad officers and prominent business men of Galveston" visited Lampasas, arriving by train within a short distance of town. But on Friday and Saturday, May 5 and 6, heavy rainstorms lashed the area, "swelling our creeks, washing away a portion of both railroad bridges across Sulphur Creek, near the town, and interfering with telegraph communication."[9]

There was another delay while bridges were repaired and the last tracks were spiked into place. Now final arrangements could be made for the official opening of the line. "Lampasas, the Saratoga of the South, sends greeting to the city [Galveston] by the Gulf, Colorado and Santa Fe, and congratulations to herself upon the completion of the iron bands which now bind her to Galveston."[10]

Before the opening ceremony took place, even before the line was completed, the boom was on in Lampasas. The Galveston businessmen who came to town before the railroad was completed were investors who intended to turn Lampasas into the "Saratoga of the South," a phrase that already was being used in promotional literature. Hotels were being built, including the three-story Globe Hotel on Western Avenue, which boasted the only elevator in Lampasas, as well as a splendid resort accommodation at Hancock Park. Two stone wings were added to the Exchange Hotel. Tourists could come by train to Lampasas and find comfortable accommodations.

The Globe Hotel on Western Avenue was the first building in Lampasas with an elevator.
—Courtesy KSM

But when visitors arrived at the depot they were a long way from any Lampasas hotel. The GC&SF planned, at a later date, to extend their Lampasas line to the west. Surveyor H. L. Higdon determined that the best approach was to skirt Lampasas from the east and build north, before angling northwest across the county. The GC&SF line never entered Lampasas proper, and the depot was a mile and a half northeast of the courthouse square. The first station was little more than a platform, and Lampasas citizens assumed that a substantial depot would be built closer to the heart of town. Despite a great deal of traffic, the GC&SF had no intention of going to the expense of building a line into town as a depot extension. Railroads all over the nation were accustomed to communities moving toward them; Lampasas would have to adjust.

"The fact that the Santa Fe will not locate its passenger depot nearer than the present depot surprises a number of citizens."[11] The correspondent to the *Galveston Daily News* was diplomatic; he could have reported that the decision disappointed as well as surprised Lampasas citizens.

Late in November work began on the passenger depot, "and the people will soon have a fine depot worthy of the town." Completed within five weeks, the passenger depot, along with a large freight depot, stood on the west side of the tracks. The surrounding area was surveyed and platted into streets and lots, but not much construction occurred, mostly a few modest houses. The little cluster of buildings, the most important of which was the GC&SF passenger depot, was called "Depot Town."[12]

Hacks carried arriving passengers to the hotels, but soon a street railway was planned. In July it was proposed to lay down tracks between the two major resort sites, Hancock and Hanna springs, a distance of about one mile. After it was learned that the GC&SF depot would remain northeast of town—more than two miles from Hancock Springs—the street railway was extended to the train station. Late in October the simple tracks for the mule-drawn trolley began to be laid, and progress was rapid. "The street railway will have the iron laid across the public square to-morrow," reported the Galveston correspondent on November 5, 1883.[13]

Soon hotel guests and Lampasans could ride the small streetcar, "drawn by a little brown mule and presided over by a very obliging conductor, who always had time to wait for a passenger, blocks away, who waved for a ride." Prima Baker Moses, as a girl, frequently rode the streetcar, "to the accompaniment of a small bell around the neck of the little mule." At the end of the line in Hancock Park, the mule was un-hitched and harnessed to the other end of the car for a return trip. Years later Prima Baker Moses was happy to learn that a "benevolent rancher gave the mule free pasturage until she died a natural death of old age. If there is a mule heaven, I am sure she is rewarded for her six or eight years of service to the patrons of old Lampasas."[14]

In November 1883 the Street Railway Company built an ice factory for additional income. In that same month, "John Farley, the iceman, of Waco, is in the city, and purchased a location on Third Street, and work will begin at once on his ice factory," reported a journalist. "This with that of the Street Railway company's factory, will be sufficient to keep us cool."[15]

Like any up and coming community of the era, Lampasas needed a telephone system. Alexander Graham Bell introduced his revolutionary invention in 1876, and by 1883 every city and large town clamored for the service, while copper mines tried to produce the metal needed for thousands of miles of new wire. By July 1883 a Lampasas company was organized to erect poles, string wire, and install telephones in doctor's offices, progressive businesses, and homes eager for the newfangled in-vention. The required 500 subscribers were signed up, and by November the telephone exchange "has opened for business, and halloo rings out on all sides."[16]

The mule-drawn trolley hauled passengers from the remote depot to Hancock Park and back.
—Courtesy KSM

With so much activity in the boomtown, so many charters to be issued, so much municipal business to conduct, it was imperative for Lampasas to organize a city government. A decade earlier the frontier village established a municipal government through "AN ACT to Incorporate the City of Lampasas," an act that was approved by the state legislature in April 1873. There would be a mayor and eight aldermen, who would appoint a city marshal, a city secretary, and a city attorney. Within three years there was an effort to abolish the corporation form of government, which ceased to function in 1876, even though it officially remained in effect. The railroad boom triggered a local election to establish a functional city government. On Tuesday, April 17, 1883, 347 men voted (many more residents were turned away because they had not yet lived in Lampasas for a year). Tillman Weaver, a seventy-three-year-old retired grocer, was elected mayor, while former Texas Ranger N. O. Reynolds was elected city marshal. The new mayor and city council immediately faced a host of pressing issues.[17]

The streets of Lampasas were hilly and packed with caliche dust. A street sprinkler wagon was put into operation by June 1883, and in October the city issued $10,000 in ten-year bonds to contract for grading Third, Fourth, Live Oak, Main, Western, and Grand streets and avenues. In December work began on a traffic bridge across Burleson Creek, just north of Hanna Springs, and a bridge spanning Sulphur Creek was under construction by Kane Brothers. In 1885 the city government issued $40,000 in bonds to build a waterworks system; the plant would be located along the north bank of Sulphur Creek, a short distance upstream and northwest of Hancock Springs.[18]

Scores of new buildings went up in Lampasas during the railroad boom: residences, commercial structures, churches, hotels. It was reported that in August 1883, nine "fine stone" commercial buildings were completed, including four on the square. In 1883 churches were built for Presbyterians and the Disciples of Christ, and the two three-story edifices of Centenary College were ready for students by the end of the year.[19]

Any community of substance during the late nineteenth century boasted an opera house. Many towns built an opera house through public subscriptions to a stock company. Investors often understood that they were performing a community service and probably would realize little or no return on their investment. During the first week of 1883 a circular was distributed on the streets announcing a meeting of citizens

The only known image of the Elks Opera House, built in 1883 on the south side of Third Street where the Lampasas City Hall later was erected. —Lampasas Leader, May 13, 1891

at the courthouse on Thursday night, January 4, to discuss the construction of an opera house. "The investment will pay 25 per cent probably more," came the optimistic promise. "Come everybody, and take part." At the meeting "an opera-house company" was organized, and "it was decided to build a $26,000 opera-house."[20]

Two lots were purchased on the south side of Third Street for $2,400. Businesses lined both sides of Third Street for three blocks leading west. The thoroughfare had become a major extension of the commercial district, and the presence of an opera house would increase the importance of Third Street. Fine Victorian houses were being built farther west on Third, which began to be called "Silk Stocking Row."

The "Elks Opera House Corporation" contracted a two-story frame building which would face north, two blocks west of the square. The front of the ground floor would produce revenue from two store spaces; on the left was a men's clothing store, and on the right was a fruit and candy shop. Upstairs the front was divided into offices for professional men. "One occupant that I recall was a popular dentist, Dr. Bierbower," reminisced Prima Baker Moses.[21]

The performance hall dominated the rear of the building. "The chairs upholstered in brown leather were elevated and arranged in tiers down to the orchestra pit," remembered Moses, "the chandeliers were most dazzling." The drop curtain was "flaming red," with a painted woodland scene dominated by an elk. Lampasas was not large enough to attract performers from the top entertainment circuit, but smaller, less renowned troupes sometimes offered such perennial favorites as *East Lynn*, *Dr. Jekyll and Mr. Hyde*, and *Ten Nights in a Barroom*. The opera house was rented for political meetings and school performances and shows presented by local amateur groups.[22]

The most famous solo performer who played the Elks Opera House was "Blind Tom," who was born sightless in 1849 in Georgia. Raised on the plantation of General James N. Bethune, Tom Wiggins was a musical prodigy who learned to play the piano by ear. The Bethune family managed his performing career, both before and after the Civil War. At ten he became the first African-American performer to play the White House. Blind Tom toured Europe, and he appeared annually in New York City. By the time he played Lampasas, Blind Tom had memorized 7,000 pieces of music—popular songs, hymns, waltzes, and classical—with the help of a professor of music who toured with him.[23]

During the flurry of construction in Lampasas there also was a flurry of destructive fires. At Depot Town, for example, on the night of July 26, 1883, E. W. Thorp's Lumber Yard, near the Santa Fe depot, was destroyed by fire, along with a nearby house. The cause was thought "to be incendiary," and the estimated loss was $9,000. The next night a small feed store just east of the square burned, and another small building was torn down to stop the blaze. A volunteer bucket brigade extinguished the fire just as flames were charring another building.[24]

At noon on Thursday, September 22, 1883, a blaze erupted in the block that formed the west side of the square. There was a strong north wind which fanned the flames southward for two blocks. J. D. Cassell's drug store was destroyed, along with Dr. Lincecum's office, a grocery store, the *Dispatch* building, A. J. Hill's mattress factory and warehouse, "the old blue front restaurant," two residences, and a boarding house. The home of the widowed Mrs. Sam Horrell was saved, along with the Globe Hotel and John Higdon's cotton gin. The loss was about $25,000, with only $10,000 worth covered by insurance.[25]

These fires of 1883 hastened construction of the waterworks system, as well as the organization of firefighters. During the first week of August 1883, only days after the fires of July 26 and 27, citizens formed "a hook and ladder company, with H. M. Burt foreman." This company

Organization of the Lampasas Fire Department began in response to destructive fires during the boom of 1883. —Courtesy KSM

was a major step in the later organization of the Lampasas Fire Department. And after each destructive fire during the boom, rebuilding was immediate and usually more substantial than the structures that had been burned.[26]

The most noble and long-lasting embodiment of the Lampasas railroad boom was the county's first substantial courthouse. A public square was included on the original town plat, but no courthouse had ever stood on it. There were shade trees and a city well, and it was used for parking wagons and hitching horses. "In the centre of the Square is a beautiful cluster of trees, principally Live Oak, that are being seriously injured by their roots being trampled around by horses and oxen," complained the *Lampasas Chronicle* in 1859. "Several beautiful trees have already been broken down by large waggons running against them. . . . The Public Well too, . . . is much exposed. Hogs are wallowing around it continually, creating a filthy, muddy place."[27]

Lampasas historian Jeff Jackson identified twelve buildings around or near the square that were used as courtrooms and county offices: "a little clapboard building" first used in 1856; "the old Commercial hotel"; a former blacksmith shop; a frame residence; commercial buildings on two sides of the square; and miscellaneous other structures. On Christmas night in 1871 a two-story frame building rented by the county burned, along with the county archives. One night the marriage record book was stolen from the former blacksmith shop. The Flood of 1873 destroyed the house being rented from Henry Hill, along with many of the county records. During the Horrell–Higgins Feud, on the night of June 4, 1877, the rented upper floor of the Hanna Building, on the north side of the square, was burglarized and district court records were stolen and presumably burned.[28]

The repeated loss of county records made it clear that a secure courthouse was needed. Furthermore, most of the rented buildings had little or no office space, so county officials often had to conduct business from their homes. In addition to a courthouse, Lampasas also needed a secure jail.

"Of all things, perhaps the most needed improvement in Lampasas town and county is a courthouse," pointed out the editors of the *Lampasas Daily Times* in one of the first editions of their newspaper. They were newcomers from Waco who did not want "to hazzard any remarks" on why the work had not been performed, "but it is evident that such an improvement is greatly needed."[29]

It was even more evident four years later in 1882, when the railroad boom began. "'Where is your court house?' is about the first question strangers ask upon arriving in our city," reported the *Lampasas Record*.[30]

Alex Northington and other progressive men were on the county board of commissioners and recognized the obvious need for both a courthouse and jail, as well as the improved ability to fund a major project. The commissioners responded promptly to a petition from District Judge W. A. Blackburn and a grand jury, employing Waco architect Wesley Clark Dodson in June 1883. The next month the commissioners selected the Kane Brothers construction firm, who had submitted a bid of $34,949. Continuing to move rapidly, the commissioners issued $40,000 in bonds in August.[31]

Site preparation began immediately with removal of trees and excavation for the foundation. The cornerstone was set on September 6, 1882, on the northeast corner. Cut from a quarry near town, the cornerstone proclaimed: "Laid by Saratoga A.F.&A.M. No. 546." Masons were present in force at the ceremony, along with members of the I.O.O.F. and the Knights of Pythias. Following custom, miscellaneous items were placed inside that cornerstone, including a Holy Bible, coins, Confed-

Site preparation for the new courthouse began in the summer of 1882. In addition to laborers, a crowd of men frequently gathered to watch the progress of the project. —Courtesy KSM

Completed in 1883, the Lampasas County Courthouse was an impressive version of Texas "Courthouse Gothic" architecture. Note the covered wagon at right. —Courtesy KSM

erate paper money, newspapers from Lampasas and other towns, and badges.[32]

Within eight months, well under deadline and budget, Kane Brothers completed the magnificent new courthouse in May 1883. There was another ceremony, featuring speeches and champagne and an enthusiastic crowd. A sturdy jail also was completed, a two-story stone structure just southwest of the square, facing Fourth Street.[33]

The imposing Lampasas County Courthouse was built during the golden age of courthouse construction in Texas. Late in the nineteenth century scores of counties erected Victorian courthouses which expressed community pride and prosperity. One of the leading courthouse architects during this era was W. C. Dodson. For his Lampasas edifice Dodson chose the popular French Empire Style of architecture, which was characterized by Mansard roofs, patterned slate shingles, bracketed cornices, and miscellaneous ornamental details. Other Victorian styles of the period that were utilized on Texas courthouses were Romanesque Revival and Renaissance Revival, although any ornate, imposing courthouse would be classified as Courthouse Gothic.

The Lampasas version of Courthouse Gothic measured ninety-six by sixty-four feet. Most of the second floor was taken up by a spacious district courtroom. On the ground floor a fireproof vault offered secure storage for county records. The building was dominated by an impressive clock tower. According to a historical plaque inside the courthouse, the bell weighs 1,300 pounds and is thirty-nine inches in diameter. The clock was operated by a 250-pound weight and a 740-pound "striking portion" which was hand wound every eight days with a large crank (the clock was electrified in 1945). In 1888 the courthouse lawn was enclosed with an iron fence (which was donated in 1917 to a World War I metal drive).[34]

For a small but growing town like Lampasas, a statuesque courthouse was like a contemporary civic center. Visitors to Lampasas would be impressed by the towering structure, whose clock bell could be heard throughout town. Lampasans finally, after nearly three decades, could take pride in their new courthouse. And, like citizens in other towns, Lampasans felt free to use their public building for unofficial purposes. Political meetings were held in the courthouse. So were church services— the Episcopalians worshipped frequently in the courtroom before their sanctuary was completed. Texas Confederate Veterans held reunions at the courthouse, and the Daughters of the Republic of Texas conducted an organizational meeting in the Lampasas County Courthouse.

The railroad boom generated rapid business expansion in Lampasas. Rickety old frame buildings—including the saloon where four State Policemen in 1873 and Merritt Horrell in 1877 were gunned down— were replaced by larger, nicer commercial buildings. Many of the new structures around the square were two-story, and most were built of native limestone. There was an aesthetic harmony to the sight of new limestone commercial structures surrounding another new, but bigger and grander, limestone building. The Lampasas County Courthouse loomed above the business district like a benevolent patriarch overseeing the life of the community below—as it still does today.

On page opposite: *The promotional map of boomtown Lampasas shows subdivisions that were surveyed but not developed. In the center of the map is Hanna Park, showing the springs and pavilion. The courthouse is a block to the southwest. Near the bridge two blocks east of the courthouse stood the stone mill built by Moses Hughes. The Park Hotel is at left, and below it is the footbridge across Sulphur Fork to the Hancock Springs bathhouse. The GC&SF passenger and freight depots may be seen at the northeastern edge of town. The mule-drawn trolley line may be traced from the depots to Hancock Park and back.* —Courtesy Jerry Goodson, Lampasas County Surveyor

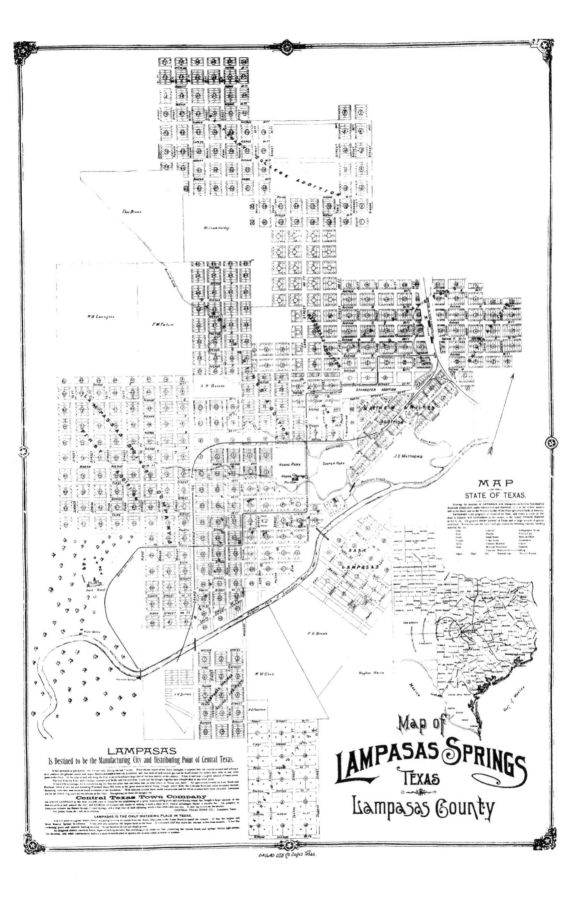

MAP
OF THE
STATE OF TEXAS.

Map of
LAMPASAS SPRINGS
TEXAS
Lampasas County

LAMPASAS
Is Destined to be the Manufacturing City and Distributing Point of Central Texas.

Central Texas Town Company

LAMPASAS IS THE ONLY WATERING PLACE IN TEXAS.

CHAPTER ELEVEN
Saratoga of the South

"Lampasas can comfortably entertain 5,000 guests."
—*Dallas Weekly Herald*, June 18, 1885

The Park Hotel was the crown jewel of the Saratoga of the South. The ornate resort hotel boasted 200 guest rooms, a dance pavilion on the front lawn, tennis courts, 200 acres of shaded grounds, boardwalks and romantic strolling paths, and spacious bath houses at Hancock Springs. In Lampasas there has never been, before or since, anything to match the elegant, glamorous Park Hotel.

The Galveston and Houston investors who built the Park Hotel understood clearly the distinction between commercial and resort hotels. Galveston was the premier resort city of Texas, and there the magnificent Beach Hotel opened in 1883, the same year that the Park Hotel was built in Lampasas. The tremendous expansion of the Texas economy and population during the 1880s produced a growing leisure class that sought recreation and pleasure. "Unlike that of the commercial hotels," explained Texas architectural historian Willard Robinson, "the character of the resort facility was intended to communicate an informal association with pleasure and fun, rather than an organized formality identified with commerce."[1]

Thus the Gracy Hotel, a block from the Lampasas square, was a no-nonsense, long, two-story, stone structure that beckoned to a business clientele. Other Lampasas hotels likewise were plain, businesslike buildings. Even the three-story Globe Hotel, although somewhat more elaborate in appearance and equipped with the town's only elevator, was located on just part of a block a short walk from the business district. There were no tennis courts or dance pavilions or bathhouses on the almost non-existent grounds of the Globe Hotel.

In April 1882 Galveston businessmen George and John Sealy and Walter Gresham, along with eight other investors from Houston, formed the Lampasas Springs Company; these eleven trustees also were investors of the Gulf, Colorado and Santa Fe Railroad. The main office of the new company was located in Houston, with a provision for a branch office in Lampasas. With a capital stock of $200,000, the Lampasas Springs Company purchased approximately 1,300 acres, including Hancock Springs, from Lewis Hancock. This land was to be subdivided and sold as lots, except for 200 acres, which was acquired for a token consideration by another corporation, the Lampasas Park and Hotel Company. This company promptly moved to develop a resort hotel worthy of the Saratoga of the South.[2]

Kane Brothers construction company of Lampasas was commissioned to build the Park Hotel. The main building of the resort was erected in the northern portion of the 200-acre park. It was two stories tall and stretched 331 feet, east to west, and was about 200 feet deep. There were three soaring towers, and galleries on both levels which encircled the building. The banisters on the galleries, or porches, were built in an eye-catching wooden pattern. Gables and tall chimneys added a picturesque appearance designed to delight guests. Inside, there were broad stairways, and "a wide elegantly carpeted hall runs the length of the building. . . ." The spacious dining room measured ninety by sixty feet, with seating for 150 guests. The music room was fifty by forty feet, while the billiard room was sixty by fifty feet with four pool tables. There was a large parlor, two small parlors, and a writing room.[3]

"The kitchen is the most perfect in Texas, has every modern convenience and . . . is kept in a state of such perfect neatness that a lady in full dress might walk across the floor without raising her train," boasted promotional literature. "The menu of the Park hotel is unexcelled, the chef and his assistants are French, and his entrees are to be tasted, they can not be described." After dinner each evening, "the gallery was crowded by gentlemen smoking their post-prandial segars. . . ."[4]

The hotel's steam laundry "is not surpassed in its perfect equipment by any in the state." Also achieving perfection were the hotel's water closets: "around the sinks and basins no order is perceptible." Sewage was piped from the hotel downhill into Sulphur Creek, with the casual sanitation practices of the day. During construction in 1883 the Lampasas Springs Company was "allowed the privilege, by our City Fathers, of building a sewer from their mammoth hotel to the Sulphur Fork of the Lampasas River."[5] Presumably the sewer emptied downstream from the Hancock Springs bath houses.

From the second-floor gallery of the Park Hotel "glimpses can be caught of the swiftly flowing Sulphur Fork of the Lampasas River." Looking to the northeast "the picturesque town of Lampasas" could be seen, especially the clock tower of the new courthouse a mile away. The four-story Beach Hotel in Galveston was larger, but Park Hotel's 331-foot length (a football field plus both end zones plus eleven more feet) made the Lampasas hostelry the longest frame building in Texas.[6]

North of the palatial hotel, two rows of cottages were built, each row running south to north. The west set of cottages accommodated single men and was called "Bachelors' Row." The row of eight cottages on the east was for families. Separate cottages were common at mineral springs resorts throughout America. The dance pavilion stood a short distance

The Park Hotel was all towers and porches and pennants, a true resort in the midst of a 200-acre park. Note the tennis game in the foreground. —Courtesy KSM

south of the hotel. The large pavilion was built without a center pole, which builders said could not be done. But Lampasas carpenter Tom Looney accomplished this construction feat.[7]

At Hancock Springs, a few hundred yards south of the hotel, a large stone bathhouse was built on the south bank, along with a footbridge for hotel patrons to cross the creek. A compartment divided the bath facility into two pools, one for women and one for men. Each pool was about forty by sixty feet wide and three to five feet deep. Bold young men sometimes swam beneath the dividing wall and emerged into the women's pool. Of course, women were fully clad in the bathing suits of the day, which could be rented from the hotel if needed. "These suits were made of a heavy material of navy blue with bloomers, blouse and sailor collars," recalled Prima Baker Moses, "with or without long black stockings, all of which when soaked with water weighed several pounds, and were the exact duplicates of the suits worn at the beaches at Galveston."[8]

Boating on the Sulphur Fork was a popular recreation, along with fishing. "Saddle horses and carriages can be provided at any time," and many hotel guests enjoyed walking in the big park. In bad weather "half a mile of galleries and halls" offered exercise. Throughout the summer a

Park Hotel letterhead. —Courtesy KSM

The Park Hotel, photographed from the east during its 1880s heyday. At 331 feet, the "Grand Park" was the longest frame hotel in Texas. The dining room seated 150 guests, and there were parlors, a music room, a writing room, and a billiard hall. —Courtesy KSM

band was employed, "giving out door concerts in the daytime and supplying dance music for the hops and germans at night"[9]

One afternoon Dr. J. N. Adkins loaded his children, Joe and Ettie Aurelia, into his buggy, driving from their home on the east of Lampasas across town to the Park Hotel. After sightseeing at the hotel, Dr. Adkins placed his children on the mule-drawn trolley for their first streetcar ride. Joe and Ettie Aurelia rode all the way back through town to the GC&SF depot. Their adventure climaxed with the arrival of the evening train, when they joined the crowd that regularly gathered to watch newcomers descend from the passenger cars.[10]

With a first-class resort hotel to go with mineral springs, an opera house, a civic center (courthouse), and an all-important railroad connection, Lampasas became—as claimed by boosters—the Saratoga of the South. Long known for its mineral waters, Lampasas now became a popular destination for tourists who enjoyed trying out the latest fashionable resort. Moreover, Lampasas boasted the facilities to host large meetings,

There were two sets of cottages facing each other behind the Park Hotel. One was for families, while this set, "Bachelor's Row," housed single men. —Courtesy KSM

and during the next several years a variety of statewide conventions and events were held at the Saratoga of the South.

In June 1883, the new Park Hotel hosted the state convention of the Knights of Pythias. Founded in 1864 in Washington, D.C., the Knights of Pythias is a fraternal organization which emphasizes high moral and religious standards and which carries on charitable work. Like other fraternal orders, the Knights of Pythias maintained a female auxiliary, the Sisters of Pythias. In America there was no government welfare until the twentieth century. Charity was local, carried on by churches and fraternal lodges.

In Texas, Lodge No. 1 was installed in Houston in 1872. By 1910 there were 378 lodges in Texas, and membership would peak at more than 30,000 members. In Lampasas the Sulphur City Lodge No. 58 was organized in March 1883 with twenty-five charter members. Three months later, in mid-June, members of the order began arriving by train from across the state.[11]

"Our city is crowded with visiting members of the order from Fort Worth, Dallas, Austin, Houston, Galveston, Cleburne, Temple and Belton," came the happy report from Lampasas. The women's auxiliary, Sisters of Pythias, had not yet been organized in Texas, but wives in large numbers came with their Pythian husbands to Lampasas and the Park

Hotel. "The great Chicago Band," which had been playing in Galveston, was engaged to entertain at the Park Hotel during the convention. On Friday evening, June 15, Pythians and their ladies marched through "the principal streets" of Lampasas to the Methodist Church, where they heard a series of addresses. The next night the hotel staged a grand ball, "which is pronounced to be the most elegant affair of its kind that ever occurred in Texas," telegraphed a reporter during that magical evening. "Swallow-tail coats and white kid gloves are to be seen on the majority of the participants, and an elegant supper is being consumed, and the whole of Lampasas seems to be enthused into pleasing the hundreds who are here."[12]

In addition to the hundreds dancing to the music of the Chicago Band at the Park Hotel, there were hundreds more who still camped or stayed at modest hotels and boarding houses to take the waters. But these were common folk who no longer received much attention from Lampasans. "Prominent ladies and gentlemen from all over the State"[13] understandably commanded notice by their mere presence, and events featuring formal dress and notable orchestras brought a glamour to Lampasas that had never before existed. But campers now were relegated to secondary status during summers at Lampasas. A key dynamic of Lampasas watering seasons, once lost, would prove difficult to recapture.

Looking from the west at the big Hancock Springs bath house. Just beyond it is the footbridge across Sulphur Fork from the Park Hotel, on a hill to the left. —Courtesy KSM

Not long after the Pythians checked out of the Park Hotel, a new crowd began to arrive for a five-day "grand shooting tournament," Tuesday through Saturday, July 17-21. All day Monday, July 16, various marksmen engaged in practice shooting, firing away at glass balls and clay pigeons. Live pigeons had been accumulated for the contest. "The 4,000 pigeons are in fine condition." J. D. Cassell and D. W. Phillips of Lampasas shot well during the practice day. There was considerable side betting, as there would be throughout the tournament.[14]

Guns were second nature to Texans of the nineteenth century, and good marksmen were widely admired. The Lampasas tournament offered a purse totaling $300, a gold prize for the overall champion, and an opportunity to visit the state's latest resort. Of course, the Park Hotel staged a grand ball for the first night of the tournament. Participants and visitors arrived in great numbers, but Lampasas was long accustomed to taking care of an overflow of tourists. "Our city proves equal to the emergency in the way of accommodating the vast crowds that are now here."[15]

The Houston Gun Club entered the tournament, along with shooting clubs from Fort Worth, Austin, Waco, Bastrop, Gainesville, Denison, Pittsburg, and Bryan, as well as the Audubon Club from Kansas City. The Lampasas shooters claimed a few honors, "though they are an infant club." Shooting went on all day for five days. "Everyone is surprised at the large number of birds killed." Betting was heavy: "side money changed hands freely on clubs as well as individual shots." Col. Robert Gribble of Waco provided a gold medal for the champion marksman. There was a tie between George Ellis of the Houston Gun Club and J. Cattraux of the Gainesville Club. But in the shootoff Cattraux accidentally discharged his rifle, enabling Ellis to win the Gribble gold medal.[16]

Two days of horse racing attracted another crowd in August. "Considerable money changed hands," while music was provided by the Commercial Saloon Band. "The races and other amusements make visitors have a jolly time here," reported a correspondent to the *Houston Daily Post*. "A ball occurs at the Park Hotel every two nights."[17]

One sad event marred an otherwise grand summer. Elisha M. Pease was a veteran of the Texas Revolution who served as governor both before and after the Civil War, 1853-57 and 1867-69. Following a long and distinguished public career, Pease spent his latter years in Austin, practicing law and engaging in business ventures. In August Pease and his wife, Lucadia Christiana, visited the new resort hotel in Lampasas.

Perhaps Governor Pease, now seventy-one, felt the need of the curative waters of Hancock Springs. While in Lampasas he suffered an attack of apoplexy, caused by a broken or blocked blood vessel in his brain. His personal physician, Dr. Wooten of Austin, was summoned to Lampasas. There was a newspaper report on Tuesday, August 21, that "Governor Pease is rapidly recovering from his brief but dangerous illness."[18]

Dr. Wooten returned to Austin, but on Wednesday night Pease took a turn for the worse "and is still in critical condition." Dr. Wooten came back to the Governor's bedside, and a few days later Pease again was thought to be improving. But on Monday evening, at 7:30 on August 27, Governor Pease died. The GC&SF provided a special train, and his body was taken back to Austin, where he was buried in Oakwood Cemetery.[19]

The tourist boom of 1883 centered on the Park Hotel and Hancock Springs. But Hanna Springs long had been attractive to those who came to Lampasas to take the waters. Located much closer to the GC&SF depot than Hancock Springs, Hanna Springs could be expected to compete for a significant share of the tourism increase with an upgrade in facilities. In February 1884 a new corporation, the Central Texas Town

The big new building at Hanna Springs boasted a vast auditorium on the second floor. —
Courtesy KSM

Company, was organized with a capital stock of $200,000. Just south of the circular, concrete Hanna Springs pool, a two-story frame building was erected, large enough to host conventions, traveling troupes, and grand balls. On the ground floor there were bathing and dressing rooms, reception parlors, concession areas, an orchestra platform, and offices. On the north and south ends wide stairways led upstairs to the great hall, 120 feet east to west, and sixty feet deep. To the east and near the streetcar tracks a stone hotel was erected.[20]

In June 1884, while the Hanna Springs facilities were under construction, the Wool Growers Association of Texas held their state convention in Lampasas. The Wool Growers Association was organized in 1881 in San Angelo. In addition to its customary hospitality, Lampasas offered an appropriate venue, because there was a growing number of sheep ranches in the country. In September Lampasas staged a "Grand Democratic Barbecue," attended by an estimated 3,000 Democrats.[21]

Statewide attention focused on Lampasas for a week in June 1885, when the Texas Volunteer Guard—forerunner of the Texas National Guard of the twentieth century—gathered at the Saratoga of the South for its first annual encampment. (There was an encampment at Houston in May 1884, but participation was limited, so the Lampasas event was the first statewide encampment.) Governor John Ireland was commander-in-chief of the Texas Volunteer Guard, and he would come to Lampasas. So would Adjutant General W. H. King, who was in charge of the daily administration of the Guard. Companies from all over Teas would go into camp at Hancock Park, while spouses and sweethearts and friends would check into the nearby Park Hotel, along with spectators drawn to the military event at the famous resort. Reporters would telegraph accounts of daily activities to newspapers throughout the state. A reporter from Dallas stated that "the people of Lampasas will be treated to a series of marches, drills, parades and maneuvers never before witnessed, even in that wide-awake and popular resort."[22]

The first Texas pioneers brought with them the early American tradition of civilian soldiery. The Texas Revolution was won by volunteer soldiers, and every able-bodied man was a member of the militia of the Republic of Texas. Militia companies from the frontier counties battled Comanche and Kiowa raiders during and after the Civil War.

The Texas Militia Act of 1879 organized local companies across the state into one brigade with three regiments, along with a separate battalion, all of which would comprise the First Division of the Texas Volunteer

Guard. By 1880 the Texas Volunteer Guard consisted of forty-seven companies of infantry, cavalry, and artillery, along with signal and headquarters units. There were thirty-eight white and nine "colored" companies. Each company elected a captain and two lieutenants. The federal government provided surplus uniforms, old rifles, artillery, and ammunition.[23]

During this period militia companies were formed in communities across the nation. There was a strong social element in most of these companies, and some units ordered their own uniforms. The young men were handsome in their military attire, and young women, along with Civil War veterans and admiring citizens, turned out to watch them drill, usually in a rented "armory." Drills usually were conducted in the evenings, and often a dance followed. Many companies staged balls at Christmas or New Year's Eve or some other holiday occasion.

Lampasas certainly had a close familiarity with militia companies, beginning with the Lampasas Guards of 1859. The Guards were succeeded by the Lampasas Minute Men of 1861 and, that same year, a company of Texas Militia. Later in the Civil War there were two companies of Texas State Troops, 2nd Frontier District. Of course, these militia companies were not social organizations. They were formed to battle Comanche raiders, and so was Company M of the Minute Men in 1872.

With such a strong background in militia units, Lampasas readily organized the "Lampasas Rifles" of the Texas Volunteer Guard. The little company was led by "Captain Cain." (There was a Joel Y. Cain living in Lampasas in 1880; he was a hotel keeper, and he was in his forties during the Civil War, so perhaps he held a wartime commission and was elected captain of the Rifles—at the age of sixty-two.) There were two lieutenants, and twenty men who were privates, corporals, and sergeants. The twenty-three-man company was issued a comparable number of rifles by the state.[24]

No state funding was provided for the encampment, nor to the participants. But from county fairs to state conventions to shooting tournaments, Lampasans knew how to stage an event. The "Lampasas Improvement Association" raised funding for the encampment, providing tents and rations for nearly 400 soldiers, as well as cash prizes for the best drilled companies. The Adjutant General felt that the cash prizes were "the main incentive to the companies to attend the encampment."[25]

The streets of Lampasas were decorated with flags. The big camp site was laid out "in the beautiful Park Hotel grounds amid a grove of gigantic oak and pecan trees, which skirt the famous Sulphur Fork," according to an admiring Dallas reporter. "The drill ground is probably the finest ever seen in Texas. . . ." Adjutant General W. H. King approved of the site because Sulphur Fork encircled the camp on three sides: "Water for both drinking and bathing purposes is to be had in the greatest abundance."[26]

"HO! FOR LAMPASAS" headlined the *Austin Daily Statesman* in a sendoff from the crack militia company, the Austin Greys. The company commander was R. P. Smythe, major and assistant adjutant general of the Texas Volunteer Guard. The Greys boarded a 10:30 train on Sunday morning, June 21, and departed for Lampasas with expectations of claiming the top prize. A total of seventeen companies, plus a five-man field band, gathered at Hancock Park on Sunday. The largest companies were the Alvarado Guards, with three officers and thirty-five men, and the Waco Light Infantry, comprised of thirty-two officers and men. No other company totaled more than twenty-eight soldiers. A few companies—the Orange Rifles, the Galveston Artillery, and the Travis Light Artillery—brought only their drill squads, one or two officers and nine men or fewer. The Palestine Brass Band arrived with eleven musicians.[27]

While the soldiers were setting up camp, tourists were unpacking in droves at the Park Hotel and every other hostelry in Lampasas. "The railroads have made the lowest rate that has ever been offered in Texas," and travelers flocked to the Saratoga of the South. Lampasas established an "intelligence office" to connect visitors with hotels, boarding houses, or private homes. The San Geronimo, a hotel of only thirty rooms, housed ninety-seven guests at the peak of this hectic week, and at one meal served 134 diners. "Our city is all stir and bustle," reported a Lampasas journalist to Austin.[28]

Major General John M. Claiborne, commander of the First Division of the T.V.G., arrived on Sunday night, and the next afternoon the Lampasas Improvement Association requested that he take command of the camp. Soon General Claiborne learned that the civilian soldiers were more civilian than soldier. The companies that brought only a squad-size drill team refused to perform their assigned camp police duties. When other companies heard of this, they balked and would only do so much. "There was no way to force them to do the duty," complained a frustrated Claiborne. But Claiborne and the Adjutant General and other ranking officers recognized many improvements that should be made for future encampments. General Claiborne asserted to Adjutant General King: "All the soldiers did well for the first trial in camp."[29]

Drills and marching maneuvers and inspections were conducted Monday through Friday. Each company took its turn on the drill field. There were many spectators, and sharp performances on the drill field "brought forth shouts of applause." There was special interest in the artillery. Battery Crawford of Dallas was commanded by Andrew Jackson Houston, son of the legendary Sam Houston; A. J. Houston had attended several military schools as a youngster, including an abbreviated enrollment at West Point. A regular army officer was present to observe and to judge the drills.[30]

At six o'clock on Wednesday evening Governor John Ireland reviewed a dress parade by the division. That night Brigadier General A. S. Roberts and two staff officers, accompanied by ladies, encountered a sentinel, who issued a challenge. But none of the officers knew the countersign, and they were arrested—a minor triumph for military discipline. On Friday afternoon the three Galveston units—Sealy Rifles, Galveston Artillery, and Galveston Artillery Light Guard—gave "a grand banquet" to the men of the encampment. Lampasas and her citizens were warmly complimented by the Galveston hosts.[31]

On Saturday the encampment climaxed with the greatly anticipated sham battle, followed by the awarding of prizes. The division was split into two battalions. At ten o'clock, with thousands of spectators watching, the Second Battalion deployed on the north bank of Sulphur Fork near Hancock Springs. Commanded by Gen. A. S. Roberts, the Second Battalion included the Lampasas Rifles, and featured Battery Crawford under Captain Houston. The First Battalion, commanded by Gen. John Claiborne, deployed uphill to the north. All guns were loaded with blank cartridges.[32]

Battery Crawford opened the firing, and a line of skirmishers advanced from the First Battalion. The Galveston Artillery blasted away "in grand style." Companies from both sides "delivered their fire in various positions, with considerable exhibition of skill." Suddenly a First Battalion force counter-attacked from behind the Park Hotel. But Captain Houston moved his battery forward, and General Roberts directed an attack against the left flank. The Galveston Artillery was overrun, and as prisoners were taken, the center of the First Battalion retreated. Seeing his forces waver, General Claiborne ordered a cease fire. The First Battalion stacked their arms, and the Lampasas Rifles celebrated victory with fellow Second Battalion companies.

The Division next formed a hollow square and prizes were awarded.

First prize was earned by the Sealy Rifles of Galveston; second prize went to the Belknap Rifles of San Antonio; the highly-touted Austin Greys won fifth prize. The judges next read their reports, and the encampment was closed with brief remarks, including an invitation to return to Lampasas in 1886. North-bound troops hurried to catch the afternoon train. Companies headed to the east or south would spend one more night in Lampasas before catching their train on Sunday.[33]

There was widespread praise for Lampasas, and the invitation for the Guard to return the next year was accepted. But the Lampasas Rifles seemed to lose interest after the encampment. Captain Cain resigned, and the company stopped meeting for drill. In September Adjutant General King traveled the state inspecting militia companies, many of which were disorganized. A constant problem that he discovered was broken firing pins, snapped when rifles were dry-fired.

When General King reached Lampasas he found the company disbanded. There had been no drills since the June encampment. The captaincy was vacant, and King could not find a single member of the company to take him to the armory. When King finally gained access to the building used as an armory, he found only fifteen rifles, although "seven were out but accounted for. Those I saw were in bad condition."[34]

Thus chastened, the Lampasas Rifles reorganized. In October a small encampment of the Texas Volunteer Guard was held in San Antonio, where regular duty soldiers could help with instruction. Only four companies came to San Antonio: the hometown Belknap Rifles, the San Antonio Rifles, the newly-formed Prairie City Guard from Weimar, and the understrength Lampasas Rifles. Lampasas brought just fourteen civilian soldiers, out of an encampment total of 101 officers and men. The Guard met for four days, October 21-24. Also in camp was a battery of the Third U.S. Artillery, and there was valuable interaction between the regulars and the State troops. Three money prizes, aggregating $1,000, were offered, but the Lampasas Rifles returned home as the only company without an award.[35]

By the following June, on the eve of the Encampment of 1886, the Lampasas Rifles were up to three officers and twenty men, the same strength as in June 1885. Once again the Lampasas Improvement Association furnished tents and rations and cash prizes; local businessmen considered it a sound investment, if thousands of tourists again were attracted to the encampment. A grandstand was built overlooking the drill field. Major R. P. Smythe of the Texas Volunteer Guard arrived early "to lay off the camp and attend to stretching the tents." The encampment was named Camp D. S. Stanley, in honor of the U.S. Army's Commander of the Department of Texas. General Stanley, a West Pointer who earned the Medal of Honor during the Civil War, planned to come from San Antonio to Lampasas during the week, and he dispatched a battery of the Third U.S. Artillery to participate in the exercises.[36]

The *Austin Daily Statesman*, recalling the previous year's experiences in Lampasas, declared that the upcoming encampment "will give the military boys a fine holiday. There will be contests in drilling and numerous other attractions and amusements for the entertainment of visitors. Special low rates will be given by the railroad company, and the militia and their guests are assured of a good time."[37]

The Austin Greys and Austin Rifles left for Lampasas on Sunday morning via the Austin & Northwestern Railroad, a narrow gauge line. The train traveled to Burnet, forty-five miles away, at eleven o'clock, after a trip of just two hours and thirty minutes. This fleet pace demonstrated "the splendid and safe condition of this road. . . ." In Burnet the two militia companies piled into hacks and covered wagons for the remaining twenty-two miles to Lampasas. The roadway was "good and the scenery fine," and the soldiers "enjoyed the trip greatly." The forty-eight men from Austin reported to camp at five o'clock. They would return to Austin the same way, for a round trip cost of only three dollars per man.[38]

Seventeen companies participated in the encampment, plus thirteen staff members of the Texas Volunteer Guard. There were fifty-eight officers and 354 men, for a total of 412 civilian soldiers in camp. Captain J. M. Lancaster and two lieutenants from the Third Artillery were on hand to assist in drilling the militia, and to participate with their guns in drills and the sham battle.[39]

At dawn on Monday, June 21, the cry of "Fall into line" echoed throughout the camp. After drilling during the morning, the companies donned their best uniforms for a dress parade through the streets of Lampasas. That evening the Houston Light Guard performed an exhibition drill that drew "shouts of applause from admiring crowds." On Tuesday morning there was another street parade, and a dress parade before 800 spectators that evening was reviewed by Governor John Ireland. General D. S. Stanley also arrived on Tuesday, and the evening train disgorged 700 tourists. That night a grand ball was held at the Park Hotel.[40]

Soldiers were given evening passes to leave camp and pursue "a good time," as encouraged by the Austin reporter. The reporter may have had in mind the Austin Greys, whose young men in tailored uniforms formed an important part of Austin's social scene. Twenty-three-year-old Will Porter, fun-loving and convivial, was one of the most popular members of the Greys. Porter worked in a bank, but in future years he would win literary fame as short story writer O. Henry. Porter and several other Greys spent an evening dancing at the Park Hotel, until they were tipped off that a corporal's guard was marching to arrest them for violating curfew. A friend met the soldiers at the hotel entrance and asked them to stack arms to avoid frightening the ladies. As the unarmed detail searched the ballroom, Porter led his comrades out the back and dashed around the building to seize the rifles and hurry toward camp. No one knew the password, but the men with rifles acted as guards of the soldiers without weapons. Pretending to be corporal of the guard, Porter snapped out, "Squad under arrest"—and the entire party was passed into camp.[41]

William Sidney Porter was a convivial member of the Austin Greys at the 1886 T.V.G. encampment in Lampasas. Later he would become famous as O. Henry, master of the short story. —Author's collection

After two more days of company and battalion drills, on Friday morning the grandstand filled by nine o'clock with spectators eager to witness the company and individual drill competitions. Two or three companies dropped out at the last minute, and the Austin Greys and Cleburne Light Guards each failed to complete their routine. Only three companies remained: The Galveston Artillery Light Guards, the Sealy Rifles of Galveston, and the San Antonio Rifles. The San Antonio company had been a favorite of bettors since the encampment started, and on Thursday morning a member of the troop telegraphed home: "We drill at 3 o'clock this afternoon, and are first choice in the pools, with no takers." The captain of each Galveston company called out errant orders while the men were marching, causing confusion and enabling the San Antonio Rifles to claim first prize.[42]

The individual competition followed, and after ten minutes Fred Cheeseman, of the Galveston Light Guards, won the fifty dollar prize as best drilled soldier. "He was borne triumphantly on the shoulders of his company from the grandstand." The exercise closed with an impressive artillery exhibition led by Captain Lancaster. "Their movements were executed with lightning rapidity and soon the air was filled with smoke from belching cannon."[43]

Lancaster's Third U.S. Artillery battery was employed in the sham battle the next morning. By nine o'clock noisy spectators jostled for positions to the accompaniment of martial music from the field band from Tyler. "The rattle of musketry, the deploying of pickets, the different movements on the field, the maneuvering for position, the deep-toned booming of artillery, all interested and excited the vast throng."[44]

Camp was broken at noon, "and all companies [were] ordered to return to their stations," reported General A. S. Roberts to Adjutant General King. "The lady friends of the San Antonio rifles" met on Saturday to plan a gala welcome for the victorious company. After a week of instruction and drill, a "very marked improvement" in the performance of militia personnel was reported to Adjutant General King.[45]

A year later, in June 1887, simultaneous encampments were staged at Paris and Houston, in the north and south areas of Texas, but that experiment was dropped. The 1888 encampment was held at Austin, the next year the Guard went to Galveston, and in 1889 the encampment was set in San Antonio. The Texas Volunteer Guard never returned to Lampasas.[46] But the first two T.V.G. annual encampments were hosted in grand style by the Saratoga of the South. There the Guard learned how to conduct large-scale encampments, while Lampasas profited considerably from two week-long invasions of thousands of pleasure-seeking tourists.

Although the Guard encampments highlighted the summers of 1885 and 1886 in Lampasas, other notable events took place at the Saratoga of the South during this period. The most historically significant was the organization of the Texas Bankers Association in July 1885.

Banking began slowly in America, with its primarily agricultural economy. As late as 1801 there were only thirty-one banks in the United

States. But the rise of industry triggered an explosion of banking, and by 1837 there were 788 banks in the nation. These banks were unregulated, and during the subsequent "wildcat period" unsound banking practices in search of profits led to frequent bank failures and the loss of depositors' money. Furthermore there was no national currency, as banks printed their own notes. By the 1860s there were 1,600 different types of notes in circulation—a counterfeiters' delight. In 1863 and 1864 Congress created a national banking system and currency, although private banks continued to function. During the post-Civil War economic boom banking flourished, and in 1875 the American Bankers Association was organized—an event which impressed two future Lampasas bankers.

Early Lampasas County had a largely agricultural economy based on farming and ranching. But with the boom that followed the arrival of the railroad, banking services were needed by an expanding Lampasas. By 1884 there were at least three unincorporated, private banks in town: the Lampasas Bank, a short-lived institution run by P. M. Hargrave; Russell, Galbraith and Sons, operated by John C. and James H. Russell, and Lewis W. Galbraith; and George T. Malone and Company, operated by brothers George, James, and Frank Malone.[47]

The Malone brothers were instrumental in organizing the first incorporated bank in Lampasas. On October 2, 1884, a meeting of local businessmen created Articles of Association for the First National Bank of Lampasas, with a capital stock of $50,000. Elected as directors were the three Malone brothers, A. H. Barnes, E. M. Longcope, Henry Exall, James W. Clark, and George R. Chastain. The next day the directors met in the offices of A. H. Barnes, a real estate developer and Lampasas businessman since 1871. The forty-eight-year-old Barnes was elected president; James Malone, vice-president; Frank Malone, cashier; and E. M. Longcope, assistant cashier. (Longcope was an experienced banker from Houston who soon would become president of the new Lampasas bank, and who married Madeline Beall, daughter of Judge William Beall of Lampasas.) The First National Bank of Lampasas opened in a substantial stone building which still stands on the northeast corner of Third Street and Western Avenue.[48]

Contemplating the American Bankers Association, E. M. Longcope conceived of a similar organization for Texas bankers. Frank Malone had previous banking experience in San Antonio and San Marcos, and he was familiar with the American Bankers Association. Malone caught

The intersection of Third Street and Western Avenue, looking east along Third toward the courthouse square. At left, is the First National Bank. —Courtesy KSM

Longcope's vision of a Texas Bankers Association, and the two young bankers began planning an organizational meeting. A letter of invitation was penned and published in the *Galveston Daily News* on May 28, 1885. "The hotel facilities are excellent," pointed out Malone, "the bathing unexcelled, and the beautiful scenery is sure to inspire grand thoughts and purposes." A printed letter was sent "to each banker throughout the State," and an ad was published in the *Galveston Daily News* from June 24 through July 23, 1885.

Thirty-one bankers from twenty-one Texas cities and towns congregated at the Park Hotel. The first meeting convened at the hotel's music room on Thursday, July 23, 1885. Wives also were in attendance, and at night everyone enjoyed "merry-making as guests of the good people of Lampasas." Business sessions were conducted in the music room from ten o'clock until noon, and in the afternoon from four to six o'clock. Frank Malone was appointed secretary of the three-day meeting, then was elected first secretary of the new organization. United States Congressman James Francis Miller, a lawyer and banker from Gonzales, was elected president for a one-year term, and he was re-elected the next year when the Texas Bankers Association met again at the Park Hotel.[49]

The main program of the Texas Bankers Association was to promote

The large pavilion in Hancock Park was the site of numerous preaching services. —Courtesy KSM

legislative and regulatory support for banking. A special objective was to remove the state constitutional restriction against the chartering of state banks. Unchartered private banks opposed this measure, and not until 1904 did Texas voters repeal the constitutional amendment that permitted the establishment of a dual system of state and national banks. The Texas Bankers Association, the oldest state bankers' association, located its headquarters in Austin, close to its founding site at the Saratoga of the South.[50]

Added to the first statewide militia encampment in June 1885 and the organizational meeting of the Texas Bankers Association the following month was the Texas Baptist State Convention in October 1885. Baptist regional association meetings often had been held in Lampasas, and later a Baptist encampment would be established in Hancock Park. But in the fall of 1885 Baptists from across the state came to the Saratoga of the South to conduct denominational business, to enjoy group singing and prayers, and to listen to sermons from the ablest and most inspiring Baptist preachers.

If Baptists and bankers and Democrats and soldiers could meet at the Saratoga of the South, horticulturalists also should find the scenery and the flora and fauna of Lampasas congenial. During the first five days of July 1891 the Texas Horticultural Society met in Lampasas. Railroads and hotels offered the customary reduced rates. There was "a wide range of most interesting topics," and participants inspected "one of the finest and most educative displays of farm and garden products, fine art and handiwork that ever charmed the eye." There was an added benefit: "The country with all its beauty, grandeurs and people are of the most charming in the state."[51]

Confederate veterans enthusiastically assembled in reunions for decades after the Civil War. Throughout the South there were statewide reunions and countywide reunions. The old soldiers proudly paraded, often in venerable uniforms, and reminisced over food and drink. In Lampasas County veterans organized R. E. Lee Camp No. 66 of the United Confederate Association. At one meeting, on April 13, 1889, a Saturday afternoon, 119 Confederate vets gathered in the courtroom of the Lampasas County Courthouse. Alex Northington was there, and so were S. T. Denson, M.V.B. Sparks, A. H. Barnes, D. W. Phillips, T. A. Casbeer, and more than one hundred other former soldiers, and they happily exchanged "pleasant recurrences to war hardships."[52]

The Texas Veterans Association held their annual reunion at Lampasas in April 1892. An organization for those who had served prior to, during, and soon after the Texas Revolution, the Texas Veterans Association was formed in 1873. Because Civil War soldiers were far more numerous, as well as at least two decades younger, membership in the Texas Veterans Association was considerably less than the Confederate Veterans of Texas. The Lampasas meeting was the twentieth annual state convention, and the Texas Veterans were able to meet comfortably in the Lampasas Courthouse. The Texas Veterans Association met again in Lampasas in 1902, but the organization disbanded five years later.[53]

Meeting in conjunction with the Texas Veterans Association in 1892 were thirteen patriotic women calling themselves "Daughters of the Lone Star Republic." Several months earlier, on November 6, 1891, sixteen ladies gathered at the Houston home of Mrs. Andrew Briscoe. Their purpose was to organize "an association to be composed of the wives, daughters, and lineal female descendants of all pioneer persons eligible for membership in the Texas Veterans Association." Mrs. Anson Jones, widow of the last president of the Texas Republic, was elected president. A committee was appointed to draw up a constitution and by-laws, two ladies were delegated to design a star-shaped emblem, and it was decided to accompany the Texas Veterans to Lampasas.[54]

The Daughters of the Lone Star Republic met in joint session with the Texas Veterans Association in the Lampasas Courthouse on Wednesday and Thursday, April 20 and 21. After the veterans adjourned, the ladies moved to the Methodist Church, two blocks from the courthouse. With Mrs. Anson Jones presiding, the ladies voted to change the name of their organization to Daughters of the Republic of Texas. The DRT grew rapidly; Lampasas ladies formed the fourth chapter, Sam Houston. Encouraging research and the preservation of records and artifacts and buildings, the DRT most famously assumed stewardship of the Alamo. The state's oldest patriotic society for women, the Daughters of the Republic of Texas held their first annual meeting, and adopted the name that would become famous across the state, at the Saratoga of the South.

Confederate veterans in Lampasas and the surrounding area gathered annually at the courthouse. —Courtesy KSM

CHAPTER TWELVE

Victorian Heyday

"Lampasas was truly the social center of the state . . ., the town was crowded with visitors. . . swimming, boating, driving and horse-back riding, and . . . dancing each evening . . . to the music of the gold-braided orchestra which played also for the noon and evening meals in the hotel."
—Prima Baker Moses, childhood memories
in *Stories of Lampasas*

In 1887, five years after the GC&SF Railroad reached Lampasas, the population reached 2,750,[1] a seven-fold increase since the arrival of iron rails transformed a frontier village into the Saratoga of the South. Every summer thousands of tourists swelled the population and increased the pace of life in Lampasas. After a quarter of a century as a dusty, slow-paced, often dangerous community of a few hundred Texans, Lampasas joined the mainstream of American life in the late 1800s.

America—and Texas—long had a predominantly rural population. As late as 1820—two centuries after American society began—only six percent of Americans lived in towns of 2,500 or more. During the next forty years Americans at last began to move from the country to towns and cities. In 1860 twenty percent of Americans lived in towns of 2,500 or more, and during the late 1800s the trend accelerated. By 1900 forty percent of the population lived in urban communities of at least 2,500, and one decade later fifty-five percent resided in towns and cities. For the first time in the nation's history less than half of the population lived on farms or in country villages.

Lampasas exemplified this transition. The community was born in a decade when only one of every five Americans dwelled in towns of

2,500 or more. During the subsequent twenty-five years the few hundred residents of Lampasas shared the same rural, small-town lifestyle as the majority of Americans. And when Lampasas finally—and rather suddenly—passed the 2,500 mark, a fast-growing percentage of other Americans also found themselves living in larger communities.

The railroad brought to Lampasas such Victorian-era amenities as toothpaste in a tube, Coca Cola, Dr. Pepper (invented in nearby Waco in 1885), peanut butter, aspirin, and phonographs. Now stylish dresses and shoes, suits and hats, could be delivered to Lampasas stores as soon as they became fashionable. The railroad brought to Lampasas hotels prominent men and women, while ambitious, visionary businessmen moved to the boomtown to seek opportunity.

Frank Malone and E. M. Longcope were experienced and enterprising bankers who came to Lampasas to help establish the first incorporated bank in the boomtown, and with vision they became the founding fathers of the Texas Bankers Association. W. T. Campbell, a native of

England who immigrated to the United States as a teenager, became a journalist and entrepreneur who moved restlessly in search of a main chance. In 1888, while still in his twenties, Campbell brought his growing family to Lampasas. Already an old hand at founding newspapers, he started the *Lampasas Leader*, while dealing in real estate and various businesses. Raised in the Anglican Church in England, Campbell affiliated with the Episcopal congregation in Lampasas. The church had begun building a stone sanctuary in 1884, but construction soon stalled. Campbell energetically took charge of the project, and St. Mary's Church was com-

W. T. Campbell founded the Lampasas Leader *and was instrumental in completing St. Mary's Episcopal Church. A busy local entrepreneur, he later helped organize the Texas Oil Company—Texaco.*
—Courtesy KSM

pleted in 1890. At six-foot-four and 300 pounds, Campbell was similar in physique to his friend and business partner, former Texas governor Jim Hogg. Hogg and Campbell were key members of a syndicate which dominated the spectacular Spindletop oil field in 1901, and which formed the powerful Texas Oil Company—Texaco.[2]

A millionaire, Campbell built a magnificent home in north Lampasas. He died prematurely, of blood poisoning, when he was only forty-seven. Campbell's funeral was held at his Lampasas residence, and he was buried in Oak Hill Cemetery. His grandson and great-grandson, Henry Villard Campbell and Henry V. Jr., each served as mayor of Lampasas.

W. T. Campbell had built a spacious and impressive Lampasas home which announced to visitors and passersby, out for a Sunday afternoon stroll or buggy ride, that the owner was a man of prosperity and prominence. Charlie and M. Y. Stokes each built such a residence, and so did Frank Malone and J. R. Key and other successful Lampasans. A number of ornate old residences, as well as buildings of other types, still stand today as reminders of the Victorian heyday of Lampasas.

Historical architecture is our most tangible link with the past. Architecture, like any art, is a reflection of life—of the people and of the period and place in which they lived. Lampasas developed from a ramshackle village to a growing, bustling town during the 1880s. The 1880s and 1890s formed the heart of the Victorian era, a time in America of explosive growth and change. American society was in upheaval after the Civil War, while industrialization and urbanization added to the turmoil. But America's unregulated economy produced vast wealth, along with a sense of power and progress and optimism.

All of these qualities were expressed in Victorian architecture. The stability of pre-Civil War society had been reflected both in the North and South by Greek Revival homes featuring stately columns and balanced, predictable floor plans—a central hallway, usually with two rooms on either side, upstairs and downstairs. In frontier Texas a rudimentary version of this "floor plan" was the "dog run" cabin, two rooms separated by a roofed breezeway, or dog run (dogs often sought shade in the breezeway). There were log cabins in early Lampasas, but most timber in the area was not suitable for building, so many dog run cabins were of board and batten construction.

After the Civil War, with slavery ended and with countless opportunities beckoning in the nation's new cities and in the last West, successful individuals turned to a new style of architecture—in their homes and churches, as well as in their commercial structures and public buildings. The expansiveness, exuberance, and vitality of the late nineteenth century found architectural expression in a multiplicity of Victorian styles: Queen Anne, General Grant, French Empire, Gothic Revival, Richardsonian Romanesque, Italianate, Shingle Style, Mansardic, Carpenter Gothic, and Gingerbread. And when components of two or three or more of these styles were combined in one building, the result was called "Bastardian." Victorian residences expressed the owners' individuality and prosperity. Shunning Greek Revival conformity, Victorian homes bristled with turrets and bay windows and decorative gingerbread. Many different materials were used, inside and outside, as a demonstration of affluence.

In Victorian Lampasas the principal public building was the 1883 courthouse, a handsome and imposing example of French Empire architecture. On a hill north of town the two three-story buildings of Centenary College featured Mansard roofs. When Lampasas finally erected its first substantial public school building, it was a two-story stone structure with Romanesque qualities and a tall cupola atop the roof.

The early churches of Lampasas were unpretentious, but in 1885 St. Mary's Catholic Church opened, a frame sanctuary with tall, narrow Gothic windows. In 1891 the growing First Baptist Church moved into a new stone building, Romanesque in style with a soaring steeple. Although slightly outside the time period of this book, in 1900 the Methodists built Lampasas' most picturesque Victorian church, an elegant frame house of worship with two steeples.

The commercial buildings of Lampasas were plain stone structures with few Victorian flourishes. But the two largest hostelries, the Park Hotel and the Globe Hotel, were big frame buildings that exhibited the romance of Victorian architecture. The Globe boasted two long, upper-level porches with ornate balustrades, and a tower perched atop the three-story section of the hotel. The Park Hotel, often called the "Grand Park," was the most elegant building in town, resplendent with towers and sweeping galleries and delicate gingerbread work.

Along "Silk Stocking Row," there were impressive Victorian residences, and others were scattered around town on other streets. Lampasas was not populous enough to support a large collection of truly splendid Victorian homes, but almost every residence built during the

1880s and 1890s boasted Victorian features. Carpenters now had the jig saw, and even modest houses were decorated with gingerbread on gables and doorways and porches. The tower, or turret, was the dominant feature of Victorian residential architecture, and many small, single-story houses at least featured a tower. On Silk Stocking Row in 1883 banker Frank Malone erected an eye-catching family home in Queen Anne style. The tower on Victorian houses usually stood to one side, dominating one front corner or the other. But Malone had a superb tower built at the center front of the house, providing an impressive entrance to the home. Malone's residence was an expression of his individuality as well as his prosperity.

If Lampasas was the site of a variety of Victorian buildings, the city streets provided the setting for another element of Victorian—and Western—urban life. On Wednesday evening, November 16, 1892, Jack Barker was driving a wagon along Third Street in the handsome neighborhood known as Silk Stocking Row. Suddenly his team of horses stampeded.

Banker Frank Malone built one of the most impressive Victorian residences along "Silk Stocking Row," and carriages frequently drove by. —Courtesy KSM

Barker lost control of the two horses, and the wagon careened down the hilly street. Prominent merchant C. N. Witcher, who lived nearby, ran to catch the horses. But he stumbled and fell onto the street, gashing his face and bruising a leg. The runaway team crashed into a buggy carrying two neighborhood ladies, who "were badly frightened but not seriously hurt." But their little vehicle "was smashed." Barker was thrown from his wagon, but he shrugged off bruises and "was able to drive home."[3]

Horse wrecks were part of life in Lampasas. Like Westerners everywhere, many Lampasas men rode horseback, along with more than a few ladies and children. In addition to saddle horses, horse-drawn vehicles plied the dung-strewn streets of Lampasas (horses eliminate more than twenty pounds of droppings a day), and there were oxen and mules as well. There were freight wagons, delivery wagons, buggies, carriages, and other light private vehicles. Even horses with placid temperaments can be startled into a stampede, while other equines with an ornery streak are constantly on the lookout for an excuse to bolt. The legions of dogs that prowled the town sometimes yapped at the heels of the larger beasts, while gusts of wind could send scraps of paper whipping in front of horses. Runaways often erupted in the streets of Lampasas, with bruises and broken bones and wrecked vehicles the inevitable result. Modern city-dwellers face the constant danger of automobile crashes, but even though life was slower paced during the nineteenth century, horse travelers also were in frequent peril.

Lampasas newspapers reported numerous runaways. In May 1889 W. L. Harris, who owned a large mercantile business on the square, was stepping out of his buggy when his horse became startled. Harris was thrown forward, and the buggy horse began kicking. Harris suffered a dislocated wrist and a broken arm. Meanwhile, the horse stampeded, jumping a fence and leaving the wrecked buggy behind.[4]

Allen Anderson, of the mercantile firm of Toland & Anderson, was driving his wife in their buggy around town on Wednesday morning, July 18, 1883. Without warning their horse became spooked and broke into a gallop. Both Anderson and his wife were thrown from the careening wagon. "Mrs. Anderson was bruised considerably but not seriously injured," reported a newspaperman. Allen toppled onto his head, and at first there were fears for his life. By the next day, however, he was said to be "resting easy." A few months later a teamster began climbing into his wagon, which was loaded with corn. Suddenly his team bolted, tossing the teamster to the ground. The loaded wagon passed over him, "and the wheels passed lengthwise over his body, bruising him considerably, but breaking no bones."[5]

In November 1888 George Russell, an African-American, rode his horse at a rapid pace across a bridge over Burleson Creek. The horse slipped and fell, and Russell broke his leg. The next year Ed Bullard, who drove the mule-drawn streetcar, was kicked in the stomach by the mule and was "quite seriously injured." On a January evening in 1893, Jasper Gracy drove a hack from his livery stable to the depot to pick up a newlywed couple to whom he was related. When the westbound train arrived Gracy went to meet the newlyweds. But the team of horses, startled by the noises of the steam engine, stampeded and dragged the hack into the night. The next morning Gracy tracked the runaways north of town, soon finding the team still hitched to the hack. The horses were peacefully grazing, and the only damage to Gracy's vehicle was "a broken hack top."[6]

Even before the arrival of the railroad swelled the Lampasas population and, consequently, traffic on the streets, summer watering seasons brought hordes of tourists who frequently rented horses or vehicles and

Women—such as this Victorian lady with a side-saddle rig—joined men in riding the streets of Lampasas. Both men and women drove horse-drawn vehicles around town, and horse wrecks became common. —Courtesy KSM

teams. In the summer of 1878, for example, "a party of ladies and gentlemen hired a hack" for a Sunday outing. At Hancock Park the vehicle somehow was run into a ditch. The hack toppled over and "was badly broken." One young lady injured her wrist, but she was taken to the tent of a vacationing physician, who "promptly reset the joint."[7]

That same summer, "Prof. Niblo" of Aten College was driving his buggy across the square on a Sunday afternoon in June when "something came loose." Spooked by the unfamiliar sensation of broken gear, the buggy horse broke into a run. "The Professor kept cool, however, and stopped him before anybody was killed." The next month Moses Hughes was thrown from his horse, breaking his collar bone and absorbing lesser injuries.[8]

Although the streets of Lampasas posed the constant possibility of danger for horsemen or buggy drivers, at least saloon shootouts and street battles no longer exploded in town. A city marshal and his deputies now provided a police force. "Where once the rowdy variety shows and the noisy dance halls thrust their disgusting presence on you there are now large stores," pointed out the first issue of W. T. Campbell's *Lampasas Leader* in 1888. "And instead of some roistering tough parading the streets discharging his six shooter an officer of the law moves quietly along."[9]

In this view of Third Street looking east toward the courthouse square, horse-drawn vehicles are moving west, and a delivery wagon is parked. Note the First National Bank right of center past the intersection. —Courtesy KSM

Riding around town in a horse-drawn vehicle was a popular Lampasas recreation. Big hats were part of the Victorian dress code. —Courtesy KSM

The most visible reminder of the gunfighter violence of early Lampasas was former feudist Pink Higgins. On Wednesday, December 6, 1882, with Lampasas bustling in the wake of the recently-arrived railroad, Pink triggered a street incident reminiscent of the rough frontier years. Pink was in Lampasas on busy Third Street when he spotted L. H. Mosty in a crowd of men in front of C. H. Ross' store. Pink held a note for $100 from Mosty, and he walked over and thrust the paper into Mosty's hand.

"There is your note," announced Pink in front of everyone. "I have paid and you must pay me."

Mosty threw the note down and tried to retreat into the store. Pink was not wearing a gunbelt nor carrying his Winchester, but he had jammed a revolver into a hip pocket, and quietly he gripped the sixgun.

"Mosty, don't make a motion or I will kill you," warned Pink, whose reputation—and sixgun—were menacing. He repeated ominously, "You have got it to pay."

"Hold up," said Mosty, raising his hands. "Hand it here—if it is properly endorsed I will pay it."

"You threw it down," growled Pink, "come out and pick it up."

Mosty walked back outside, picked up the note, and examined it.

"By God," said Mosty, realizing he was cornered, "I want to inform you I have got the money."

Producing a wallet, Mosty counted out ten ten-dollar bills. "You have got your money." Mosty stepped back into the store and muttered, "I am robbed."

Mosty filed a complaint, and in May 1883 a grand jury indicted Pink for aggravated assault. More than a year later, on June 13, 1884, Pink was charged in district court—in the new courthouse—with robbery of $100 by "unlawfully, willfully and feloniously" making an assault upon Mosty.

Pink pled not guilty, and the case came to trial in December 1884—two years into the boom of the Saratoga of the South. After hearing witnesses and arguments, Judge W. A. Blackburn presented a lengthy charge to the jury, focusing upon the definition of robbery. Pointing out that theft by violent assault demanded a prison sentence of two to ten years, Judge Blackburn added significantly: "While no man has any legal right to collect a debt due him by assault or by violence, and putting in fear of life or bodily injury, yet it does not necessarily follow that a collection thus made is robbery, but might be some other offense. . . ." Therefore aggravated assault would demand a fine of $25 to $1,000, or confinement in the county jail from one month to two years.[10]

The jury declared Pink guilty of aggravated assault, and assessed his punishment as a fine of $100—the amount he had extracted from Mosty. There certainly was an element of fairness in this decision, but Pink—and Judge Blackburn—could recall a time when he probably would never have been brought to court over such an incident. And if Pink was struck by the local change in attitude over his rough methods—methods embraced by frontier Lampasas when he rode in pursuit of war parties and rustlers—within a few years he would learn just how far public opinion had turned.

Several years after his trouble with L. H. Mosty, Pink traded horses for cattle through an agent, inadvertently coming into possession of a "wild stag" (hair had grown over the brand). When Pink tried to sell the animal to a meat market in Lampasas, rancher Sam Jennings revealed the overgrown brand and stated that the beast had been stolen from his spread, which was north of Higgins Gap. Charged with cattle theft, Pink pled not guilty. But the jury was not favorably inclined toward this forty-year-old relic of the rowdy frontier period of Lampasas. Pink Higgins—Indian fighter, feudist, mankiller—was the most intimidating reminder of the wild old days, and Lampasans of the 1890s regarded him more with disapproval than nostalgia. The trial was held in district court in Lampasas in November 1891, and the jury delivered a guilty verdict on the flimsiest of evidence. Pink was sentenced to two years in the state penitentiary.[11]

Pink's conviction and sentence were upheld on January 16, 1892, and his confinement dated from that point. He was jailed for a few weeks in Lampasas, then delivered to the Rusk Penitentiary in East Texas. (The penitentiary at Huntsville opened in 1849, but overcrowding was a problem by the 1870s, and a larger facility was constructed in Rusk, which began receiving prisoners in 1883.) John Higgins, Pink's father, brought Cullen and Tom Higgins to East Texas to attend school and to visit their dad at Rusk. Cullen went on to become a lawyer and district judge in Scurry County, while Tom would stay in Lampasas, teaching school and serving as county judge.[12]

Pink's friends submitted petitions on his behalf to Governor James Hogg, and he was released in November 1893. Back in Lampasas County Pink was uncomfortable, and perhaps he felt a pioneer's urge to move to a less settled land. One of his old riders, Jess Standard, already had relocated northwest to a small spread below Abilene. Pink's long-time friend, Bill Wren, served two terms as sheriff of Lampasas County, 1892 to 1896, then moved to Scurry County. When Pink was offered a job in the same vicinity, working for the vast Spur Ranch as a range rider, he and his family left Higgins Gap, and he resumed his lifelong battle against rustlers.

Trouble with rustlers in Lampasas County was a major condition that led to the organization of a farmers' alliance which would spread throughout much of the nation. In turn, this Farmers' Alliance of the South was instrumental in the formation of one of the most important third political parties in the nation's history. The People's Party elected state legislators and congressmen, and was a major factor in the presidential election of 1892. The People's Party was supported by the *People's Journal*, published in Lampasas in 1892 and 1893.

Lampasas County was plagued by stock theft and by the Horrell–Higgins Feud in 1877. In September 1877 a group of frustrated farmers and small ranchers met at a one-room frame schoolhouse on Donaldson Creek about nine miles northwest of Lampasas. There already was a farmers' organization throughout America. The Patrons of Husbandry, popularly known as the Grange, was formed in 1867, and six years later the first Grange in Texas was organized at Salado, about fifty miles east of Lampasas. A minimum of fifteen members made up a neighborhood Grange. Traveling organizers collected one dollar for each male Granger and fifty cents for women. Soon more than one million farmers belonged to the Grange.

During the 1870s there were at least two Grange lodges in Lampasas County. The Lampasas Patrons of Husbandry met at the Aten College building at nine o'clock on the second and fourth Saturday mornings per month (farmers and their families habitually came to town on Saturdays), while the School Creek Grange gathered one Saturday per month.[13] Masons were instrumental in establishing the Patrons of Husbandry, so a fraternity format was followed: there were special handshakes, badges, segregation—even a National Worthy Master. The Grange emphasized agricultural education through lecturers, county fairs, state fairs, and agricultural and mechanical colleges—all to improve and economize farming and ranching methods. But a more important focus of the Grange was co-operative buying and selling: Montgomery Ward was established in 1871 to sell to Grangers, and the retail catalogue was a primary tool. In 1876 the Texas State Grange claimed 40,000 men, women, and children as members of 1,275 lodges.

But the Grange did not focus upon stock theft, which was a major problem in Lampasas County during the 1870s. In the fall of 1877 there were three meetings within a few weeks at the Donaldson Creek school. Knights of Reliance was chosen as a name, then rejected in favor of Farmers' Alliance. Officers were elected, including L. S. Chavose, President, and Grand Smokey, Jacob Childress. The Grand Smokey was assigned to investigate stock thefts and pursue rustlers.[14]

The Farmers' Alliance did not adopt fraternal trappings such as rituals and secrets, but embraced co-operative buying and selling, as well as social activities for isolated farm families and political involvement. One typical Alliance picnic saw nearly 300 farmers, ranchers, and family members gather at Rock Creek Church. Late in the morning speeches began to be delivered by politicians running for the state legislature, county judge, and district attorney, followed by dinner on the grounds. "Such a dinner as was spread defies our powers of description," rhapsodized a *Lampasas Leader* reporter. After feasting the children played while adults held an Alliance business meeting.[15]

The Farmers' Alliance proved to have considerable appeal. Within a year there were fourteen sub-alliances of the Farmers' Alliance in

Lampasas County, as well as a growing number in nearby counties. In July 1878 Farmers' Alliance No. 1 on Donaldson Creek hosted a "State Alliance" meeting, attracting representatives from the Lampasas County alliances and from eleven sub-alliances outside the county.[16]

Growth of the Farmers' Alliance soon slowed, while the Grange declined rapidly into insignificance, in Texas and across America. But farmers needed help in a nation that was steadily industrializing and urbanizing. In 1883 the Texas State Farmers' Alliance was reorganized, moving forcefully along the economic and political lines pioneered a few years earlier in Lampasas. From 1870 until 1895 farm prices steadily declined throughout the country, and farmers were desperate to claim a share of American prosperity. Leaders of the Farmers' Alliance were young and aggressive, and the organization exploded with growth—nearly three million members—as American farmers embraced the hope of reforming the system.

Factory workers were going through the same process, behind unions such as the Knights of Labor, National Labor Union, and the American Federation of Labor. Soon a political party was formed to champion the causes of the unions' and farmers' organizations. The People's Party, or "Populists," crusaded for federal ownership of rail-

Farmers' Alliance members are meeting at the rural schoolhouse where the influential organization was born. —Courtesy KSM

roads, regulation of banks, direct election of senators, government loans to farmers, and other reforms designed to return power to working people of the factories and of the farms. In 1888 and 1890 Populists from farm states were elected to legislatures and to Congress.

In the Presidential Election of 1892, Gen. James B. Weaver of the People's Party ran a strong race, attracting more than one million votes. During the excitement of the election campaign, in the summer of 1892, the *People's Journal*, "Devoted to the Development of Lampasas County and the People's Party," was launched in Lampasas.[17] Democrat Grover Cleveland won re-election, but the Democratic Party prudently adapted many Populist reforms. While the People's Party thereupon entered permanent decline, Populist policies and the reform urge became part of the Democratic fabric. And an important element of this movement was born in a frame school building a few miles from Lampasas. The historic little school was taken by rail to the Chicago World's Fair of 1893 and dismantled. Plank by plank, piece by piece, shingle by shingle, the building was sold for souvenirs.[18]

"Lampasas Leads and Always Will Lead in Everything," trumpeted a headline in the *Lampasas Leader* of March 16, 1889. "Lampasas was the first town in Texas to start a creamery," explained the opening sentence of the story. "She saw the advantages to be derived from it and concluded to have one. This was three months ago:—it is now in operation."

In October 1888 "The Lampasas Creamery" incorporated with a capital stock of $5,000. Among nearly forty listed stockholders were E. M. Longcope, J. M. Malone, A. H. Barnes, Judge W. B. Abney, J. I. Campbell, and the Texas Trading Company. "Milk your cows farmers!" announced an article in the *Leader*. The creamery was built at the end of Western Avenue overlooking Sulphur Fork. The building was seventy-five feet long, twenty feet wide, and it was painted creamy white. Inside were conductor pipes, "a fine strainer, to remove all lumps," two big cream tanks, large churns (which made 400 revolutions per minute), the engine room ("Every thing is done by steam"), a large refrigerator, and other equipment. Area farmers were given 5½-gallon cans to bring their milk to the creamery, which had a cleansing facility for the cans. The floors were inclined, with a gutter in the center, for easy rinsing-cleaning. The waste from the process "is the finest fattening in the world for hogs."[19]

On Tuesday, January 29, 1889, the stockholders and numerous citizens gathered "to see the first butter made in the first creamery in Texas." The butter "smelled of sweet spring grass, and fresh milk just from the cow; . . . butter that tasted like butter clear away down to your toes." Samples were shipped to newspapers around the state. The *Austin Statesman* declared that the Lampasas butter "is rich in color and of very superior flavor." "In complexion and flavor it is the equal of the best Holland butter," boasted the *Dallas News* of "the first creamery butter ever made in the state."[20]

As Lampasas businessmen continued to seek profitable opportunities, their wives and sons and daughters enjoyed a social life typical of Victorian communities. For example, during the same week that the Lampasas Creamery was organized, a young man about town, D. M. Dunkum, "entertained, in his elegant way, at the Globe parlors last Friday evening." Dunkum, who was manager of the Globe Hotel, hosted ten friends and their dates, as well as his future bride, eighteen-year-old Settie Anderson, and two "stags." The party featured cards, music, and refreshments.[21]

Two weeks later Dunkum and several of his friends were at the Victorian residence of merchant T. W. Toland for the wedding of his daughter, Simmie, to another popular Lampasan, Bev. A. Harris. Dunkum was an usher, and he gave the newlyweds a "beautiful silver water pitcher." Dunkum's sweetheart, Settie Anderson, was a bridesmaid and gave a "Silver, Pickel Castor colored glass bowl." Harry J. McIlhany, who brought one of the bride's sisters to Dunkum's recent party, also gave a "Silver Pickel Castor, colored glass bowl." It was customary everywhere for Victorian newspapers to describe the wedding ("The bride was one of the most attractive and accomplished belles of Lampasas. . . ."), then to list the attendees and their gifts: "Life size portraits of the bride and groom by Miss Mary Toland" (sister); "Laid Work Quilt by Mrs. N. S. Toland"; "Family Bible by Mr. and Mrs. W. D. Harris"; etc.[22]

Earlier in the year W. B. Abney opened his handsome residence to a "largely attended" social given by the ladies of the Methodist Church. That fall another prominent Lampasan, J. D. Cassell, opened his home for "a very pleasant sociable given by the young folks." During the Christmas season of 1892 there was a "bachelor's supper." On the night after Christmas in 1888 a "very pleasant Christmas sociable" was held at the home of Mr. and Mrs. D. G. Price. D. M. Dunkum and Settie Anderson headed the guest list, and Miss Ettie Adkins was another guest. Mr. and Mrs. Price had given their daughter, Helen, a new piano for Christmas, and the instrument made "its debut in elegant style." Half an hour before midnight "the company marched into the dining room, where two large tables were loaded down with cakes, nuts, and edibles of every kind." The revelers agreed that this party was "the most pleasant one they had participated in this year. . . ."[23]

Every Christmas season brought a round of parties, but during the Victorian era another fixture of Christmas became an increased focus upon Santa Claus and gifts. During the season of 1892, for example, Key Brothers proudly advertised "the largest assortment of Christmas goods ever before seen in Lampasas. . . ." Elsewhere in the newspaper the firm pointed out that "Santa Claus has opened a new store in the city, all for the children, and appointed Key Brothers, agents."[24]

In 1890, the December 10 issue of the *Lampasas Dispatch* was filled with large ads by merchants. The front page was dominated by "Your Friends, SPARKS BROS. DRUG and STATIONERY COMPANY." A great miscellany of goods was listed, emphasizing "TOYS, TOYS, TOYS, for Girls and Boys." At the top of the page was a reminder that "Santa Clause consigned to us this year the biggest stock of Christmas goods ever before exhibited in Lampasas."

Inside, the eighty verse lines of "The Cow Boys Christmas Ball" at "Anson City" was reproduced. The Key Brothers ran a half-page ad, and so did several other firms. J. D. Cassell, "The Popular Druggist," displayed two images of Santa Claus at the top of his ad, and urged customers to "see his elegant line of holiday presents, such as. . . ."

The Red Star Racket House emphasized, "We have made special arrangements with Santa Claus to fill the stockings of the children with suitable gifts at prices that surprise our opposition." J. D. Townsen, shoe dealer, pointed out: "You can't enjoy Christmas if your feet are not Warmly and Neatly Clad. . . ." Former sheriff N. O. Reynolds, now the owner of the Brunswick Saloon, issued an important reminder to the public:

> The Holidays are approaching and good
> PURE LIQUORS
> Will be wanted for Egg Nog, Mince Pies
> Fruit Cakes, table use, etc.

The approaching holidays included New Year's. On the last night of

1892, groups of young people went to each church in Lampasas, and as midnight approached, church bells broke the silence of the night all over town. A moment or so into 1893 a more lively ringing commenced. "This, they say," reported the *People's Journal*, "is ringing out the old year and ringing in the new one." It was customary for many women to "keep open house" on New Year's Day, and for the *Leader* to publish "their names, residence and assistants who will receive with them" (usually a daughter, niece, or friend).[25]

The Thanksgiving celebration of 1888 was a true expression of the holiday by Lampasans. At nine o'clock on Thursday morning, November 29, the community's church bells began tolling, reminding the populace of approaching events. At ten o'clock merchants closed their doors and made their way to the courthouse. "By eleven the large court room was filled with willing worshipers," related the *Leader*. "A table loaded with gifts of food, clothing and money told it was a 'Thanksgiving day' and the display of stars and stripes said it was 'National.'"

Church choirs had united into a large combined choir, accompanied by an organ (probably a little harmonium or pump organ, or a portable "telescope" organ—more homes had small organs than pianos during this period). The combined choir "grandly sang an opening anthem of praise," followed by the reading of Psalms 103 and 105 by a local pastor, who "led the worshippers in prayer." There was another resounding hymn, and Professor Marshall McIlhaney, president of Centenary College, read the Thanksgiving Proclamation of President Grover Cleveland. A sermon of Thanksgiving by Elder J. C. Midyett climaxed the service, and the charity committee was elated by "the thank offerings" left for the poor. That evening there was another service in the courtroom, complete with hymns, prayers, and Bible readings, and concluding with the singing of "Praise God from whom all blessings flow. . . ." The *Dispatch* reported the Thanksgiving events in detail, including a long list of "nuggets of gold" gleaned from the sermons and readings of the day.[26]

The efforts of a large combined choir singing to the accompaniment of an organ lugged up the long, steep stairway of the Lampasas courthouse indicated the community's "intense musical activity." In her meticulous study of musical activity in Lampasas, Gloria Geren Steelman discovered an impressive combination of professional musicians (Park Hotel orchestras and traveling opera house performers), local amateurs (singers, pianists, church choirs), and competent music teachers

(Centenary College faculty members and private instructors). For twelve years Centenary College offered solid, often advanced musical instruction, complete with recitals and other performances. Many students were young ladies from Lampasas, some of whom stayed in their home town and themselves taught future generations of local girls. Berta Cassell, wife of merchant J. D. Cassell, was a music teacher at Aten College by 1881, and within five years she began offering quality private lessons, as well as student recitals in her home. One recital in 1889 featured a dozen pupils performing sixteen musical numbers—"a most excellent entertainment."[27]

Newspaper ads during the late 1880s and 1890s reveal several merchants who sold pianos, organs, violins, guitars, banjos, accordions, and sheet music. The Lampasas social scene often included parlor musicales. Churches offered local musicians the opportunity to perform as choir members, and occasionally at church fund-raisers. The growing number of women's organizations brought regular music performances as entertainment at club meetings. Cultivated guests at the Park Hotel sometimes staged concerts in the hotel's music room.[28] When the popular Christie Minstrels played Lampasas in April 1891, they were greeted by a standing-room-only crowd.[29] Lampasans had learned to appreciate and enjoy music of many types. The cultural atmosphere of Lampasas was enriched, and the town moved closer to the mainstream of Victorian America.

Another cultural reflection of the Victorian era was baseball, which became America's first team sport after the Civil War. The game spread rapidly to cities and towns, and during the 1870s and 1880s professional teams organized "major" and "minor" leagues. The "Texas Base Ball League" opened play in 1888, and by the next season the state's premier cities offered fans (called "kranks") regular professional play. Austin, Dallas, Fort Worth, Galveston, Houston, and Waco comprised the early Texas League. The Austin Senators and Waco Navigators were the closest teams to Lampasas.

Lampasas boys played baseball on empty lots, and like almost every other community in America, Lampasas fielded a "town team." During the spring of 1891 "the Lampasas base ball club was organized . . . and will be known as the 'Leaders,'" reported the *Lampasas Leader*. "The *Leader* will champion the cause of the boys every time." The Leaders booked games at Burnet and Llano in May, and these two teams would be expected to return the contests in Lampasas.[30]

By the late 1800s, uniformed teams were playing baseball, America's first team sport, at Hancock Park before large crowds. —Courtesy KSM

Another sport that remained popular in Lampasas was horse racing. Horse races had been held since the earliest years of Lampasas Springs, amid avid enthusiasm and considerable betting. The same conditions prevailed more than three decades later. Early in November 1888 the *Lampasas Leader* touted "The Finest Gathering of Racing Stock Ever Put on a Track in Texas." A long article listed the types of races and horses, citing the sires and dams of the most famous animals, and listing the betting odds (200 to 1 in a couple of matchups). Judge W. A. Blackburn entered a champion trotter. "The track is in elegant condition," reported the *Leader*, "smoothly rolled and well turfed."[31]

The next month, two days after Christmas, another set of races was staged. The following summer, in August 1889, a horse show and races were held in conjunction with the county fair. The mile track was "well laid out and graded," and the grandstand was "comfortably arranged." Reduced railroad rates were arranged. The hotels and boarding houses of Lampasas also promised "rates to satisfy every purse," while those who wanted to "can find free camping ground at the Hanna or Hancock springs." The Lampasas Fair Association already was looking ahead to next year's event: "the fair and stock show . . . will be the largest, most attractive and best attended, of any ever held in Western Texas."[32]

There was an urgency to the efforts to draw a major crowd for the

fair and races of 1889, and for the fair of 1890. The railroad had resumed its march from Lampasas westward in 1885, building northwest
across Lampasas County. Tracks missed the old Senterfitt village, but a
new town, Lometa, was founded. No longer the railhead, Lampasas experienced an economic change with two-way rail traffic. Many
Lampasans believed that the rail line to the west cost Lampasas business
when travelers went through town without stopping for a visit. But the
Texas Trading Company and, later, the Stokes brothers, capitalized on
the extended rail lines to expand their business operations.

The train that now passed through Lampasas on its way to San
Angelo was referred to derisively in the *Leader* as a "tap-rackety" which
was fortunate to stop off "at the center of civilization, culture and
health" (Lampasas, of course). When the westbound schedule was
changed to reach Lampasas at 8:05 P.M. the *Leader* expressed disdain:
"We think it should have been made 4:30 P.M. and then it might possi-
bly arrive at about eight o'clock."[33]

A more important problem than the tap-rackety for Lampasas was
the continuing lack of a public school, a problem which mirrored a larger
difficulty facing the Lone Star State. By the 1880s, despite remarkable
growth of population and prosperity, Texas did not have a public school
system worthy of the name. Lampasas embodied the state's educational
condition: there was notable growth after the railroad arrived in 1882,
but the town languished without a public school. The community always
had a private school or two, taught by a "professor" or "schoolmarm,"
or by a husband and wife team, either in a rented building or at the
teacher's home. In 1883 an amendment to the Texas Constitution of
1876 created a twenty-cent ad valorem school tax, while permitting district voters to supplement this sum with local taxes. The next year a law
created an elective state superintendent of instruction and directed
county judges to supervise county school districts. Public education was
provided for a school term of at least four months for children ages eight
(it was thought unwise to require children of six or so to walk a mile or
two or three to school) to sixteen. Teachers were required to hold certificates, often acquired and maintained at summer "normals."

But even under these modest requirements, educational progress
was slow. Across the state the school-age population grew rapidly, but
local voters usually were reluctant to approve local taxes to build school
houses. Lampasas remained a case in point. In 1889, several years after
the school legislation of 1883 and 1884, there still was no public school

in Lampasas, and repeated requests for a local school tax never even came to a vote. In 1889 the son of Dr. J. N. Adkins, J. M. Adkins, along with his wife, operated a two-room school in the old Aten College building. There also were three or four single-teacher schools, including one in Depot Town and one for African-American children. An important step came in 1892, when Professor W. W. Chandler, assisted by three or four women teachers in various locations in town, introduced a graded school system for Lampasas children.[34]

Two years later the Lampasas city aldermen authorized Mayor J. W. Townsen to sell school bonds for a long overdue public school building. Bids were opened on December 20, 1894, and the contract was awarded to Ed Parker. The school was erected four blocks northwest of the square. The cornerstone was laid in May 1895, progress was rapid, and the big limestone building welcomed students before the end of the year.[35]

Enclosed by a wrought-iron fence, the Lampasas Public School housed all eleven grades. Elementary grades were one through seven, and high school freshmen began in grade eight. W. W. Chandler was installed as school superintendent during construction of the building, and Superintendent Chandler headed the Lampasas High School faculty. Lampasas therefore became part of a surge of secondary education throughout the United States. In 1860 there were merely 311 public high schools in America, none in Texas. Secondary schools spread slowly after the Civil War, but by 1890 there were 2,500 public high schools in America. Less than seven percent of young Americans between the ages of fourteen and seventeen attended high schools in 1890. As urbanization advanced during the 1890s, so did secondary education. There were 6,000 high schools in 1900, more than double the total of 1890 (and by 1910 there were 14,000). Lampasas became part of this extraordinary expansion of high schools in 1895.

Ironically, the same year that Lampasas High School opened its doors, Centenary College abruptly ended twelve years of quality education in Lampasas. In 1894, after more than a decade in the two three-story buildings atop College Hill north of Lampasas, Centenary College moved into the now-vacant Park Hotel building. Following its first busy, exciting years as a resort hotel, the Grand Park experienced a severe drop in patronage. The Park Hotel tried closing in the winter, then reopening during the tourist season. But fashionable tourists tried the Park Hotel one year, or two or three, then traveled to the next new vacation spot.

The big hotel, with a large staff and 200 acres of grounds, simply cost too much to maintain after business declined. For a time in 1891 the Keeley Institute leased space to treat people with drinking problems, and there were two summer normals for teachers. The hotel's Hancock Springs facilities were "closed because of the lack of patronage."[36]

In 1894 Centenary College Trustees, including M. Y. and Charlie Stokes, J. A. Abney, J. I. Campbell, and Methodist minister S. E. Burkhead, decided to move the college operation to the Park Hotel and grounds. The rambling structure was leased for fifty dollars per month, plus $1.25 per student, beginning in September 1894. The college's equipment and furniture was moved in, leaving the College Hill buildings vacant. The trustees felt that the western part of town "was building up very rapidly and it was much more accessible to the majority of students." No longer would the college have to bear the expense of hack transportation to and from the isolated campus on College Hill."[37]

The fall semester of 1894-95 featured a fine arts concert, "which was most excellent and well attended and appreciated by the audience." Prima Baker Moses later described this memorable evening, and she also recorded an even more unforgettable event early in the spring semester and shortly before her fourteenth birthday. "On the night of February 27, 1895, a bitter cold night, when everything was covered with ice and

The first Lampasas Public School building opened in 1885, serving the community's students for more than 80 years. —Courtesy KSM

water pipes frozen, which rendered the Fire Department helpless in controlling the fire, the building burned to the ground, illuminating the town and country-side for miles around. . . ."[38]

Centenary College, like most small, denominational colleges, was underfunded. With music instruments destroyed, along with other classroom equipment and furniture, Centenary College never reopened. Most Victorian resort hotels were frame structures that fell victim to fires, a fate shared by the Park Hotel. Fourteen years after it was erected on a tree-shaded hillside near Hancock Springs, the grandiose symbol of the Victorian heyday of Lampasas vanished.

But memories of the Park Hotel and of the Victorian glamor of Lampasas Springs proved vivid and tenacious, and so did recollections of the community's long frontier period. Comanche raids, cattle drives, gunfights—with the passage of years, frontier dangers and hardships were remembered as adventurous and heroic and exciting. Indeed, the formative decades of Lampasas offered a rich buffet of memories, and Lampasans embraced their colorful, historic heritage with pride and nostalgia. Decades later, a prominent elder statesman of Lampasas decided to host a major reunion, while old-timers still were around to tell—and probably embellish—familiar stories, and to pass down first-person accounts of a time and a town that were worth remembering.

CHAPTER THIRTEEN

Reunion

"God be with us till we meet again."
—Kate Hoy Longfield

Change was in the air in the early 1900s, and not solely because a new century had begun. By the start of the twentieth century the United States had become the wealthiest nation in the world. In 1900, for example, America produced as much steel as its next two competitors combined, England and Germany. The American population doubled within just thirty years, from 38,500,000 to 76,000,000 in 1900, and Americans felt a sense of pride and destiny. The national sense of destiny was spurred by war and unintended consequences that thrust America onto the world stage at the turn of the century.

In 1898 the United States trounced Spain in the brief but triumphant "Splendid Little War." After the U.S.S. *Maine* exploded in Havana harbor in February 1898, Spain was blamed and war was declared in April. There were only 28,000 officers and men in the U.S. Army, and a call went out for volunteers. The War Department organized 182,000 volunteers—including a company from Lampasas—into seven corps, and scrambled to provide rudimentary training.

Following a local tradition that went back forty years, more than eighty Lampasans responded to the call to arms, organizing a military company called the Mabry Guards, in honor of Texas Adjutant General

Woodford H. Mabry. The Mabry Guards became Company A of the Second Infantry Regiment of the Texas Volunteer Guard.[1] While the Mabry Guards were organizing, drawing uniforms and weapons, and hurriedly training with their new regiment, the most famous unit of the war was going through the same process in San Antonio. The First Volunteer Cavalry Regiment—popularly known as "Teddy Roosevelt's Rough Riders"—soon departed San Antonio for Florida and subsequent transportation to Cuba. Units of the Texas Volunteer Guard, including the Second Infantry and Mabry Guards, made their way to Florida as soon as possible.

In July 1898 the U.S. Navy destroyed a Spanish fleet at Santiago, Cuba, while the American invasion force—featuring Colonel Roosevelt leading a charge outside Santiago—overwhelmed Spanish land forces. A great many American units, including the Second Infantry Regiment of the T.V.G., were unable to secure transportation in time for the invasion. East of Cuba the small Spanish island of Puerto Rico fell in August to a swift campaign expertly led by Gen. Nelson A. Miles.

In a Miami hospital on August 13, Corporal Willie Bean of the Mabry Guards died of typhoid fever. While 400 American servicemen were killed in action during the Spanish-American War, another 5,200 died of typhoid fever, malaria, yellow fever, and similar diseases. Corporal Bean was the oldest son of William Bean, who came with his brothers Mark and Tilford "Snap" Bean to Lampasas after the Civil War. William married Julia Stilwell of Lampasas, and Willie was born in 1874. Willie was raised on the Bean ranch five miles west of Lampasas, and he volunteered for the Mabry Guards when he was twenty-three. Corporal Bean's body was shipped by train to Lampasas and deliv-

Tombstone of Cpl. Willie Bean, who died in service during the Spanish-American War, and was interred in the family plot at Oak Hill Cemetery. —Photo by the author

ered to the home of his maternal grandmother. Laid to rest near his father in the city cemetery, "a very large cortege followed the body to its last resting place, and amid tears and floral offerings the last sad rites were performed. . . ."[2] General Mabry also was a victim of disease, dying of malaria while on occupation duty in Cuba in 1899 at the age of forty-two.

Meanwhile, the United States took possession of Puerto Rico while working to stabilize Cuba. During the first battle of the war, in May 1898, Commodore George Dewey destroyed a Spanish fleet in Manila Bay. With poverty-stricken Filipinos in rebellion against their longtime Spanish masters, President William McKinley decided to "uplift and civilize" the Philippines, consisting of 7,000 islands and 8,000,000 people. Reluctantly, but with little other choice, Spain agreed to cede the Philippines in exchange for $20,000,000. Thus the United States had defeated an age-old European power in battle, and at the dawn of the twentieth century assumed responsibility for a major possession on the other side of the world.

And so Americans marched into the twentieth century proud of their new status as a major player on the world stage. American power and wealth grew steadily during the twentieth century, while the increasingly distant 1800s became tinged with nostalgia. The proliferation of Western novels and films—Hollywood churned out 300 Western movies per year during the early decades of the twentieth century—emphasized the adventure and heroism of frontier life. Surviving pioneers everywhere sensed a growing appreciation from younger generations.

In 1934 Charlie Stokes, robust and wealthy at sixty-nine, conceived of a Lampasas County pioneers' reunion. Charlie was an accomplished host; much of his business success had been achieved by hosting large or small groups of associates. He decided to sponsor a fifty-year reunion, for anyone who had been born in or moved to Lampasas County by 1884 or earlier. Charlie himself moved to Lampasas with his mother and older brother in 1880 when he was fifteen. Charlie cowboyed for a few years before settling down to help the Stokes Bros. firm expand into an enormous success, Lampasas' largest employer. Charlie Stokes came to Lampasas before the railroad arrived, and he spent a few memorable years engaging in a classic frontier occupation. He understood the pioneers who settled Lampasas County, and he was in a position to host a suitable celebration for these aging stalwarts.

Charlie organized several committees to handle arrangements. Soon it was decided to hold the reunion on Wednesday, October 10, 1934, at the new Lampasas State Park that opened in June just east of town. The Chamber of Commerce had raised $2,500 to purchase 140 acres, and a Civilian Conservation Corps company built a native stone entrance, stone picnic tables, barbecue pits, a "concession house," gravel roads, a baseball park, a polo field, and a low water dam across Sulphur Creek.[3]

Mrs. Kate Hoy Longfield, seventy-three, agreed to handle publicity, and newspapers in Lampasas and other communities ran articles from her about the upcoming event. People who had moved to other towns or states were invited. Charlie Stokes paid for the barbecue meal. On the morning of the reunion, Lampasas business houses, as well as the post office and courthouse, displayed Old Glory as the old-timers made their way through town toward the park.

Only fifty-year qualifiers were to be admitted for the morning reunion and the noon meal, although everyone was welcome during the afternoon. At the park gate Charlie Stokes stationed Will Standard, born in Lampasas County in 1879, and John Brandon, born in 1886. Standard and Brandon "knew everybody and were not to be fooled by some who looked older than their years, in order to join the exclusive company inside the park," reported the *Leader* with tongue in cheek.[4]

Inside the gate Mrs. John C. Abney, chairman of the badge committee, along with "her coterie of young lady helpers, decorated over six hundred persons with badges. . . ." The ladies also recorded the names of everyone who received badges—except for one independent old settler who insisted on writing his own name. The final list included more than 660 names. Mrs. Abney and her committee members continued to say to each other, "I never had such a good time in my life."

The senior attendee on the grounds was ninety-five-year-old Kate Gilbreath of Kempner. Mrs. Gilbreath, along with Mrs. W. R. Hughes, ninety-one, and Mrs. F. C. Frasier, eighty-four, were unable to mingle with everyone, but many friends came to them to visit. "Neil McAnelly and Will J. Smith, first and second white children born in the county, are no longer vigorous," observed the *Leader*, "and they held separate receptions, their friends clustering about them." McAnelly, now seventy-eight, had become feeble and had not left his home in three months, but he made the effort to come to the reunion. Mrs. J. M. Townsen of Adamsville was eighty-three and had lived in Lampasas County for more

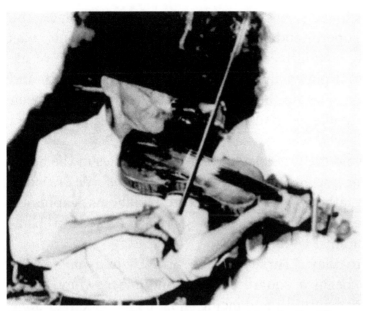

Old-time fiddler June Cox was the lead musician for the 50-year Lampasas County pioneer reunion of 1934. —Courtesy KSM

than eighty years, a record in 1934. Mrs. Townsen was unable to travel to Lampasas, but a silver badge was sent to her. Lucile Standard, wife of Will and owner of a photography studio on the square, was present with a camera to photograph the most venerable of the pioneers.

There was no agenda so that the old-timers would be free to visit. Lively interaction was continual as men and women eagerly moved from one group to another. The *Leader* said that "it was like a three-ring circus, if you watched one ring, you missed what was going on in the other two."

In the background was music from an earlier time. The lead musician was fiddler June Cox, who moved into Lampasas County with his parents in the early 1880s when he was a little boy. Cox was a renowned country fiddler, and he often played with Hosea Bailey, who was present with his guitar. Charlie Stokes had lined up five fiddlers, two banjoists, Bailey on guitar, and a mandolin player. This fine band added just the right musical atmosphere to a nostalgic occasion.

Finally Charlie Stokes announced that dinner was ready to be served ("dinner is correct" asserted the *Leader*). He told his guests that it was a pleasure to be with them, and insisted that the party was theirs not his. Then he quoted lines from poet Edgar Guest:

> You are the folks that my thoughts agree with,
> You are the folks that I like to be with;
> Whatever life sends me of weal or woe,
> You are the folks that I'm glad to know.
> And my old heart blithely pens this line,
> God bless you! Glorious friends of mine!

Sarah Jane Campbell-Scott, widow of W. T. Campbell and later the wife of George Scott, superintendent of Lampasas Public Schools, was chairman of the serving committee. Campbell-Scott and "a score of assistants began passing out plates already filled with abundant food, and continued to do so until over six hundred and sixty persons had been served." Rev. Lawrence Williams returned thanks for the meal, and asked divine protection for all who were present.

After the meal two old settlers rose to thank "Mr. Stokes in the name of all members present for his magnificent hospitality." W. T. Bean (called "Snap," like his father), who had moved to Oklahoma, expressed gratitude for everyone, like himself, "who gladly returned to Lampasas . . . for this reunion."

The band began to play "Turkey in the Straw," and an "expert caller" joined them to begin a square dance. Longtime cowboy Lonce Mitchell, now eighty-one, started the dancing—just as he once had done at the end of a trail drive in a Kansas cowtown dance hall. Others quickly came forward "and the years fell away, and they were boys and girls again, dancing the old beautiful square dances. . . ."

Kate Hoy Longfield, a one-time schoolmarm, was sought out by former students who were eager to visit with "Miss Kate." Like a schoolteacher checking roll she asked them to sign a list—the total was seventeen. Kate was the widow of Lampasas County sheep rancher Frank Longfield, who had sold 200 acres for the Lometa townsite. As the crowd of old-timers finally began to disperse at the end of an incomparable day, Miss Kate was heard to say, "God be with us till we meet again."

Throughout the day hundreds of early settlers—pioneer farmers, cowboys, urban pioneers, wives and now-grown children of the frontier—swapped thousands of stories. These thousands of reminiscences, large and small, often were exaggerated into the tall tales characteristic of old frontiersmen everywhere. And these stories covered every element of the founding decades of Lampasas.

The founder of Lampasas, Moses Hughes, had died in 1903. But several of his descendants came to the reunion, and they knew much about his adventures and his four wives and fifteen children. Bill Bradley was present, at eighty-three the only surviving member of the famous pursuit and fight with Comanches in 1872. Mrs. F. C. Frasier told about attending a dance in Lampasas during the early 1870s that was abruptly halted because of Comanche raiders. The young men ran out to chase the warriors—only to find that their horses had been stolen.

W. T. Bean's father had owned "the noted horse, Tornado." During the Flood of 1873 the elder Bean "rode Tornado into the seething flood and rescued several persons by taking them one at a time behind him on the horse, until all were carried to a place of safety."

This anecdote brought memories of the exciting celebration of the Fourth of July in 1873. Twenty-five young horsemen from Lampasas and the countryside had trained their favorite mounts for a "Knights Tournament." Each participant represented "a knight of old" and, on the Fourth, donned "brilliant suits made of velvet." One observer recalled with relish that "it was a sight to remember as they rode through the square on the way to [Hancock] park on those beautiful horses." At the park the "knights," riding at full gallop, tilted with lances "at a long row of high hung rings." Sir John Sparks lanced the greatest number of rings, giving him the privilege of crowning Miss Rachel Knight queen of the tournament.

Although she could not attend the reunion, Emma Hastings Payn wrote a reminiscence which was published in the *Leader*:

My father, John R. Hastings, brought his family to Lampasas in the fall of 1873. Mr. Vance was the first person to bid us welcome; when we stopped at Hancock Springs, he gave us a drink, and it was good white sulphur then. The wooden troughs and bath tubs looked like they were lined with white velvet. Mr. Vance was in charge of the springs for Mr. Hancock. One landmark that I remember was a big tree in the center of Third Street, between the Mackey Drug Store and the People's National Bank. Court was held in the large room over Toland and Anderson's store, fronting east. The tree was a hitching rack for horses, and during court, it would be surrounded by them. . . .[5]

P. J. Leatherwood also mailed in a memoir:

I came to Lampasas during the fall of 1878, and I called it home until 1932. When I first came, one was seldom, if ever, out of sight of covered wagons along the Round Rock and Lampasas road, some loaded with freight, while others were loaded with families and household effects, bound for the new country. Many of these wagons were drawn by oxen, while others used mules or horses. Then, too, was the day of the old stagecoach, drawn by four to six strong horses, and to gain time, the horses were driven at high speed, and changed every 10 to 15 miles. I have seen . . . horses changed in 3 minutes. I was at the old Santa Fe depot and saw the first work train come in before the passenger service had begun. Then came the boom, and the building of the Park Hotel . . .; I watched the construction as a boy usually does. Many of my early school days were spent in the old Aten College. . . . It was during these days that the courthouse was built, and I well remember how Mrs. Emma C. Aten stopped every activity in the school room, that all might listen to the big clock toll out the hour for the first time. The large old bell that used to call us to school at the Aten College was later used by the city for the fire alarm, atop the fire station . . ., and if I could hear that old bell ring today, I would reach for my books.[6]

All of these topics and others were rehashed by the hundreds of old settlers at the reunion. Lampasas businessman F. J. Harris recounted his Confederate service as a messenger boy, because he was too young to enlist as a soldier. Charlie Stokes was just past boyhood when he drove cattle up the trail, and Harry Taylor happily reminisced about his own experiences as a trail driver. Lonce Mitchell had a fund of stories about his years on the cattle trails, often working with Pink Higgins. Jess Standard also rode for Pink, but he was absent; at eighty, within a few months he would die at Tuscola. But gatekeeper Will Standard was well-versed in his father's tales and passed them on with gusto. Will himself was a teenaged cowboy in the 1890s, but when he married Lucile Mauldin he sought steady employment in town to support their large family. For a quarter of a century Will was the only paid fireman in Lampasas, training horses on the side to keep in touch with cowboy life.

Simmie Toland Harris came from Temple to see friends from her days as a young Lampasas socialite. At the reunion she encountered J. D. and Berta Cassell, both in their seventies. The Cassell home was frequently the scene of socials for young people, as well as musical evenings which often demonstrated the accomplishments of Berta's many piano and violin pupils.

From Comanche attacks to musicales. From Confederate veterans to schoolmarms. From cowboys to urban pioneers. From the Flood of '73 to the Knights Tournament—both in the same year. From Lampasas Springs to the Saratoga of the South. During a single day in 1934, more than six hundred men and women discussed, described, debated, defended, amplified, relived, expounded, exaggerated, and laughed about almost every aspect, every notable character and event, of Lampasas during the 1800s. The formative decades of Lampasas were brought back to life by an aging regiment of proud Texas pioneers.

Today, nearly eight decades later, the Lampasas pioneers are all gone, and so are their sons and daughters. But grandsons and grand-daughters still abound, as well as members of subsequent generations. Many pioneer descendants live in Lampasas, but wherever they reside there is a healthy interest in the deeds, in the lives, in the history of their ancestors and the town they built.

There are reminders of the historic past all over Lampasas. The superb 1883 courthouse still looms above downtown Lampasas. The 1870 Northington building continues to occupy its corner of the square, and the Star Hotel, built in the same year, stands stout but empty. The original home of the First National Bank on Third Street has been handsomely refurbished, and other stone commercial buildings from the nineteenth century remain in use. The two-story rock home built by Dr. J. M. Adkins continues to dominate a hill east of downtown. Fine Victorian residences are still occupied on the onetime "Silk Stocking Row" and elsewhere around town. Sturdy St. Mary's Episcopal Church, begun in the 1880s, continues to serve a faithful congregation. Hancock Springs and Hanna Springs are maintained and still flow.

Many key structures from the 1800s have vanished, but informative historical markers indicate their original location. Active local historians—individuals and members of the DRT (which adopted its name

Ruins of the old Park Hotel bathhouse have been stabilized as a tangible reminder of the Saratoga of the South era. —Photo by the author

while meeting in Lampasas), the Lampasas County Historical Commission, and the Keystone Square Museum—labor constantly to promote and preserve the unique and picturesque past of Lampasas. A treasure trove of documents and photos and artifacts are on file or display at the museum.

Spring Ho is a community celebration that is staged each summer in Lampasas. Great numbers of citizens work on committees to stage this popular annual event—just like Lampasans of the 1870s, who worked together to stage county fairs, or of the 1880s, who brought the Texas Volunteer Guard encampments to town.

If Lampasans of the 1800s could be transported to a modern Spring Ho event, they would enjoy themselves hugely—just like the 1934 reunion. And when looking around town, they would be elated to see the courthouse, the First National Bank building, St. Mary's Church, the home of Dr. Adkins, surviving Victorian houses on Third Street, and—always—the springs.

Endnotes

Chapter 1

1. Moses Hughes told his story in a letter written to a relative on January 29, 1885, and published in Jonnie Ross Elzner, *Relighting Lamplights*, 75-76, and in an interview with the *Leader* published on October 14, 1898. Also see the account of Hughes and his family by descendant Nancy Franklin in the county history complied by the Lampasas County Historical Commission, *Lampasas County, Texas—Its History and Its People*, 216-217, as well as the Hughes obituary in the *Lampasas Leader*, May 1, 1903.

2. The most informative single source about the springs is *Lampasas Springs*, a brochure prepared by Jeff Jackson, a resourceful local historian whose knowledge of Lampasas history is unsurpassed.

3. "Lampasas," *Texas Almanac 1859*, 177. The *Almanac* article on Lampasas was written by "H. R.," probably Dr. Hillary Ryan, the town's first physician.

4. Letter from Hughes in Elzner, *Relighting Lamplights*, 75-76.

5. Hughes letter in *Relighting Lamplights*, 75-76.

6. Ibid.

7. See the biographical account of McAnelly in *Lampasas County, Texas*, 265. Frontier Texas, surveying techniques were described to the author by Jerry Goodson, Lampasas County Surveyor and an avid local historian.

8. See the biographical sketches of "John Burleson, I" and "John Burleson, II" in *Lampasas County, Texas*, 128.

9. The description of the pioneer community in 1855 was written by a reporter and published in the *Austin State Times*. It appeared on August 18, 1855, and was reprinted in *Lampasas County, Texas*, 408. Jonnie Ross Elzner related that Reverend Childers preached the first sermon, *Rebuilding Lamplights*, 23.

10. Descendants of Pleasant Cox continually research and exchange information about their Lampasas County ancestor. See, for example, "When the Pleasant Cox Family Moved to Lampasas Springs In March 1855," a family publication shared with me by Joe Cox, a former student of mine at Lampasas Junior High School and a treasured friend. The biographical sketch of Pleasant Cox in *Lampasas County, Texas*, 152, was written by W. Pleasant Cox.

11. *Austin State Times*, August 18, 1855.

12. F. M. Cross, *Early Days in Central Texas*, 30-31.

13. *Austin State Times*, August 18, 1855.

14. Ibid. For the price of lots see Elzner, *Relighting Lamplights*, 19.

15. "Moses Hughes," *Lampasas County, Texas*, 217.

16. *Austin State Times*, Austin 18, 1855.

17. Jackson, *Lampasas Springs*; Elzner, *Relighting Lamplights*, 178-180.

18. Prima Baker Moses, *Stories of Lampasas*, 14-17.

19. *Austin State Times*, August 18, 1855.

20. Petition and signatures reproduced in *Lampasas County, Texas*, 409-410.

21. Mention of Dr. Ryan as the first physician and Bill Willis as first county surveyor is in Elzner, *Relighting Lamplights*, 22-23.

22. Discussions of the origin of the name "Lampasas" are in *Lampasas County, Texas*, 1, and Elzner, *Relighting Lamplights*, 11-12, 291.

23. *Lampasas County, Texas*, 1.

Chapter 2

1. Letter from Hughes in Elzner, *Relighting Lamplights*, 75-76.

2. *Lampasas Dispatch*, September 13, 1877.

3. The Comanche story has been powerfully told by T. R. Fehrenbach in *Comanches, The Destruction of a People and in Lone Star, A History of Texas and the Texans*. Also see Rupert Norval Richardson, *The Comanche Barrier to South Plains Settlement* and S. C. Gwynne, *Empire of the Summer Moon*.

4. Mrs. A. D. Gentry, "Reminiscences of Mrs. J. J. Greenwood," *Frontier Times*, 1924, 12-13.

5. Each of the initial line of frontier forts is described and pictured in Herbert M. Hart, *Old Forts of the Far West*, 13-27.

6. Fehrenbach, *Lone Star*, 424-425.

7. T. H. Espy to Sam Houston, February 15, 1860, *Texas Indian Papers*, Vol. IV, 8-10.

8. Lt. Thomas C. Frost to Gov. H. R. Runnels, Feb. 8, 1858; Petition from Citizens of Lampasas County to Gov. H. R. Runnels, September 28, 1858; Pettion for Ranger Company for Lampasas County to Governor H. R. Runnels, October 18, 1858; Petition from Citizens of Lampasas County, October 25, 1858; Letter from H. R. Runnels to Lampasas County, October 27, 1858; Letter from H. R. Runnels to Gen. D. E. Twiggs, October 27, 1858. *Texas Indian Papers*, V, 220-221; 285-286; 288-290, 291, 292.

9. Williamson Jones to H. R. Runnels, October 17, 1858; B. S. Whitaker to H. R. Runnels, October 25, 1858. *Texas Indian Papers*, III, 297; 299-300.

10. Hillary Ryan to H. R. Runnels, October 30, 1858. *Texas Indian Papers*, III, 301-302.

11. Ibid., November 13, 1858, 307-308.

12. N. D. McMillan to Capt. John Williams, January 3, 1859. *Texas Indian Papers*, V, 301-302.

13. Hillary Ryan to H. R. Runnels, May 14, 1859. *Texas Indian Papers*, III, 327-328. *Lampasas Chronicle*, October 1, 1859.

14. Military Muster Rolls in *Lampasas County, Texas*, 417-418. Also see Military Activities on page 17.

15. The history of the 27th Brigade and the other frontier units is detailed in Smith, *Frontier Defense in the Civil War*. "Military Activities" in Lampasas County are described in *Lampasas County, Texas*, 17.

16. The gravestone of John Higgins, at Rock Church Cemetery east of Lampasas, states that he was a private in the 27th Brigade.

17. Clifford B. Jones, "Notes on the Life of 'Pink' Higgins, 3-4.

18. This incident is described by Brown, *Indian Wars and Pioneers of Texas*, 114-115, and Wilbarger, *Indian Depredations of Texas*, 623-624.

19. Statement of Indian Depredations on the Texas Frontier, 1865—July 19, 1867. *Texas Indian Papers*, IV, 232-234.

20. Gentry, "Reminiscences of Mrs. J. J. Greenwood," *Frontier Times*, 1924, 12-13.

21. Biographical sketch of Charles Calhoun Carter, *Lampasas County, Texas*, 133; Report from Judge W. B. Pace to J. W. Throckmorton, February 15, 1867. *Texas Indian Papers*, IV, 161-162.

22. T. H. Adams to Gov. J. W. Throckmorton, July 7, 1866; Petition from Lampasas County to J. W. Throckmorton, July 15, 1866; Mary E. Cochran to J. W. Throckmorton, July 1866. *Texas Indian Papers*, IV, 94-95, 96-97, 101.

23. Letter from Lampasas Citizens to Senators Burney and Cooley, August 15, 1866. *Texas Indian Papers*, IV, 103-104.

24. Hart, *Old Forts of the Southwest*, 189.

25. *Lampasas County, Texas*, 19, and *Lampasas County Cemeteries*, 15.

26. "Indian Fighters," and Dr Garret Townsen, "First Settlers North of School Creek," both in *Adamsville Through Their Eyes*, 243 and 316-318.

27. *Austin Daily State Journal*, August 15, 1870; *Lampasas Dispatch*, October 17, 1871.

28. Margaret McCrea Aynsworth to "sister," March 23, 1859; Sarah McCrea to Mary Frances McCrea Supple, February 19, 1861.

29. Sarah McCrea to Mary Frances Supple, April 14, 1862; Margaret Aynsworth to Mary Frances Supple, July 14, 1863; Len McCrea to brother and sister, "Jim" and "Maggie" (Margaret), October 1865

30. Margaret Aynsworth to "Brother & Sister," January 28, 1870; Len McCrea to John McCrea, September 26, 1871; Sarah McCrea to "children," October 1871.

31. *Lampasas Record*, October 11, 1934. This edition published Bradley's detailed reminiscence.

32. Heitman, *Historical Register and Dictionary of the United States Army*, 2 vols.

33. The Company M rosters of August 9, 1872, February 22, 1873, and September 12, 1873, are listed in *Lampasas County, Texas*, 418.

34. *Lampasas Leader*, undated, quoted in *Lampasas County, Texas*, 20.

Chapter 3

1. Valenza, *Taking the Waters in Texas*, 17.

2. The story of watering resorts in Texas is told in Valenza, *Taking the Waters in Texas*. Also see Fowler, *Crazy Water: The Story of Mineral Wells and Other Texas Health Resorts*.

3. *Austin State Times*, August 18, 1855.

4. *Texas Almanac, 1859*, "Lampasas County," 177-178.

5. Ibid., 178.

6. Cross, *Early Days in Central Texas*, 30.

7. *Austin State Times*, August 18, 1855. The author lived in Lampasas for three years during the 1960s. The city water supply was Sulphur Creek, and drinking the sulphur water was a difficult adjustment. But once I became accustomed to Lampasas water, I disliked other drinking water. The reporter from LaGrange got it right, for 1855 and long thereafter.

8. Dawson diary reproduced in *Lampasas Record*, January 24, 1924.

9. *135th Anniversary Celebration, 1856-1991*. First Baptist Church, Lampasas, Texas, October 13, 1991. Scott's Hotel ad in *Lampasas Chronicle*, October 1, 1859.

10. Penn, *Life and Labors of Major W. E. Penn*, 172-174.

11. Valenza, *Taking the Waters in Texas*, 45, 58-63, 148, 152-153.

12. Adkins, *One Texas Old Maid*, 18.

13. Lincecum, ed., *Science on the Texas Frontier*, 174.

14. Ibid.

15. Jeff Jackson, "The History of Hanna Springs," *Lampasas Dispatch* Record, January 5, 2001.

16. Adkins, *One Texas Old Maid*, 12-16.

17. Ibid., 15-16.

18. Interview with Webber in the *Lampasas Leader*, March 16, 1920.

19. *Lampasas Dispatch*, May 10 and June 28, 1877.

20. Ibid., June 28, 1877.

21. Ibid., May 28, 1877.

22. Ibid., June 28, 1877.

23. Ibid., June 28, July 26, and August 16, 1877.

24. D. W. Phillips to J. E. Lankford, June 9, 1878, reprinted in the *Lampasas Daily Times*, June 11, 1878; also see the first issue of the *Daily Times*, June 1, 1878.

25. *Daily Times*, June 23 and 29, 1878.

26. Ibid., July 19, 1878.

27. Ibid., July 13, 16, 27, and August 10, 1878.

28. Ibid., June 1, 6, 8, and 12, 1878.

29. Ibid., June 11, 13, 14, and 15, 1878.

30. Ibid., June 16, 1878.

31. "Northington Building: A true survivor," *2011-2012 Guide to Lampasas*; *Daily Times*, June 11, 12, 13, July 14, 26, and 31, 1878.

32. *Daily Times*, June 22, 23, 28, 30, July 16, and August 2, 1878.

33. Ibid., August 6, 1878.

34. Ibid., July 4, 7, 10, 26, 28, and August 23, 1878.

35. Ibid., June 30, July 1, 7, 16, 20, 27, and 28, 1878.

36. Ibid., July 20, 1878.

37. Ibid., June 15, 16, 18, 20, 23, 25, 27, 30, and July 7, 1878.

38. Ibid., June 11, 15, 22, July 6, August 2 and 17, 1878.

39. Ibid., July 16, 1878.

40. Ibid., August 18, 1878.

41. Ibid., July 6, 1878.

42. Ibid., August 1, 3, 18, 20, and 27, 1878.

43. Ibid., June 5, 26, July 17, 19, 23, 27, and August 20, 1878.

44. Ibid., June 9, July 13, 14, 19, and 26, 1878.

45. Ibid., August 3 and 4, 1878.

46. Ibid., August 6, 7, 8, 9, and 10, 1878.

47. Ibid., August 21 and 22, 1878.

48. Ibid., August 29, 1878.

Chapter 4

1. Billington, *Westward Expansion*, 6-7.

2. *Lampasas County, Texas*, 217-218; *Lampasas Dispatch*, May 10, 31 March

14, 1878; *Lampasas Leader*, March 14, December 29, 1888, and June 15, 22, September 28, 1889.

3. *Lampasas County, Texas*, 409, 414, 417, 418, 420; "Lampasas," *Texas Almanac 1859*, 177.

4. Adkins, *One Texas Old Maid*, 12-13.

5. Ibid., 20.

6. Ibid., 35, 50-51, 55-58.

7. Ibid., 40-41, 46-47, 50, 140-141, 170-171.

8. Ibid., 170-171.

9. Ibid., 40, 77, 84.

10. *Lampasas County, Texas*, 288-289.

11. Billington, *America's Frontier Heritage*, 78, 88.

12. *Lampasas Leader*, January 13, 1899.

13. Moses, *Stories of Lampasas*, 12.

14. *Lampasas County, Texas*, 59, 346; Adkins, *One Texas Old Maid*, 54.

15. Moses, *Stories of Lampasas*, 12-13.

16. Moses, *Stories of Lampasas*, 12-13; Adkins, *One Texas Old Maid*, 109111, 129, 140-142.

17. *Lampasas Dispatch*, November 9, 1872.

18. Moses, *Stories of Lampasas*, 12-13.

19. *Lampasas Dispatch*, July 26, August 9 and 16, September 13 and 20, November 8, and December 20, 1877.

20. There is an excellent article on the Gracy family, written by descendants, in *Lampasas County, Texas*, 185-186.

21. *Lampasas County, Texas*, 20-21.

22. Ibid., 20.

23. The best accounts of the Flood of 1873 are in the *Lampasas Dispatch*, September 29, 1873, and a fourth anniversary story in the *Dispatch*, September 27, 1877.

24. *Lampasas Dispatch*, September 29, 1873.

25. Ibid., September 29, 1873.

26. Ibid., September 29, 1873, and September 27, 1877.

27. Ibid., September 29, 1873; Moses, *Stories of Lampasas*, 15-16.

28. **Lampasas County Texas**, 390; J. Kay Richardson (great-granddaughter) to Jane McMillin; *Lampasas Leader*, October 5, 1917 (obituary).

29. *Lampasas Leader*, October 20, 1888.

30. Stokes, "Observations on the Background and History of the Firm of Stokes Bros & Co."

31. Stokes, "Observations on the Stokes Bros."; and *Lampasas County, Texas*, 354.

32. Ibid.; Charles Stokes interview.

33. Stokes, "Observations on the Stokes Bros"; *Lampasas County, Texas*, 88.

34. Charles Stokes interview.

35. Walker, *Home to Texas*, 72-73.

36. Stokes, "Observations on the Stokes Bros."

37. Ibid.

38. Ibid.

Chapter 5

1. Fehrenbach, *Lone Star*, 554.

2. The Townsen story is told in biographical essays on Jasper and Perry in *Lampasas County, Texas*, 368-370.

3. *Lampasas Leader*, July 27, 1934; *Lampasas County, Texas*, 368-370.

4. *Lampasas County, Texas*, 105-108.

5. *Lampasas County, Texas*, 220-21; Census of 1860, Lampasas County.

6. Gentry, "Reminiscences of Mrs. J. J. Greenwood," *Frontier Times*, 1924, 12-13.

7. Ibid.

8. Mary H. Richardson to General H. L. Burkitt, in *Adamsville Through Their Eyes*, 338.

9. *Lampasas County, Texas*, 288-289.

10. Skaggs, *Cattle-Trailing Industry*, 1-11, 123-125.

11. Walker, *Home to Texas*, 58.

12. *Lampasas County, Texas*, 16, 368-369.

13. Jones, "Notes on the Life of 'Pink' Higgins," 2; *Lampasas Leader*, July 27, 1934.

14. Jones, "Notes on the Life of 'Pink' Higgins," 2; *Lampasas County, Texas*, 209.

15. Dobie, *The Longhorns*, 110.

16. Lampasas newspapers that were searched for stray notices: *Chronicle*, October 1, 1859; several available issues of the *Dispatch* for 1871, 1872, 1876, 1877, 1878, and 1882; the three-month run of the *Daily Times* in 1878; several issues of the *Leader* in 1882 and 1883; and the *People's Journal* of 1892 and 1893. All prominently displayed stray notices.

17. An extensive history of extralegal violence was presented by Richard Maxwell Brown in *Strain of Violence, Historical Studies of American Violence and Vigilantism*. Also see Frank Richard Prassel, *The Great American Outlaw, A Legacy of Fact and Fiction*; W. Eugene Hollon, *Frontier Violence, Another Look*; and Wayne Gard, *Frontier Justice*.

18. Brown, *Strain of Violence*, 59-60.

19. List of sheriffs in Lampasas County, Texas, 420.

20. Jones, "Notes on the Life of 'Pink' Higgins," 4-5.

21. Ibid., 5.

22. Charles Van Trease, "Horse Thief Story," in *Adamsville Through Their Eyes*, 319.

23. John Nichols, interview by J. Evetts Haley, May 15, 1927.

24. Webb, *The Great Plains*, 280-318.

25. *Lampasas Leader*, October 13, 1888.

26. *Lampasas Dispatch*, June 8, 1882.

27. *Lampasas Dispatch*, April 6, 1882; *Galveston Daily News*, April 15, 1882.

28. Russell, *Bob Fudge*, 20-23, 41.

29. O'Neal, *Pink Higgins*, 72-102.

30. Standard family genealogical and archival collection

31. *Lampasas Daily Times*, June 9, 1878

Chapter 6

1. O'Neal, *Encyclopedia of Western Gunfighters*, 3-17.

2. Lampasas historian Jeff Jackson collected information about gunfights, lynchings, and other violent incidents in "Lawlessness" on pages 24-29 of *Lampasas County, Texas*. The killing of Nixon by Willis is described on page 27.

3. Gillett, *Six Years with the Texas Rangers*, 73; *Lampasas County, Texas*, 24.

4. Jeff Jackson, "Shadrick T. Denson," *Lampasas County, Texas*, 159.

5. *Lampasas Dispatch*, November 9, 1872.

6. Nichols interview, 8.

7. Ibid., 7-8.

8. *Lampasas County, Texas*, 25.

9. Nichols interview, 6, 42-43. A mine of information about the Horrells was compiled by the noted author Frederick Nolan in *Bad Blood, The Life and Times of the Horrell Brothers*, and by historian David Johnson in a book not yet published as of this writing. Johnson graciously permitted me to read his manuscript, which should be in book form by the time this book is published.

10. Nichols interview, 43.

11. Nichols interview, 6-7; Nolan, *Bad Blood*, 11-12.

12. Nichols interview, 42-43.

13. *Lampasas County, Texas*, 24.

14. Accounts of the bloody encounter between Williams's force and the Horrell faction are in Gillett, *Six Years with the Texas Rangers*, 73-75; the Nichols interview, 7-9; and a newspaper article, based largely on the testimony of fatally wounded Officer Andrew Melville, that was circulated statewide and that was found by the author in the *Cleburne Chronicle*, March 29, 1873.

15. Gillett, *Six Years with the Texas Rangers*, 74.

16. *Lampasas County, Texas*, 24; *Cleburne Chronicle*, March 29, 1873.

17. Gillett, *Six Years with the Texas Rangers*, 74; Nolan, *Bad Blood*, 27-28; *Lampasas Dispatch*, November 9, 1872.

18. Gillett, *Six Years with the Texas Rangers*, 75.

19. The story of the Horrell War is detailed in Rasch, "The Horrell War," *NMHR*, and Nolan, *Bad Blood*, 47-95. Another meticulous account will be available in David Johnson's forthcoming book about the Horrells.

20. Sonnichsen, *I'll Die Before I'll Run*, 132-134.

21. Gillett, *Six Years with the Texas Rangers*, 77; *Lampasas County, Texas*, 25.

22. Cox, "Lampasas County's Longmeadow Cemetery," *Texas Tales*, and *Lampasas County, Texas*, 27.

23. *Lampasas County, Texas*, 27.

24. Nichols interview, 24-25.

25. DeVos, et al, eds., *Anthology of the Hoo Doo War*, 149-151.

26. Johnson, *Mason County "Hoo Doo" War*, 157, 160-161.

27. *Lampasas Dispatch*, January 3, 1878.

28. *Lampasas County, Texas*, 27.

29. *Lampasas Dispatch*, September 27, 1877.

30. *Lampasas Daily News*, June 5 and July 17, 1878.

31. Ibid., July 23 and 27, 1878.

32. *Lampasas County, Texas*, 57.

Chapter 7

1. *Lampasas Leader*, January 26, 1889.

2, Ibid., January 26, 1889.

3, Nichols interview, 10.

4. *Lampasas Leader*, January 26, 1889; *Galveston Daily News*, April 15, 1882.

5. Nichols interview, 21-22.

6. Sonnichsen, *I'll Die Before I'll Run*, 135.

7. *Lampasas County, Texas*, 26; Sonnichsen, *I'll Die Before I'll Run*, 136. Sonnichsen interviewed elderly Lampasans in 1944 regarding the feud.

8. Gillett, *Six Years with the Texas Rangers*, 78.

9. Nichols interview, 13-14; Gillett, *Six Years with the Texas Rangers*, 77.

10. *Lampasas Leader*, January 26, 1889; *Lampasas County, Texas*, 26.

11. Nolan, *Bad Blood*, 112, 115; *Lampasas County, Texas*, 26.

12. Jones, "Pink Higgins," *Atlantic Monthly*, 86.

13. *Lampasas Leader*, January 26, 1889.

14. *Galveston News*, June 15, 1877.

15. Northington, "I Saw Them Stack Their Guns," *Frontier Times*, 18.

16. Nichols interview, 23.

17. Jeff Jackson has conducted the most detailed study of the battle in Lampasas, presenting his findings in *Lampasas County, Texas*, within an excellent article on "The Horrell–Higgins Feud," 25-27, and in an informative brochure, *Historical Guide to the Shootout on the Public Square*. A thorough account which rings with the authority of eyewitnesses was published twelve years after the gunbattle in the *Lampasas Leader* on January 26, 1889. Also see the eyewitness description by John Nichols on pages 11-12 and 23-24 of his interview by J. Evetts Haley.

18. Nichols interview, 11-12.

19. Ibid., 11 and 23.

20. *Lampasas Leader*, January 26, 1889.

21. Nichols interview, 24.

22. *Lampasas Leader*, January 26, 1889.

23. Northington, "I Saw Them Stack Their Guns," *Frontier Times*, 18.

24. *Lampasas Leader*, January 26, 1889.

25. Northington, "I Saw Them Stack Their Guns," *Frontier Times*, 18.

26. Maj. John B. Jones to Adjutant General William Steele, July 10, 1877.

27. Sgt. N. O. Reynolds described this daring and bloodless arrest in a detailed letter to the editor of the *Lampasas Dispatch*, dated August 4, 1877, and published in the August 9 issue. The *Lampasas Leader* account, January 26, 1889, was based on eyewitnesses, and C. L. Sonnichsen, *I'll Die Before I'll Run*, 140-142, interviewed family members. Other contemporary accounts are available in Gillett, *Six Years with the Texas Rangers*, 78-79, and Roberts, *Rangers and Sovereignty*, 167-169.

28. Gillett, *Six Years with the Texas Rangers*, 79.

29. Ibid., 80.

30. Nichols interview, 14-15.

31. The murder and lynching at Meridian may be studied in: Nichols interview, 14-15, 25-26; Jackson, "Vigilantes: The End of the Horrell Brothers," *NOLA Quarterly* (April-June 1992), 13-19; Sonnichsen, *I'll Die Before I'll Run*, 147-149; Nolan, *Bad Blood*, 136-150.

32. *Lampasas County, Texas*, 26.

33. The quotes in this paragraph are taken from essays C. L. Sonnichsen wrote about feuding in *I'll Die Before I'll Run*, 3-11 and 316-324, and in *Ten Texas Feuds*, 3-8. During the late 1980s I was privileged to associate with Doc, who discussed with me feuding in general and the Horrell–Higgins conflict in particular.

34. Jeff Jackson related the murders of James Collier, Bill Vanwinkle, and William Kinchelo in *Lampasas County, Texas*, 27.

35. Jeff Jackson learned from Higgins family members the circumstances of Betty's affair and departure.

36. J. P. Higgins vs. Delilah E. Higgins, in Lampasas District Court Minutes, Vol. 4, 235.

37. Jeff Jackson compiled the history of Albertus Sweet in "Victim of Circumstance: Albertus Sweet, Sheriff of Lampasas County, Texas, 1874-1878," *NOLA Quarterly*, Vol. 20, 14-21.

38. Details about Pink's family life are in O'Neal, *Pink Higgins*.

Chapter 8

1. *Texas Almanac 1859*, 177-178.

2. O'Neal, *Cattlemen vs. Sheepherders*, 1-16.

3. Adams, *Western Words*, 275.

4. Adams, *Western Words*, 275-276; Holt, "Woes of the Texas Pioneer Sheepman," *Southwestern Sheep and Goat Raiser*, 73.

5. O'Neal, *Cattlemen vs. Sheepherders*, 15-16; Shirley, *Shotgun for Hire*, 56.

6. *San Saba News*, quoted in *Austin Democratic Statesman*, February 6, 1880; Holt, "Sheep Raising in Texas in 1881-1882," 40.

7. Holt, "Woes of the Texas Pioneer Sheepman," 62; Gard, "The Fence-Cutters," *Southwestern Historical Quarterly*, July 1947; and Holt, "The Introduction of Barbed Wire Into Texas," 65-79.

8. Gard, "The Fence-Cutters," 11; Gammel (comp.), *Laws of Texas*, 9: 566-567, 569.

9. Gentry, "Reminiscences of Mrs. J. J. Greenwood," *Frontier Times*, 1924, 13.

10. *Lampasas Leader*, December 1, 1888.

11. *Lampasas Dispatch*, February 7, 1878; D. W. Phillips to J. E. Lankford, published in the *Dispatch*, June 11, 1878.

12. Biographical article on William Mark Wittenburg in *Lampasas County, Texas*, 393.

13. In addition to the federal censuses of 1880 and 1940, the *Forgotten Texas Census, 1887-88*, was a report by the state's Department of Agriculture. The report on Lampasas County is on pp. 132-133.

14. *Lampasas Leader*, December 1, 1888.

15. *Lampasas Dispatch*, May 11, 1889.

16. *Galveston Daily News*, October 2, 4, 8, and 21, 1883; *Lampasas County, Texas*, 28.

17. *Galveston Daily News*, September 7, October 15 and 27, 1883.

18. Ibid., October 27, 1883.

19. Ibid., December 10, 1883, and January 2, 1884.

20. Ibid., March 24, 1884.

21. Aten, "Fence-Cutting Days in Texas," *Frontier Times*, July 1939, 441-442. Also see Preece, *Lone Star Man*, 127-129.

22. The killing at the Feild ranch was related to the author in an interview with Mark Feild on February 10, 1978, and on other occasions. Mark was the grandson of Andy Feild, who shot a cowboy to death on the Feild sheep ranch in 1889. Mark was a 1926 graduate of Lampasas High School, and a star on the undefeated, unscored-on district championship LHS football team of 1925. By the time the United States entered World War II, Feild had taken over the family ranch. Although he had started a family, like so many other Texans Feild attempted to enlist in the armed forces. But because the wool he produced was critical to the war effort, Feild was sent back to his ranch. So were other Lampasas area woolgrowers.

23. *Lampasas County, Texas*, 273-274, 288.

24. Ibid., 248-249.

Chapter 9

1. The denominational facts and figures are textbook material, available in such reliable texts as Richardson, et al, *Texas, The Lone Star State*, 163-164, 280, and Fehrenbach, *Lone Star*, 599-600.

2. McBeth, *Texas Baptists*, 45, 51-52, 61.

3. Fehrenbach, *Lone Star*, 600-601.

4. Mullins, et al, *135th Anniversary Celebration*, 1856-1991. This booklet is crammed with information, lists, and statistics about the First Baptist Church of Lampasas.

5. Stokes, Paisano; Sparks, "A Winner of the West," *Frontier Times*, vol. 16, no. 7 (April 1939).

6. Stokes, Paisano, 19.

7. Ibid., 23.

8. Ibid., 23-24.

9. Ibid., 24.

10. Ibid., 25.

11. Ibid., 32-34.

12. Ibid., 31-32.

13. Ibid., 17.

14. *Lampasas Daily News*, June 8 and 16, July 11, 1878.

15. *Lampasas Daily News*, June 16, July 11, August 11, 1878.

16. An excellent biographical article on Carroll is available online at the Baptist History Homepage. Carroll's denominational work is described in McBeth, *Texas Baptists, A sesquicentennial History*.

17. Mullins, et al., *135th Anniversary Celebration, 1856-1991*.

18. McBeth, *Texas Baptists*, 110-111.

19. *Lampasas Dispatch*, June 8 and September 14, 1889; Mullins, et al., *135th Anniversary Celebration, 1856-1991*.

20. When the venerable First Baptist Church burned in 1937, Jessie Standard, a reporter for the *Leader* and later mother of the author, called in the alarm to the Lampasas Fire Department. Will Standard, her father and the only fulltime employee of the LFD, took the call and drove the fire truck two blocks to the church. Lucile Standard, his wife and Jessie's mother and a professional photographer, snapped photos of the conflagration.

21. Elzner, *Relighting Lamplights*, 183; Methodist Church Centennial Edition, *Lampasas Record*, March 13, 1980.

22. Ibid.

23. Descriptions of Centenary College are offered by: Prima Baker Moses, whose family boarded students in their home, in *Stories of Lampasas*, 32-37; and by Gloria Geren Steelman in her Master's Thesis, "Musical Activity in Lampasas, Texas; 1880-1929," 118-124.

24. Moses, *Stories of Lampasas*, 34-36.

25. Steelman, "Musical Activity in Lampasas," 68-69, 121, 123; Moses, *Stories of Lampasas*, 36.

26. Adkins, *One Texas Old Maid*, 172-175.

27. Bonilee Key Garrett, interview by author.

28. "Historical Sketch of St. Mary's Episcopal Church," unpublished manuscript last revised in 2000, and another unpublished manuscript, "A Brief History of St.

Mary's Episcopal Church." Those manuscripts, as well as a file of miscellaneous materials, were loaned to the author by Jane McMillin, a lifelong member of St. Mary's.

29. *Lampasas County, Texas*, 68; Elzner, *Relighting Lamplights*, 186.

30. Hatley, *Our First 100 Years, 1881-1981, First Presbyterian Church, Lampasas, Texas*; Elzner, *Relighting Lamplights*, 184-185.

31. Elzner, *Relighting Lamplights*, 187-188; *Lampasas County, Texas*, 76.

32. *Lampasas County, Texas*, 63; Moses, *Stories of Lampasas*, 38.

33. *Lampasas Record*, July 18, 1963.

Chapter 10

1. Adkins, *One Texas Old Maid*, 153.

2. Ibid., 151-153.

3. Ibid., 153.

4. Mrs. Effie Osburn Greenwood, quoted in *Lampasas Dispatch*, July 9, 1973, from a letter to the paper first printed on August 23, 1931.

5. Werner, "Gulf, Colorado and Santa Fe Railway," *Handbook of Texas*, Vol. 3, 376-377.

6. Dodge, *How We Built the Union Pacific*, 53-54.

7. Bell, *New Tracks in North America*, 254.

8. *Galveston Daily News*, May 26, 1883.

9. Ibid., March 15, April 5 and 14, May 5 and 8, 1882.

10. Ibid., May 11, 1882.

11. Ibid., October 28, 1883.

12. Ibid., November 26 and December 30, 1883.

13. Ibid., July 15, October 28, November 6 and 7, 1883.

14. Moses, *Stories of Lampasas*, 59.

15. *Galveston Daily News*, November 4, 6, 7, and 17, 1883.

16. *Galveston Daily News*, July 31 and November 27, 1883; Adkins, *One Texas Old Maid*, 146-147.

17. The fourteen sections of the 1873 incorporation act are reproduced in Elzner, *Relighting Lamplights*, 313-316; *Lampasas County, Texas*, 20. For the election see *Galveston Daily News*, April 19, 1883.

18. *Galveston Daily News*, June 2, October 28, December 30, 1883; *Lampasas County, Texas*, 20.

19. *Galveston Daily News*, January 3, June 13, August 13, November 4, 1883.

20. Ibid., January 3 and 6, 1883.

21. Moses, *Stories of Lampasas*, 60-61

22. Ibid., 61.

23. Southall, *Blind Tom*.

24. *Galveston Daily News*, July 27 and 28, 1883.

25. Ibid., September 22, 1883.

26. Ibid., July 28, August 7, September 22, 1883.

27. *Lampasas Chronicle*, October 1, 1859.

28. Jackson and Jackson, *Lampasas County Courthouse*, 4-5.

29. *Lampasas Daily Times*, June 7, 1878.

30. *Lampasas Record*, June 8, 1882.

31. Jackson and Jackson, *Lampasas County Courthouse*, 6; *Galveston Daily News*, July 20, 1883.

32. Jackson and Jackson, *Lampasas County Courthouse*, 6-7; *Galveston Daily News*, July 24 and 25

33. Jackson and Jackson, *Lampasas County Courthouse*, 7.

34. Jackson and Jackson, *Lampasas County Courthouse*, 22-24; courthouse clock plaque.

Chapter 11

1. Robinson, *Gone from Texas*, 178-179.

2. Abstract of Deed, loaned to the author by Sue McMillin Faulkner, City Attorney of Lampasas; *Articles of Incorporation of the Lampasas Springs Company*, April 29, 1882.

3. The Park Hotel was described in detail in promotional literature. See the *Lampasas Leader*, May 11, 1889. Another fine description was left by Prima Baker Moses, who was deeply impressed as a child by the elegant hotel. See Moses, *Stories of Lampasas*, 53.

4. *Lampasas Leader*, May 11, 1889.

5. *Lampasas Leader*, May 11, 1889; *Houston Daily Post*, May 25, 1883.

6. *Lampasas Leader*, May 11, 1889.

7. Moses, *Stories of Lampasas*, 53.

8. Moses, *Stories of Lampasas*, 54-55; interview with Bonilee Key Garrett, who was told by her grandfather that he and his friends swam beneath the separating wall to the women's pool.

9. *Lampasas Leader*, May 11, 1889.

10. Adkins, *One Texas Old Maid*, 160.

11. Frantz, "Knights of Pythias," *Handbook of Texas*, III, 1147; *Galveston Daily News*, March 29, 1883.

12. *Houston Daily Post*, June 16, 1883.

13. Ibid., June 16, 1883.

14. Ibid., July 17, 1883.

15. Ibid.

16. The tournament is described in detail, including complete lists of top finishers in each category, in the *Galveston Daily News*, July 18 and 20, 1883, and the *Houston Daily Post*, July 17 and 20, 1883.

17. *Houston Daily Post*, August 21, 1883.

18. Ibid.

19. *Galveston Daily News*, August 23, 26, 27 and 28, 1883; *Austin Daily Statesman*, August 23, 1883.

20. *Lampasas County, Texas*, 5.

21. Files of Dr. Rush McMillin of Lampasas, provided to the author by his daughter, Jane McMillin.

22. *Dallas Weekly Herald*, June 25, 1885.

23. For information about the Texas Volunteer Guard see the *Year Book for Texas*, Vol. II, 1902, 101-106; *Year Book for Texas*, Vol. I, 1901, 107-109; "Texas National Guard," *Handbook of Texas*, VI, 366-370. Also see Cooper, *The Rise of the National Guard: The Evolution of the American Militia, 1865-1920*.

24. *Dallas Weekly Herald*, June 18, 1885; Census of 1880 for Lampasas County, Precinct 1, entry 90, p.11; Report of the Adjutant General, July 8, and September 29, 1885, 32-33, 36-38.

25. Report of the Adjutant General, June 29, 1886, 35

26. *Dallas Weekly Herald*, June 18, 1885; Report of the Adjutant General, June 29, 1886, 35.

27. *Austin Daily Statesman*, June 21, 1885; Report of the Adjutant General, July 8, 1885, 32-33.

28. *Dallas Weekly Herald*, June 18, 1885; Austin Daily Statesman, June 25, 1885.

29. Report of the Adjutant General, July 8, 1885, 32-33.

30. *Austin Daily Statesman*, June 24, 1885; *Dallas Weekly Herald*, July 2, 1885.

31. *Austin Daily Statesman*, June 25 and 27, 1885.

32. There are two accounts of the sham battle in the *Austin Daily Statesman*, June 28, 1885.

33. *Austin Daily Statesman*, June 28, 1885.

34. Report of the Adjutant General, December 1886, 45.

35. Ibid., October 27, 1885, 33-34.

36. Ibid., June 29, 1886, 35.

37. *Austin Daily Statesman*, June 22, 1886, 35.

38. Ibid., June 22, 1886.

39. Report of the Adjutant General, June 29, 1886, 35.

40. *Austin Daily Statesman*, June 22 and 23, 1886.

41. Langford, *Alias O. Henry*, 41; Long, O. Henry, 51-53; Nolan, *O. Henry*, 112.

42. *Austin Daily Statesman*, June 26, 1886; *San Antonio Daily Light*, June 24, 1886.

43. *Austin Daily Statesman*, June 26, 1886.

44. Ibid.

45. Report of the Adjutant General, June 29, 1886, 36; *San Antonio Daily Express*, June 25, 1886; Report of the Adjutant General, June 29, 1886, 36.

46. The list of Guard encampments, along with competition winners, is in the *Year Book of Texas*, Vol. I, 1901, 107-113.

47. Dr. Rush McMillin wrote an excellent article, about the "Financial Institutions" of Lampasas in *Lampasas County, Texas*, 29-30.

48. *First in Lampasas*, 1884-1885.

49. Philpott, "The Texas Bankers Association—A History," *Texas Bankers Record*, January 1917, 30-34, and February 1917, 20-23.

50. Gatton, *Texas Bankers Association*.

51. *Lampasas Leader*, May 23, 1891.

52. Ibid., April 20, 1889.

53. Kemp, "Texas Veterans Association," *Handbook of Texas*, VI, 440; "Texas Veterans Association," *Year Book of Texas*, Vol. II, 1902, 8-13.

54. Rash, "Daughters of the Republic of Texas," *Handbook of Texas*, II, 517-518; "Daughters of the Republic of Texas," *Year Book of Texas*, Vol. I, 129-148, and Vol. II, 13-18.

Chapter 12

1. Foster, *Forgotten Texas Census*, 132.

2. McMillin, "The Spindletop Connection," *Lampasas Dispatch*, January 19, 2001. Lampasas historian Jane McMillin wrote a lengthy and carefully-researched article relating the life and career of W. T. Campbell, with special emphasis on his role in the Spindletop oil boom and the formation of the Texas Oil Company—Texaco.

3. *People's Journal*, November 18, 1892.

4. *Lampasas Leader*, June 1, 1889.

5. *Galveston Daily News*, July 19 and November 27, 1886; and *Houston Daily Post*, July 20, 1883.

6. *Lampasas Leader*, November 17, 1888, and June 15, 1889; *People's Journal*, January 27, 1893.

7. *Lampasas Daily Times*, August 6, 1878.

8. Ibid., June 4 and July 28, 1878.

9. *Lampasas Leader*, October 6, 1888.

10. The account of this incident was drawn from documents about Case No. 1268, *The State of Texas vs. J. P. Higgins*, Lampasas County District Court. Copies of these documents were provided to the author by Jeff Jackson.

11. Interview with Jeff Jackson, September 29, 1998.

12. J. P. Higgins, Certificate of Prison Conduct, December 3, 1893; Dr. John Higgins of Lampasas told the author about the sojourn in East Texas during which Cullen and Tom Higgins attended business colleges. Tom's obituary lists his matriculation at Tyler Commercial College and at "summer normals" for teachers.

13. *Lampasas Dispatch*, February 14, 1878.

14. *Lampasas County, Texas*, 79-80.

15. *Lampasas Leader*, October 6, 1888.

16. *Lampasas County, Texas*, 79.

17. *The People's Journal*, Masthead, July 29, 1892.

18. Cole, "Farmers Alliance Was Founded in Lampasas," *Lampasas Dispatch*, July 9, 1873.

19. *Lampasas Leader*, October 27, 1888; January 19, 1889.

20. Ibid., February 2 and 16, 1889.

21. Ibid., October 27, 1888.

22. Ibid., November 10, 1888.

23. Ibid., December 29, 1888; April 20 and September 7, 1889; *People's Journal*, December 16, 1892.

24. *People's Journal*, December 23, 1892.

25. *People's Journal*, January 6, 1893; *Lampasas Leader*, December 22, 1888.

26. *Lampasas Leader*, November 24, and December 1, 1888.

27. Steelman, "Musical Activity in Lampasas, Texas, 1880-1929." Master's Thesis, University of Texas of Teas. The Cassell recital is described in the *Lampasas Leader*, June 8, 1889.

28. See, for example, the *Lampasas Leader*, May 25 and June 15, 1889.

29. *Lampasas Leader*, April 27, 1891.

30. Ibid., April 27, 1891.

31. Ibid., November 3, 1888.

32. Ibid., December 29, 1888; July 6 and August 3, 1889.

33. Ibid., October 27, 1888.

34. *Lampasas County, Texas*, 59.

35. Ibid.

36. Moses, *Stories of Lampasas*, 36, 56.

37. Ibid., 36-37.

38. Ibid., 36-37.

Chapter 13

1. A list of Mabry Guards is provided in *Lampasas County, Texas*, 418-419.

Records of the Guards during the Spanish-American War are available in the Texas Volunteer Guard collection at the Texas State Archives.

2. *Lampasas Leader*, August 19, 1898.

3. The Lampasas "State" Park is described in *Lampasas County, Texas*, 33. The City of Lampasas owned the park, and sold it for $5,000 in 1941. The property soon was purchased by Leo K. Gunderland, who operated it as "Gunderland Park" for a number of years.

4. The reunion was described in detail in two articles in the *Lampasas Leader*, October 12, 1934. In the next issue, October 19, the *Leader* printed a list of 600-plus attendees. Also see the description in *Lampasas County, Texas*, 33.

5. The letter of Emma Hastings Frazier is most readily accessible in *Lampasas County, Texas*, 33.

6. Leatherwood's letter also may be read in *Lampasas County, Texas*, 33.

Bibliography

Books

Adams, Ramon F. *Western Words: A Dictionary of the American West*. Norman: University of Oklahoma Press, 1968.

Adkins, Ettie Aurelia. *One Texas Old Maid*. Dallas: William T. Tardy, Publisher, 1938.

Alexander, Bob. *Rawhide Ranger, Ira Aten: Enforcing Law on the Texas Frontier*. Denton, Texas: University of North Texas Press, 2011.

Bell, William A. *New Tracks in North America*. New York: Scribner, Welford & Co., 1870.

Billington, Ray Allen. *America's Frontier Heritage*. New York: Rinehart and Winston, 1966.

Billington, Ray Allen. *Westward Expansion: A History of the American Frontier*. Fourth Edition. New York: The Macmillan Company, 1963.

Book Committee, Adamsville Heritage Association. *Adamsville Through Their Eyes, History & Reflections*. Killeen, Texas: Spectrum Printing, 2008.

Brown, Richard Maxwell. *Strain of Violence, Historical Studies of American Violence and Vigilantism*. New York: Oxford University Press, 1975.

Burkhalter, Lois Wood. *Gideon Lincecum, 1793-1874: A Biography*. Austin: University of Texas Press, 1965.

Carlson, Paul. *Texas Woollybacks, The Range Sheep and Goat Industry*. College Station: Texas A&M University Press, 1982.

Caro, Robert A. *The Years of Lyndon Johnson: The Path to Power*. New York: Alfred A. Knopf, Inc., 1982.

Carpenter, Glynda. *Carpenter. The History of Hancock Springs, 1852-1992*. Lampasas: Privately Published, 1992.

Cotner, Robert C. *James Stephen Hogg, A Biography*. Austin: University of Texas Press, 1959.

Cross, F. M. *A Short Sketch-History from Personal Reminiscences of Early Days in Central Texas*. Brownwood, Texas: Greenwood Printing Company, 1910.

Day, James M., comp. *The Texas Almanac, 1857-1873: A Compendium of Texas History*. Waco: Texian Press, 1967.

DeVos, Julius, *et al*, eds. *The Anthology of the Hoo Doo War*. Mason: Mason County Historical Commission, 2006.

Dobie, J. Frank. *The Longhorns*. Boston: Little, Brown and Company, 1941.

233

Dodge, Grenville M. *How We Built the Union Pacific Railway*. Denver: Sage Books, 1965.

Elzner, Jonnie. *Relighting Lamplights* of *Lampasas County, Texas*. N.p., 1974.

Fehrenbach, T. R. *Comanches: The Destruction of a People*. New York: Alfred A. Knopf, 1974.

Fehrenbach, T. R. *Lone Star, A History of Texas and the Texans*. New York: The Macmillan Company, 1968.

Fowler, Gene. *Crazy Water: The Story Of Mineral Wells and Other Texas Health Resorts*. Fort Worth: Texas Christian University Press, 1991.

Franklin, Nancy Dillard. *Moses Hughes and His Family*. Baltimore, MD: Gateway Press, Inc., 2004.

Gard, Wayne. *Frontier Justice*. Norman: University of Oklahoma Press, 1949.

Gatton, T. Harry. *Texas Bankers Association: First Century, 1885-1985*. Austin: Texas Bankers Association Historical Committee, 1984.

Gillett, James B. *Six Years with the Texas Rangers*. New Haven: Yale University Press, 1925.

Gwynne, S. C. *Empire of the Summer Moon: Quanah Parker and the Rise and Fall of the Comanches, the Most Powerful Indian Tribe in American History*. New York: Scribner, 2010.

Hart, Herbert M. *Old Forts of the Far West*. Seattle: Superior Publishing Company, 1965.

Hatley, Minnie Piper. *Our First 100 Years, 1881-1891, First Presbyterian Church, Lampasas, Texas*. Lampasas: Hill Country Publishing Co., Inc., 1981.

Heitman, Francis B., comp. *Historical Register and Dictionary of the United States Army*. 2 vols. Washington, D. C.: Government Printing Office, 1903.

Hollon, W. Eugene. *Frontier Violence, Another Look*. New York: Oxford University Press, 1974.

Hunter, J. Marrin. *The Trail Drivers of Texas*. Austin: University of Texas Press, 1992.

Johnson, David. *The Mason County "Hoo Doo" War, 1874-1902*. Denton: University of North Texas Press, 2006.

Lampasas County Historical Commission. *Lampasas County Cemeteries, 1856-1995*. Austin: Eakin Press, 1995.

Lampasas County Museum Foundation, Inc. *Images of America: Lampasas County*. Charleston, S. C.: Arcadia Publishing, 2009.

Lampasas History Book Committee, compilers. *Lampasas County, Texas, Its History and Its People*. Marceline, Missouri: Walsworth Publishing Company, 1991.

Langford, Gerald. *Alias O. Henry, A Biography of William Sidney Porter*. New York: The Macmillan Company, 1957.

Lincecum, Jerry Bryan, Edward Hake Phillips, and Peggy A. Redshaw, eds. *Science on the Texas Frontier, Observations of Dr. Gideon Lincecum*. College Station: Texas A&M University Press, 1997.

Long, E. Hudson. *O. Henry, The Man and His Work*. New York: Russell & Russell, 1949.

Marhon, Richard C. *The Last Gunfighter, John Wesley Hardin*. College Station, Texas: Creative Publishing Company, 1995.

McBeth, Harry Leon. *Texas Baptists, A Sesquicentennial History*. Dallas: Baptistway Press, 1998.

Moses, Prima Baker. *Stories of Lampasas*. N.p., n.d.

Mullins, Wilda. *135th Anniversary Celebration, 1856-1991*. Lampasas: First Baptist Church, 1991.

Newcomb, W. W., Jr. *The Indians of Texas, from Prehistoric to Modern Times*. Austin: University of Texas Press, 1961.

Nolan, Frederick. *Bad Blood: The Life and Times of the Horrell Brothers*. Stillwater, Oklahoma: Barbed Wire Press, 1994.

Nolan, Jeannette Covert. *O. Henry, The Story of William Sydney Porter*. New York: Julian Messner, Inc., 1943.

O'Neal, Bill. *The Bloody Legacy of Pink Higgins, A Half Century of Violence in Texas*. Austin: Eakin Press, 1999.

O'Neal, Bill. *Cattlemen vs. Sheepherders: Five Decades of Violence in the West, 1880-1920*. Austin: Eakin Press, 1989.

O'Neal, Bill. *Encyclopedia of Western Gunfighters*. Norman: University of Oklahoma Press, 1979.

Parsons, Chuck, and Donaly E. Brice. *Texas Ranger N. O. Reynolds, The Intrepid*. Honolulu, Hawaii: Talei Publishers, Inc., 2005.

Penn, W. E. *Life and Labors of Major W. E. Penn: "The Texas Evangelist."* St. Louis: C. B. Woodward, 1896.

Prassel, Frank Richard. *The Great American Outlaw, A Legacy of Fact and Fiction*. Norman: University of Oklahoma Press, 1993.

Preece, Harold. *Lone Star Man: Ira Aten, Last of the Old Texas Rangers*. New York: Hastings House, Publishers, 1960.

Raines, C. W., State Librarian. *Year Book For Texas, 1901*. Austin: Gammel Book Company, Publishers, 1902.

Raines, C. W., State Librarian. *Year Book For Texas*, Vol. II. Austin: Gammel-Statesman Publishing Company, 1903.

Report of the Adjutant General of the State of Texas, December, 1886. Austin: Triplett & Hutchings, State Printers, 1886.

Richardson, Rupert N. *The Comanche Barrier to South Plains Settlement*. Austin: Eakin Press, 1996.

Richardson, Rupert N., *et.al. Texas, The Lone Star State*. 10th edition. New York: Prentice Hall, 2010.

Richardson, Willard B. *Gone from Texas, Our Lost Architectural Heritage*. College Station: Texas A&M University Press, 1981.

Roberts, Capt. Dan W. *Rangers and Sovereignty*. San Antonio: Wood Printing & Engraving Co., 1914.

Russell, Jim. *Bob Fudge, Texas Trail Driver, Montana-Wyoming Cowboy, 1862-1933*. Aberdeen, S. D. : North Plains Press, 1981.

Shirley, Glenn. *Shotgun for Hire*. Norman: University of Oklahoma Press, 1970.

Smith, David Paul. *Frontier Defense in the Civil War*. College Station: Texas A&M University Press, 1992.

Sonnichsen, C. L. *I'll Die Before I'll Run*. New York: Devin-Adair Company, 1962.

Sonnichsen, C. L. *Ten Texas Feuds*. Albuquerque: University of New Mexico Press, 1957.

Southall, Geneva Handy. *Blind Tom, The Black Pianist-Composer: Continually Enslaved*. Lanham, Maryland: Scarecrow Press, 2002.

Sowell, A. J. *Early Settlers and Indian Fighters of Southwest Texas*. Austin: State House Press, 1986.

Stokes, Katy. *Paisano: Story of a Cowboy and A Camp Meeting*. Waco: Texian Press, 1980.

Tyler, Ron, ed.-in-chief. *The New Handbook of Texas*. 6 vols. Austin: Texas State Historical Association, 1996.

Valenza, Janet Mace. *Taking the Waters in Texas: Springs, Spas, and Fountains of Youth*. Austin: University of Texas Press, 2000.

Walker, Stanley. *Home to Texas*. New York: Harper & Brothers, 1956.

Webb, Walter Prescott. *The Great Plains*. New York: Grossett & Dunlap, 1931.

Wilbarger, J. W. *Indian Depredations in Texas. 1889*; reprint Austin: The Pemberton Press, 1967.

Winfrey, Dorman H., and James M. Day, eds. *The Indian Papers of Texas and the Southwest*, Vols. III, IV, and V. Austin: Texas State Historical Association, 1995.

Wolfe, Peggy Smith, compiler. *Lampasas County, Texas: Timeline of Early Events*. N.p., 2010.

Articles

Aten, Ira. "Fence Cutting Days in Texas." *Frontier Times*, July 1939.

Canfield, Bruce N. "Something Different, The Ward-Burton." *American Rifleman*, 154 (January 2006), 48-49, 72, 81, 82, 83, 84.

Cox, Mike. "Lampasas County's Longmeadow Cemetery." *Texas Tales* column, May 26, 2011.

Cox, Mike. "O. Henry." *Texas Tales* column, June 2, 2005.

Gard, Wayne. "The Fence-Cutters." *Southwestern Historical Quarterly*, July 1947.

Holt, R. D. "The Introduction of Barbed Wire into Texas and the Fence Cutting War." *West Texas Historical Association Year Book*, 1928.

Holt, R. D. "Sheep Raising in Texas in 1881-1882." *West Texas Sheep and Goat Raiser*. December 1956.

Holt, R. D. "Woes of the Texas Pioneer Sheepman." *Southwestern Sheep and Goat Raiser*, December 1940.

Jackson, Jeff. "Victim of Circumstances: Albertus Sweet, Sheriff of Lampasas County, Texas, 1874-1878. *Quarterly of the National Association for Outlaw and Lawman History*, vol. XX, no. 3 (July-September, 1996), 14, 16-21.

Jackson, Jeff. "Vigilantes: The End of the Horrell Brothers." *NOLA* Quarterly, XVI, no. 2 (April-June 1992), 13-19.

Jones, Charles Adam. "Pink Higgins, The Good Bad Man." *Atlantic Monthly* (July 1934), 79-89.

"Legend of C. D. Stokes Still Lives in Texas." *Texas Sheep and Goat Raiser*. June, 1951.

McMillin, Jane. "The Spindletop Connection." *Lampasas Dispatch*, January 19, 2001.

Northington, M. G., as told to Curtis Bishop. "I Saw Them Stack Their Guns." *Frontier Times*, Spring, 1962.

"Northington Building: A true survivor." *2011-2012 Guide to Lampasas*. *Lampasas Dispatch Record*, 2011.

Werner, George C. "Gulf, Colorado and Santa Fe Railway." *Handbook of Texas*, 3, 366-367.

Philpott, W. A., Jr. "The Texas Bankers Association—A History." *The Texas Bankers Record*, January, February, and April, 1917.

Rasch, Philip J. "The Horrell War." New Mexico Historical Review, vol. 31, no. 3 (July 1956), 223-231.

Sparks, John. "A Winner of the West," *Frontier Times* 16, no. 7 (April 1939).

Documents

Federal Census Records. Lampasas County, Texas: 1860, 1870, 1880, 1890, 1900.

Foster, L. L., Commissioner. *Forgotten Texas Census: First Annual Report of the Agricultural Bureau of the Department of Agriculture, Insurance, Statistics, and History. 1887-88.* Austin: State Printing Office, 1889. Reprint by Texas State Historical Association, Austin, 2001.

Gammel, H. P. N., comp. *The Laws of Texas, 1822-1897.* Vols. 8 and 9. Austin: The Gammel Book Company, 1898.

Higgins, J. P. Certificate of Prison Conduct, December 3, 1893. Texas State Archives, Austin.

Higgins, J. P., vs. Delilah E. Higgins. Lampasas District Court Minutes, Vol. 4, 235.

Petitions to the Governor. Lampasas County Collection, Texas State Archives, Austin.

The State of Texas vs. J. P. Higgins. Case No. 1268, Lampasas County District Court.

Texas Volunteer Guard Collection. Texas State Archives, Austin.

Newspapers

Austin Daily State Journal
Austin Democratic Statesmen
Austin State Times
Cleburne Chronicle
Dallas Weekly Herald
Galveston Daily News
Houston Daily Post
Lampasas Chronicle
Lampasas Daily Times
Lampasas Dispatch
Lampasas Leader
Lampasas Record
(Lampasas) *People's Journal*
San Antonio Daily Express

Miscellaneous

Articles of Incorporation of the Lampasas Springs Company. N.p., April 28, 1882.

Jackson, Jeff. "Historical Guide to the Shootout on the Public Square." Pamphlet. Lampasas, Texas: 1990.

Jackson, Jeff. "Lampasas Springs," brochure. Lampasas County Chamber of Commerce and Courtyard Square Association, 2003.

Jones, Clifford B. "Notes on the Life of 'Pink' Higgins." Unpublished typescript.

Richardson, J. Kay, to Jane McMillan, n. d.

Steelman, Gloria Geren. "Musical Activity in Lampasas, Texas, 1880-1929: A Socio-Historical Study." Master's Thesis, University of Texas at Austin, 1971.

Stokes, Charles E., Jr. "Observations on the Background and History of the Firm of Stokes Bros & Co in the Lampasas Area, 1880s through 1951." Unpublished manuscript, files of Jane McMillan, Lampasas.

"When the Pleasant Cox Family Moved to Lampasas Springs in March 1855." Cox family publication

Index

239

About the Author

BILL O'NEAL is the author of more than thirty books and 300 articles and book reviews. He was selected as *True West Magazine*'s "Best Living Non-fiction Writer, 2007." Bill's book, *The Johnson County War*, was voted 2005 Book of the Year by the National Association for Outlaw and Lawman History (NOLA) and in 2007 he was inducted into NOLA's Hall of Fame. Bill has appeared on TV documentaries about the Old West on TBS, The History Channel, A&E, The Discovery Channel, and TNN. He is regularly featured on the nationally syndicated radio show *Chronicles of the Old West*.

Bill is a member of the Western Writers of America and of numerous historical organizations. He taught history for thirty-three years at Panola College in Carthage, Texas, where his teaching awards included a Piper Professorship in 2000. Bill's wife, Karon, teaches in Panola's math department and assists with research and manuscript preparation for each of his books.

Shortly before this book went to press, Bill was appointed State Historian of Texas by Governor Rick Perry. Bill is the third historian to receive this honor. As State Historian he will travel extensively around the state as ambassador for the incomparably rich and colorful history of Texas.

CPSIA information can be obtained
at www.ICGtesting.com
Printed in the USA
BVHW02s2055071117
499763BV00017BA/1009/P